Lafayette

THE LIFE

OF THE

GENERAL LAFAYETTE,

Marquis of France, General in the United States Army, Etc.

BY

P. C. HEADLEY,

AUTHOR OF "WOMEN OF THE BIBLE," "LIFE OF JOSEPHINE," "LIFE OF MARY QUEEN OF SCOTS," "LIFE OF KOSSUTH," ETC.

NEW YORK:

C. M. SAXTON, 25 PARK ROW.

1859.

PREFACE.

In offering the public another biography of Lafayette, the motives are similar to those which induced the author to write the "Life of Josephine." It is true, the history of this great man has been given in various memoirs, but not a full and chronologically correct record of his eventful and brilliant career. Besides, his *character* may be more carefully analyzed and studied in the light of recent developments, which add a new interest to portions of his history, formerly involved in a good deal of obscurity.

Lafayette's name is inseparably associated with that of George Washington; and he should be known as familiarly to every American citizen. To make this acquaintance with him in his manifold spheres of activity more completely attainable by all, is the design of this volume. European and American authorities have been consulted, but their opinions often deemed not strictly legitimate in view of facts. Especially is the part he acted in the French Revolution discussed freely, and the patriotic designs of the unsuccessful Hero seen, it is believed, through all that bloody tragedy.

The theme is a *national* one — and the book will have this feature to commend it to those readers, whose *reverence* for the Bible has brought down wholesale condemnation upon an expansion or illustration of the brief descriptions of the heroes and heroines of the sacred volume.

It is believed that the accuracy of the work will not be impeached. Information has been sought from a great variety of sources, Foreign and American.

The disinterested philanthropy and panting for freedom which animated the Marquis in his youth, and engaged his riper thought when a venerable hermit at La Grange, appeal to the heart and aspirations of the successors of the illustrious dead as the guardians of a Republic, which has passed from the stormy deep of physical combat, to the less awakening, but equally perilous sea of moral and political conflict.

CONTENTS.

CHAPTER IV.

CHAPTER V.

CHAPTER VI.

CHAPTER VII.

features, while the retainer was kept in the most degrading bondage, and the lord was looked upon universally as the absolute despot of the yielding serf, we find the house of Lafayette regarding the wants of its vassals, and improving the condition of that class, upon whom nearly all the nobility were wont to look down with haughty contempt. As early as the fifteenth century, when France was subjected to a hostile invasion, and the security of its government threatened, a Lafayette became the terror of the foe, and contributed more than any other to drive out the enemy from the land. In the seventeenth century Louis de Lafayette was especially instrumental in defeating the plans of Richelieu, and in reconciling Louis XIII to his queen. The family is not without favorable notice in the literary annals of France. Madeline Countess de Lafayette is the authoress of several works of much celebrity which have come down to the present time. In all the annals of this illustrious line, there are no unworthy deeds, and no stain of dishonor tarnishes its escutcheon. It is an instance of that transmitted worth and renown, of which there are but few examples in history. Ancestral honors seem to have been made perennial, and adorn with acknowledged right, the brow of him to whom by the law of the realm they descended.

The birth place of young Lafayette, was in the province of Auvergne, situated in the central part of the southern division of France. The Chateau de Chavagnac, where he first saw the light, is about one hundred and twenty leagues from Paris, and is an exceedingly romantic spot. The country seat stands amid an amphitheater of mountains, commanding a magnificent and ample view of encircling summits. This region was probably thrown up by the same convulsion that elevated the Auvergne range, and exhibits all the varied and picturesque scenery of a surface, which has been broken into broad undulations and solemn peaks, by the upheaving of volcanic fires. The chateau was built in 1701 on the ruins of one that had long been the family residence, but was swept away with its ancient associations and pleasant memories, by a conflagration that left only the blackened fragments of the fine old homestead.

Interesting as the home of Lafayette is to the traveler, it contains but few memorials of himself. Even the room in which he was born cannot be identified, and a single portrait of him, taken in his boyhood, is almost the only evidence that these walls formed the field of his juvenile pastimes, and echoed to the unheeded and merry voice of "the heroic defender of liberty in two hemispheres."

The first seven or eight years of his life, were passed in Chavagnac. His father, a Colonel in the French army, having fallen in the battle of Minden a few months before his birth, the care of his infancy was left entirely to his mother, a woman of excellent qualities and rare attainments.

By her unwearied devotion, the frail form of this only son, survived the debility which, for awhile, indicated a brief career. She watched with maternal solicitude and joy the hue of health stealing so gradually over his pale features, and marked the increasing strength of his attenuated frame; although it gave but slight promise of the vigor which sustained the fatigues and arduous duties of his subsequent life. His mind, however, gave early indications of its power. He seemed to leap over infancy at a stride, and was a mature man in thought and feeling, while others of his age were only children. The same generosity and nobility of soul; the love of liberty and enthusiastic hatred of oppression; the self-sacrificing spirit and warm hearted devotion to whatever he espoused, which rendered his after life so illustrious, characterized also his early history. At the age of about twelve years he was entered at the college of Louis le Grand in Paris, where, under a course of excellent training, he zealously pursued his studies. His mind was well formed for a student, and, had his attention been continued in that direction, he might easily have become one of the most accurate scholars of his time. Of study he was passionately fond, to the exclusion, for awhile, of all other demands upon the precious hours. In the Latin and Greek classics he became especially proficient, and lost neither his love nor knowledge of them in later years. The foundation of that mental force and precision which he subsequently displayed, was firmly laid by this close discipline during the early part of his residence in Paris. He was, however, afterwards subjected in his literary pursuits to frequent interruptions. His high rank gained him the attention of royalty, and the attractions of the gay French court drew him away from his course of intense application. A passion for brilliant society, together with an increasing desire for military exploits, began to stir his youthful spirit. By the death of his mother, in 1770, and of his grandfather a short time after, he became the heir to immense wealth, which, being entirely at his own control, surrounded him with a crowd of parasites and flatterers, whose fawning and constant attendance checked, at once, the scholar's progress. The mildness and affability of his manners, moreover, made him a great favorite at court, where the gentle but unfortunate Marie Antoinette took him under her special care. He became a page to the queen, and at the age of fifteen, in the year 1770, he was enrolled a member of the *Mousquitaires du Roi*, a body of soldiers whose particular duty it was to protect the person of the king, and which was composed solely of the descendants of the noblest families of France. Through the direct influence of the queen, he was promoted to the rank of a commissioned officer in this corps; and, though he says that his military services "only interrupted his studies on review days," it is evident that the alacrity and zest with which he was wont to engage in intellectual culture had already subsided under the pressure of engagements of quite a different nature.

He was fond of the social circle, but rarely joined in the frivolous amusements and trifling talk prevalent in the saloons of the metropolis He was habitually silent when discussion turned on topics which he thought unworthy attention; while yet his amiable manner made him a favorite, whenever his fine figure moved amid the thronged apartments of wealth and fashion.

His own conversational powers were of a high order, and their activity varied much with his moods — sometimes mild and winning, and again ardent and enthusiastic. In this he would resemble the musical rivulet moving to the measures of an inward melody; and then, perhaps the same hour, remind one of the rapid and sounding torrent dashing on in its wild and stirring march. When he spoke of liberty, or listened to a tale of oppression, his eye kindled with a glow, that disclosed the pure and intense flame on freedom's hidden altar. His soul, from earliest boyhood, was fired with the themes of human well-being, and despotic cruelty. While at Chavagnac, his delicate and sensitive frame would often tremble, and his lips quiver, to the agitation awakened by a contemplation of the destiny designed for a struggling race, and his pantings for an atmosphere untainted with the breath of tyranny. He uses the following language, long afterwards, to a friend:

"You ask me at what period I first experienced my ardent love for liberty and glory;—I recollect no time of life anterior to my enthusiasm for anecdotes of glorious deeds, and to my projects of traveling over the world to acquire fame. At eight years of age, my heart beat when I heard of an hyena that had done some injury, and caused still more alarm in our neighborhood, and the hope of meeting it was the object of all my walks. When I arrived at college, nothing ever interrupted my studies, except my ardent wish of studying without restraint. I never deserved to be chastised; but, in spite of my usual gentleness, it would have been dangerous to have attempted to do so. I recollect with pleasure that, when I was to describe in rhetoric a perfect courser, I sacrificed the hope of obtaining a prize, and described the one, who, on perceiving the whip, threw down his rider. Republican anecdotes always delighted me, and when my new connections wished to obtain for me a place at court, I did not hesitate displeasing them to preserve my independence." How plainly, in all this, is his character seen. The steed, gentle when well treated, but throwing his rider at sight of the whip, had spirit which chimed in well with that of the youthful *hater* of oppression.

In his seventeenth year* Lafayette was married. The object of his choice was first selected by him from considerations of family interest, but the marriage was consummated, as there is every reason to believe, with the purest affection. His lady was the Comptesse Anastasie de Noailles, daughter of the Duke d'Ayen ; and brought to his own, a heart full of virtue, courage, and conjugal affection. Her life is one of the brightest in the annals of female heroism, conspicuous alike for gentleness, disinterested devotion,

---

*April, 1774.

and patient endurance of every privation which attends deepest misfortunes. In the progress of this history, we shall have occasion to notice and admire her worth. She brought her husband a fortune, which together with his ample inheritance, gave him a revenue of 200,000 francs, or 37,500 dollars, per annum. But *she* was a richer treasure than it all. Lafayette gave abundant evidence that he cherished for her the highest esteem, and her character and history show that she reciprocated fully his affection. "At this period of his life, the Marquis de Lafayette was a man of commanding figure and pleasing features, notwithstanding his deep red hair. His forehead, though receding, was fine; his eyes clear hazel, and his mouth and chin delicately formed, exhibiting beauty rather than strength. The expression of his countenance was strongly indicative of a generous and gallant spirit, with an air of conscious greatness. His manners were frank and amiable—his movements light and graceful. Formed, both by nature and education, to be the ornament of a court, and already distinguished by his varied and attractive qualities in the circle of his noble acquaintance, his free principles were neither withered by the sunshine of royalty, nor weakened by flattery and temptation."

Amid the enjoyments of an effeminate court, and surrounded by all the delights of his newly made domestic alliance, Lafayette was dreaming of a very different future. Visions of military life, which were ever dancing before his mind, were painted in still more glowing colors by the camp-scenes through which he was wont to pass. He was a soldier by profession, but he had *chosen* the sword, and now carried it that he might wield it for the *right*, and not alone to blazon his own name with renown. A fire burned in his breast, and a lofty enthusiasm was there; and he longed for some opportunity to give scope to the inward flame — some arena on which he could stand and battle for the wants of the struggling millions. This became an absorbing theme of thought. To have quelled the mighty impulse would have wrecked the man, as truly as to still the throbbing heart forever would have left only a motionless and expressionless form. This desire to behold an uprising of the oppressed — a rending of fetters; and to hear the knell of despotism the world over, had deepened into a fixed purpose, ripening with his powers, and was now the very breath of his life. It had risen above all other passions, till it was now the guiding one of his being. He was waiting only for some brilliant opportunity in which he might re-realize his cherished dreams; and this was soon presented.

In the summer of 1776, he was stationed on military duty as an officer of the French army, in the citadel of Metz. It was the summer distinguished as the greatest modern epoch in the progress of humanity — the summer of the declaration of AMERICAN INDEPENDENCE. He was at this time but little more than eighteen, but, as we have before noticed, his maturity was far beyond his years. The Duke of Gloucester having been exiled from the court of Great

Britain on account of his impolitic marriage, was then at Metz. He was a brother of the King of England, and was constantly receiving advices relating to the progress of the opening struggle in America. The first tidings of the kind which he communicated to the French officers there, struck the key note to Lafayette's fiery ardor; and the more vividly the Duke described the plans of the British ministry to crush the efforts of the colonists, the more firmly settled in his breast became the plan, which he seems to have immediately formed, of going to their rescue. America fighting for its independence appealed strongly to his imagination, but America oppressed and likely to be crushed in the struggle, enlisted every sympathy of his heart. Throwing up his office at Metz, he returned to Paris. He knew that the earnest opposition of his family and friends would be brought to bear against his designs, but he had determined to throw himself into the struggle, and no human barrier could defeat the purpose. His first steps, however, were taken with great caution. With the utmost secrecy he made his inquiries and preparations, carefully concealing his intentions from the wife of his bosom and most of his intimate friends. At length he disclosed his determination to his relative the Count de Broglie, but received from him the strongest opposition. The Count pictured to him, in glowing terms, the difficulties and dangers of the undertaking, and endeavored by every means to dissuade him from the enterprise — "Your uncle perished in the wars in Italy," said he, "your father fell in the battle of

Minden, and now I will not be accessory to the ruin of the only remaining branch of the family.' Notwithstanding, Lafayette was not disheartened. The secretary of the Count, Mr. Duboismartin, entered at once into all his plans, and approved them. His position and skill enabled him to render the Marquis important aid, both in the way of advice and active assistance. Lafayette, not for a moment dissuaded from his romantic and perilous scheme by his interview with the Count de Broglie,* soon laid open all his plans to the Baron de Kalb, to whom he had been attracted by a kindred sympathy. The Baron's heart beat with the same enthusiasm which animated the young Marquis, and his love of liberty was equally ardent. De Kalb zealously seconded his design, and opened to him new methods for carrying it forward. Mr. Silas Deane, an agent sent out by the American Congress to negotiate with the French government, was at this time in Paris. To him De Kalb introduced the Marquis, and spread before him the generous offer of his personal service in the American war. Mr. Deane was at first unfavorably impressed with the boyish appearance of Lafayette, (he was at this time scarcely nineteen years of age,) but the earnestness with which the young volunteer pleaded his cause; the ardor which he manifested in the enterprize, and the probable effect which his departure would have throughout France in awakening a more intense sym-

---

* Lafayette afterwards states, that the Count withdrew his opposition after all his efforts to turn him from his project had proved in vain.

pathy with the American States overcame his first hesitation. A mutual agreement was made, and Lafayette left him with his youthful spirit bounding to the music of freedom's battle. The following paper, which he had obtained from Mr. Dean, was to him a richer treasure than his ancestral domain. It was given in virtue of Lafayette's stipulation to depart as early as circumstances should permit, and engage personally in the struggle for the Independence of the United States.

"The desire which the Marquis de Lafayette shows of serving among the troops of the United States of North America, and the interest which he takes in the justice of their cause, make him wish to distinguish himself in this war, and to render himself as useful as he possibly can. But not thinking that he can obtain leave of his family to pass the seas and to serve in a foreign country, till he can go as a general officer, I have thought that I could not better serve my country, and those who have entrusted me, than by granting to him, in the name of the very honorable Congress, the rank of Major-General, which I beg the states to confirm and ratify to him, and to deliver him the commission to hold and take rank from this day with the general officers of the same degree. His high birth, his alliances, the great dignities which his family hold at this court, his considerable estates in this realm, his personal merit, his reputation, his disinterestedness, and above all, his zeal for the liberty of our provinces, are such as to induce me alone to promise him the rank of Major-

General in the name of the United States. In witness of which I have signed the present this 7th day of December, 1776.

SILAS DEANE."

"The secrecy," says Lafayette, "with which this negotiation and my preparations were made, appears almost a miracle; family, friends, ministers, French spies and English spies, all were kept completely in the dark as to my intentions."

In the midst of his preparations, unforeseen difficulties arose. A ship was fitting out in which he was to take his departure, when news of disastrous defeats in the revolutionary army reached France. Hearts throbbing with hope were hushed at the tidings of these sad reverses on the field of conflict for liberty. The intelligence which flew across the Atlantic and made the bells of London ring for joy, fell like a funeral knell upon many a circle in Paris and other parts of the kingdom. The court of Versailles had not yet openly espoused the American cause, but Louis XVI was looking upon the struggle with anxious eye, and discerning politicians were already predicting that France would soon be joined in fraternal league with the United States, against England. Dr. Franklin had joined Mr. Deane at Paris, with more definite instructions, and both, though not publicly acknowledged, were yet secretly received by the king; and while they were assured of his approval of the revolution, they also had reason to believe that he would soon openly espouse it. In receiving the American agents, and giving them encouragement of future assistance, Louis XVI did not see the mine which he was laying deep beneath his own feet and the Bourbon throne. His ministers clearly saw that the American declaration was no less hostile to the principals of the French, than to those of the English monarchy; but their arguments and persuasions with the king, were unavailing before the strong representations of Dr. Franklin, and the cherished desire to humble the pride of his hereditary foe. He was on the point of an official proclamation of the Independence of the thirteen colonies, and just ready to unsheath the sword in their behalf, when their sudden misfortunes reached his ear. He paused awhile to wait the issue of the fearful crisis. The aspect of affairs in the new world was indeed gloomy. The battle of Brooklyn had been fought, resulting in the total route of the continental forces, and the evacuation of Long Island. New York, after a desperate resistance, had been given up to the British. General Howe was master of Forts Washington and Lee. The heroic army was fast becoming disbanded; the militia throwing down their arms, and returning home in despair. General Washington with the remnant who remained, ill clothed and scantily fed, was retreating before the British, through a desponding country. It was rumored in France that thousands were daily flocking to avail themselves of the pardon which Lord Howe had offered to the rebels; and though Washington was still unyielding, yet the last reasonable hope of liberty had well-nigh expired. So dark were the prospects, that the American commissioners at Paris ceased for a time from their representations to the king, and even urged Lafayette to abandon his project of enlisting in their service. They told him that the late unhappy news had so deranged their affairs, that they could not now offer him even a passage to America, nor assure him of any ground of success should he be able to go. They had, however, mistaken their man. Lafayette was not yet known. With a generosity which has no parallel, he replied to their attempts to dissuade him from the enterprise, by assuring them that if their country was indeed reduced to such an extremity, that was the very hour when his embarking to join her armies would render the most essential aid. "I thank you for your frankness," said he, "but now is precisely the moment to serve your cause; the more people are discouraged, the greater utility will result from my departure. Until now you have only seen my ardor in your cause, but that may not prove at present wholly useless. If you cannot furnish me with a vessel, I will purchase one and freight it at my own expense, to convey your despatches and my person to the shores of America."

Neither of the three* commissioners was prepared for this noble offer. They had supposed that the Marquis, in common with others who had gone from Europe to enlist in the American struggle, was actuated more by youthful impulses and a passion for adventure

---

* Arthur Lee was the third commissioner.

or military glory, than by any genuine sympathy with an oppressed people panting for freedom. But a romantic zeal, or love of excitement, would have given way before the difficulties which now tried the spirit of Lafayette. With unbending resolution he instantly set himself at work, to carry out his proposal. From his own estates he raised the money necessary for the expedition, and without delay prepared to purchase and equip a vessel for his use. His preparations were necessarily matured with the utmost privacy, so as to escape the vigilance of his domestic circle, the French government, and English spies. He was fully aware of the resistance with which he would meet if his plans became known, and therefore kept them almost wholly within his own breast. British jealousy had been aroused by the assistance which France rendered to the colonies, and Lord Stormont strongly represented the case to Louis. The king, owing to the recent reverses in America, began to distrust the expediency of an open alliance, and to make some demonstrations against the interest awakened in behalf of transatlantic freedom. Lafayette, being suspected, was constantly under the espionage of his own and a foreign government, but the same calm forethought which he afterwards displayed upon the field of battle, was manifested during the progress of this, his conflict with unseen foes. With heroic fortitude he pressed on, surmounting each obstacle as it arose, looking as tranquilly upon the difficulties that environed him at home, and the dangers awaiting him abroad, as one would gaze upon the quiet sea, or watch the bright clouds as they wandered over a summer sky.

To his wife, whom he tenderly loved, Lafayette revealed nothing of his plans. He knew perfectly her affection, and that the delicate situation in which she was placed would increase her unwillingness to bear the separation. This latter circumstance especially affected him. But his mind was fully decided, and he bowed to the necessity which seemed laid upon him. He knew that she would bear the stroke better, should it come when no power could avert it, than if she were for a long time to see the impending doom. To escape her knowledge and the surveillance of royalty, his ship was purchased and preparations made for his departure through his friend Mr. Duboismartin, the secretary of the Count de Broglie. Lafayette controlled every thing, but the secretary was the visible channel through which all his directions flowed.

In the midst of his preparations, the French government wished to send Lafayette on a diplomatic mission to London. His associate was the Prince de Poix, and though the journey, occurring at this time, was eminently distasteful to him, he was aware that it would only excite suspicion to refuse, and accordingly submitted to the journey with as much suavity as he could command. Dr. Franklin, who clearly saw the difficulties which the Marquis would encounter, should his contemplated sailing for America become known to the government, advised his visit to London, in the hope that this would divert the inquiries which he knew were constantly and busily made in reference to all his operations.

More from this consideration than any other, Lafayette went. His rank gained him attention at once, at the court of St. James; but on reaching London, before paying his respects to the British Majesty, he sought an interview with Bancroft, *the American.* The distinction with which he was received by the nobility, and his flattering reception at court, did not change his sentiments at all respecting the struggle between England and her colonies. His design of enlisting personally in the strife was concealed, but his opinions were openly avowed. He expressed them even at the house of Lord Germain, who was minister for the colonial domain; and while at Lord Rawdon's, who had just returned from New York, he signified his joy at the news of the victory at Trenton. Offers were made him to visit the sea ports, and inspect the vessels which were fitting out against the *rebels*, but all these invitations were invariably refused. His stay in London was short, for his restless spirit was anxious to get back to Paris and superintend his movements there. "At the end of three weeks," he writes, "when it became necessary for me to return home, while refusing to accompany my uncle, the ambassador to court, I confided to him my strong desire to take a trip to Paris. He proposed saying that I was ill during my absence. I should not have made use of this stratagem myself, but did not object to his doing so."

Hastening back thus early to the capital, concealment was necessary, lest his sudden return should give rise to unwelcome suspicions. Repairing to the house of the Baron de Kalb, he spent three days in secret interviews with Americans and a few of his friends, in whom he could confide. The confinement and the restraint under which he felt himself placed in these circumstances, were irksome to his bold and frank nature, which could work at daylight in the very face of danger, generally with far greater success, and always with far more ease, than when engaged in secret intrigue, and desirous to escape the observation of all. Through one of his agents, a ship had been bought, and was now in progress of equipment for him at Bordeaux. Unwilling to trust the whole management of it to others, and anxious to see the progress made, he hastily left Paris and set out for that city. His scheme, however, began to be known. It was impossible that the extensive outfit which he was actively making, should for a long time escape the observation of spies with whom he was surrounded. It is probable that the vigilance with which he was watched had already detected his absence from London, and conjectured, if it had not learned with certainty, his return. There is reason to believe that this was immediately laid before Louis by the English ambassador, together with an earnest remonstrance against the plan of Lafayette, the outline of which was disclosed. It is, at least, certain that information was communicated to the court of Versailles, and representations made to the king, which led to an order for the arrest of Lafayette, soon after he had reached Bordeaux. Tidings of this were at once communicated to the Marquis, and, flying from France to Spain, he resolved to complete his arrangements at Passage,* and to embark for America from that port. Disguise was now at an end. He openly avowed his intentions, as well as his purpose that no mortal power should prevent their accomplishment.

At Passage his firmness was put to the severest test. Letters arrived from his family, which were not only urgent in their entreaties for him to remain, but violent in their denunciations of his project. He was reproached for his want of parental care, and even taunted for faithlessness to her whom he had sworn to love. This was a terrible trial to his sensitive spirit, but he resolutely bore it. The Countess Anastasie was tenderly beloved by him, and it was his bitterest struggle to tear himself from her without a parting adieu. To be charged with want of affection, when it was burning intensely on its secret altar, was subduing; but he endured this, and more. Letters came, under kingly authority, peremptorily forbidding his embarkation for the new world. Louis signified his highest displeasure should he disobey this order; and Lafayette well knew the meaning of the threat. Disobedience to the commands of his sovereign was, for one in his position, no trivial affair. It made him liable to the confiscation of all his immense estates, and subjected him to outlawry and

* A Spanish port.

disgrace. Should he persevere, he might land on a foreign shore penniless and forsaken, under a monarch's frown, and with nothing but his sword to aid the cause which he had so zealously espoused. Nothing, however, could daunt him, or change his indomitable will. Feigning obedience, for the purpose of seeking a more favorable opportunity for weighing anchor, he returned to Bordeaux, and wrote to the ministry, asking leave to consummate his plans. He frankly owned their nature and design, but plead as a reason why he should be allowed to go, the benefit which would accrue to France could the pride of England be humbled by wresting the transatlantic possessions from her hand. Cogent as these reasons were, and deedply as they were felt, the king was not then willing to afford the slightest umbrage to his powerful rival, and accordingly the petition of Lafayette was refused. This he learned through a friend, as no direct answer was ever sent. At Bordeaux he received orders to proceed to Marseilles and join himself to the Duke d'Ayen who was going into Italy. Upon pretence of obeying he set off from Bordeaux; but instead of taking the road to Marseilles, passed directly southward to Bayonne. His steps were closely watched, and before he had proceeded many hours, he found that pursuers were on the track. Changing his dress for that of a courier, and concealing himself in a stable while the coach in which he was traveling stopped at Bayonne, he hoped to elude detection. He had the start of the messengers, and could easily distance them. At St. Jean de Luz, a village near the boundary line of France and Spain, he was recognized by one who observed him while on his previous tour from Passage to Bordeaux. It was a woman, however, and a single sign from Lafayette for her to keep silent, made the secret safe. He reached Passage in safety, found his vessel in readiness, and March 26th, 1777, with sails outspread, the prow of his gallant Victory was turned toward the strand hallowed by the footsteps of freedom. By way of signifying his disapprobation, Louis XVI immediately granted permission to a Major General in the French army,* to offer his services to the king of Great Britain to assist in subduing his rebellious subjects. Despatches were instantly sent to the national forces at the West Indies to arrest Lafayette, should his vessel, as was expected, stop there on its way. The sagacity of the Marquis was, however, equal to the emergency. Suspecting that he might be detained should he touch at the Islands, as soon as he got fairly to sea, he ordered the captain to steer directly for the American coast. This officer at first refused, but the Marquis was peremptory and unyielding, and the course of the vessel was accordingly changed. The voyage was long and tedious. The ship was heavy, and its slow sailing and rolling motion soon added sea sickness to the trials of the young soldier. Recovering, he addresses the following letter to his wife, which, as it breathes the language of affection, will be interesting to the reader:

---

* The Count de Bulkely.

"On board the Victory, May 30, 1777.

* * "How many fears and anxieties enhance the keen anguish I feel at being separated from all that I love most fondly in the world! How have you borne my second departure? Have you loved me less? Have you pardoned me? Have you reflected that, at all events, I must equally have been parted from you — wandering about in Italy, dragging on an inglorious life, surrounded by the persons most opposed to my projects and to my manner of thinking? All these reflections, did not prevent me from experiencing the most bitter grief when the moment arrived for quitting my native shore. Your sorrow, and that of my friends, all rushed upon my thoughts, and my heart was torn by a thousand painful feelings. I could not, at that instant, find any excuse for my own conduct. If you could know all that I have suffered, and the melancholy days that I have passed, while thus flying from all that I love best in the world! Must I join to this affliction the grief of hearing that you do not pardon me? I should, in truth, my love, be too unhappy."

His ardor for liberty, is well exemplified in the following extract from another letter, dated

"On board the Victory, June 7th.

"I am still floating upon this dreary plain, the most wearisome of all human habitations. To console myself a little, I think of you and of my friends. I think of the pleasure of seeing you again. How delightful will be the moment of my arrival! I shall hasten to surprise and embrace you. I shall, perhaps, find you with your children. To think, only, of that happy moment is an inexpressible pleasure to me; — do not fancy that it is distant; — although the time of my absence will appear, I own, very long to me, yet, we shall meet sooner than you can expect. While defending the liberty I adore, I shall enjoy perfect freedom myself; I but offer my services to that interesting Republic from motives of the purest kind, unmixed with ambition or private views; her happiness and my glory are my only incentives to the task. I hope, that for my sake, you will become a good American, for that feeling is worthy of every noble heart. The happiness of America is intimately connected with the happiness of all mankind. She will become the safe and respected asylum of virtue, integrity, toleration, equality, and tranquil happiness."

After a tedious voyage of almost two months in duration, the Victory came in sight of the American shores. A thrill of unspeakable emotion passed over the frame of the heroic stranger, as the long, low, sand-plains of the eastern coast of South Carolina, spread away before his vision. This was the land, towards which all the earnest yearnings of his soul had gone forth; over which hung his most radiant hopes and anticipations. What fortunes awaited him there; — what reception would he meet; — what were now the prospects of the glorious conflict, upon whose triumph he had staked his all; — what would be his fate; — should he fall early in battle, or live to see the victorious issue of the struggle, and go back to France, himself covered with glory, and bearing in his heart the gratitude of a free people, for his timely aid in breaking their fetters? These, and similar inquiries thronged his mind; but all vanished before the rapture of his arrival. He landed at Winyau Bay, about sixty miles northeast from Charleston, on the 14th of June, 1777

CHAPTER II.

LAFAYETTE IN AMERICA—RECEPTION—VISITS CHARLESTON—LETTER TO HIS WIFE—PROCEEDS NORTHWARD TO PHILADELPHIA—HIS RECEPTION THERE—DISTRUST OF CONGRESS—RESOLUTIONS PASSED—LAFAYETTE MEETS WASHINGTON—FRIENDSHIP OF THE TWO—DARK PROSPECTS OF THE REVOLUTION—BATTLE OF BRANDYWINE—HEROIC CONDUCT OF LAFAYETTE—IS WOUNDED—AT BETHLEHEM—LETTERS—AGAIN AT CAMP—ACCOMPANIES GEN. GREENE TO NEW JERSEY—ENGAGEMENT AT GLOUCESTER—LAFAYETTE IS APPOINTED TO A COMMAND—WINTER QUARTERS AT VALLEY FORGE—THE CONWAY CABAL—EXPEDITION AGAINST CANADA—LAFAYETTE RETURNS TO VALLEY FORGE.

LAFAYETTE and the Baron de Kalb, who accompanied him, stepping on liberty's soil mutually swore to conquer, or die in the contest upon which they were entering. It was midnight when the canoe, which had conveyed them from the ship to the landing place up the bay, rested on the silent beach. The Marquis was in high spirits, now that he was fairly across the monotonous sea; and he could look confidently forward to the fruition of his hopes. Beneath that midnight sky, with the stars looking calmly down upon him, and the land he had come to defend slumbering at his feet, the patriotic self-devotion of the young adventurer was a romantic and beautiful beginning of a brilliant career. At the house of Major Benjamin Huger* he met with a hearty welcome, and received all the attention which generous hospitality, and a due appreciation of his

* This officer fell, covered with wounds, during Provost's invasion.

magnanimity, could bestow. Lafayette was charmed with every thing that he saw about him. "The novelty of all that surrounded him the next morning when he awoke — the room, the bed covered with mosquito nets, the black servants who came to ask his commands, the beauty and foreign aspect of the country which he beheld from his windows, and which was covered with a rich vegetation, all united to produce on his mind a magical effect, and excite in him a variety of inexpressible emotions."

Remaining but a short time amid the pleasures of this attractive retreat, he set out for Charleston, to make arrangements for the return of his vessel to France, before he should go northward to Philadelphia. He here met with General Moultrie, and was so delighted with his recent gallant defence of the fort on Sullivan's island, that he at once presented him with clothing, arms, and accoutrements, for one hundred men. From Charleston he writes to his wife, dated June 19th.

"I landed at Charleston, after having sailed for several days along a coast swarming with hostile vessels. On my arrival here, every one told me that my ship must undoubtedly be taken, because two English frigates had blockaded the harbor. I even sent, both by land and by sea, orders to the captain to put the men on shore, and burn the vessel, if he had still the power of doing so. *Eh bien!* by a most extraordinary piece of good fortune, a sudden gale of wind having blown away the frigates for a short time, my vessel arrived at noon-day, without having encountered friend or foe. At Charleston I have met with General Howe, a general officer, now engaged in service. The governor of the state is expected this evening from the country. All the persons with whom I wished to be acquainted, have shown me the greatest attention and politeness, (not European politeness merely.) I can only feel gratitude for the reception I have met with, although I have not yet thought proper to enter into any detail respecting my future prospects and arrangements. I wish to see the Congress first. I hope to set out in two days for Philadelphia, which is a land journey of more than two hundred and fifty leagues. We shall divide into small parties. I have already purchased horses and light carriages for this purpose.

"I shall now speak to you, my love, about the country and its inhabitants, who are as agreeable as my enthusiasm had led me to imagine. Simplicity of manner, kindness of heart, love of country and of liberty, and a delightful state of equality, are met with universally. The richest and the poorest man are completely on a level ; and although there are some immense fortunes in this country, I may challenge any one to point out the slightest difference in their respective manner toward each other. I first saw and judged of a country life at Major Huger's house. I am at present in this city, where every thing somewhat resembles the English customs, ex cept that you find more simplicity here than you would do in England. Charleston is one of the best built, handsomest, and most agreeable cities that I have ever seen. The American women are very pretty, and have great simplicity of character. The extreme neatness of their appearance is truly delightful. Cleanliness is every where even more studiously attended to here than in England. What gave me most pleasure is to see how completely the citizens are all brethren of one family. In America there are none poor, and none even that can be called peasants. Each citizen has some property, and all citizens have the same rights as the richest individual or landed proprietor in the country. The inns are very different from those in Europe ; the host and hostess sit at the table with you, and do the honors of a comfortable meal, and when you depart, you pay your bill without being obliged to tax it. If you should dislike going to inns, you may always find country houses, in which you will be received, as a good American, with the same attention that you might expect to find at a friend's house in Europe.

"My own reception has been most peculiarly agreeable. To have been merely my traveling companion suffices to secure the kindest welcome. I have just passed five hours at a large dinner, given in compliment to me by an individual of this town. Generals Howe and Moultrie, and several officers of my suite, were present. We drank each others' health, and endeavored to talk English, which I am beginning to speak a little. I shall pay a visit to-morrow, with these gentlemen, to the governor of the state, and make the last arrangements for my departure. The next day, the commanding officer here will take me to see the town and its environs, and I shall then set out to join the army.

"From the agreeable life I lead in this country, from the sympathy which makes me feel as much at ease with the inhabitants as if I had known them twenty years, the similarity between their manner of thinking and my own, my love of glory and of liberty, you might imagine that I am very happy; but you are not with me, my dearest love; my friends are not with me; and there is no happiness for me when far from you and them. I often ask you if you still love; but I put that question still more often to myself, and my heart ever answers yes;—I trust that my heart does not deceive me. I am inexpressibly anxious to hear from you, and hope to find some letters at Philadelphia. My only fear is, lest the privateer which was to bring them to me, may have been captured on her way. Although, I can easily imagine that I have excited the special displeasure of the English, by taking the liberty of coming hither in spite of them, and landing before their very face, yet, I must confess that we shall be even more than on a par if they have succeeded in catching that vessel, the object of my fondest hopes, by which I am expecting to receive your letters. I entreat you to send me both long and frequent letters. You are not sufficiently conscious of the joy with which I shall receive them. Embrace, most tenderly, my Henriette; may I add, embrace our children? The father of those poor children is a wanderer, but he is, nevetheless, a good, honest man—a good father, warmly attached to his family, and a good husband, also, for he loves his wife most tenderly. The night is far advanced, the heat intense, and I am devoured by gnats; but the best countries, as you perceive, have their inconveniences. Adieu, my love, adieu."

This letter is full of interest. It adds a fresh coloring to the character of its author; all the exciting circumstances attending his advent on a new continent, did not create forgetfulness of the duties home-affections imposed. Upon the same altar glowed conjugal and parental love, with the deepest devotion to a bleeding and ravaged country. The manner in which he speaks of the equality of American society, and his delight in contemplating a country without *peasantry*, show that aristocratic prejudices of rank and titles were entirely in abeyance to an expansive and unrivaled philanthropy. In all his intercourse with others, he was ready to forget himself and his position, and be one of the plain people by whom he was surrounded. But he longed for the stirring scenes of the battle-field. His delay at Charleston was wearisome to him. Though at a great distance from the seat of war, he caught up every rumor and vague report, with his eye kindling like the eagle's, when, imprisoned, he hears from afar the cry of his fellow. Young in years, he was yet mature in every point of character. He astonished ordinary men no more, by his adherence to the doubtful fortunes of freedom, than he did veteran soldiers by the sagacity and breadth of his views. Here, as ever, he won the admiration, respect, and love, of all who came within the atmosphere of his magical presence. As soon as practicable, leaving Charleston, Lafayette was on his way to Philadelphia. The travel was exhausting, though he hardly knew it in the fine excitement his enterprize awakened. In our day, railroads and steam boats make this passage a pleasant excursion. Then, the roads were new and bad, the weather often unfavorable, and every outward circumstance contributed to make the journey toilsome and discouraging. In a letter to his wife, written at Petersburgh, Va., July 17th, 1777, he says:—"I am now eight days' journey from Philadelphia, in the beautiful state of Virginia. All fatigue is over, and I fear that my martial labors will be very light if it be true that General Howe has left New York, to go, I know not whither. But all the accounts I receive are so uncertain, that I cannot form any fixed opinion until I reach my destination.

"You must have learned the particulars of the commencement of my journey. You know that I set out in a brilliant manner, in a carriage, and I must now tell you that we are all on horseback—having broken the carriage according to my usual praiseworthy custom—and I hope soon to write to you that we have arrived on foot. The journey is somewhat fatiguing; but, although several of my comrades have suffered a great deal, I have scarcely, myself, been conscious of fatigue. The captain who takes charge of this letter will, perhaps, pay you a visit. I beg you, in that case, to receive him with great kindness.

"The farther I advance to the north, the better pleased am I with the country and its inhabitants.

There is no attention or kindness that I do not receive, although many scarcely know who I am. But I will write all this to you more in detail from Philadelphia."

Congress was now in session at Philadelphia; and immediately upon his arrival, Lafayette presented himself before it. The time was in many respects inauspicious. A crowd of foreign adventurers who had made the same stipulations with Mr. Deane as himself, had recently been importuning that body to fulfill the agreements which their minister at Paris had rashly made. Many of those whom Mr. Deane had sent over came simply to follow their profession, without the slightest regard to the right of the cause in which they were to take up arms. It was with them, simply a *quid pro quo*. They gave a certain amount of service, for which they were to receive a certain amount of pay, and degree of rank in the army. If this were done, they had no farther concern. Many of them would have as soon drawn the sword for the enemy, provided they could have expected an equal return for their employment. We would not, however, in this list, include all the foreigners who contributed so materially by their military skill and aid to final victory. Many of them were brave men and true—who bitterly hated oppression. These will always be remembered with gratitude, while those who fought from mercenary motives or love of glory, will be forgotten. Congress thus embarrassed from the numerous applications already received, was unprepared for farther solicitation.

Much dissatisfaction was felt towards Mr. Deane for encouraging expectations which could not be realized. Many American officers began to express discontent at seeing themselves suddenly superseded in rank by their foreign allies. So many were the complaints, and manifold the difficulties, that the legislative assembly had almost come to the determination not to receive farther requests of the kind; and when Lafayette appeared he was treated with coolness, which amounted well nigh to neglect. The young Marquis, who had been hailed with joy upon his arrival, and treated with unbounded respect until now, could not have anticipated a change so marked, and undesignedly cruel. Here was displayed anew that moral heroism, which shone in every hour of trial. Having laid his stipulations with Mr. Deane before Congress, with the confidence of unsullied motives, he learned from the Chairman of the Committee on Foreign Affairs, that owing to such circumstances as we have detailed above, there was little hope that his request would be granted. Seizing a pen, he immediately directed to Congress the following brief but *meaning* note:

"After the sacrifices I have made, I have a right to exact two favors: — one is, to serve at my own expense — the other is, to serve as a volunteer."

Such a note, in beautiful contrast with the proud demands of many who had lately claimed appointments, was an affecting surprise. It disclosed the man — assured them he was a benefactor, whose offers should not be lightly esteemed. They soon learned his worth, and, with astonishment, the generous sacrifices he had made. Accordingly, upon the 31st of July, 1777, they passed the following preamble and resolution :

"WHEREAS, The Marquis de Lafayette, out of his great zeal in the cause of liberty in which the United States are engaged, has left his family and connexions, and, at his own expense, come over to offer his service to the United States, without pension or particular allowance, and is anxious to risk his life in our cause ;

"RESOLVED, That his services be accepted, and that in consideration of his zeal, illustrious family and connexions, he have the rank and commission of a Major-General in the army of the United States."

On the 1st of August, Lafayette was presented to Washington. The tide of war seemed now to be moving towards Philadelphia, and the Commander-in-Chief had left Germantown, that he might place the city in a posture of defence. The majestic figure, the noble deportment and affability of manners which characterized Washington, won the whole soul of Lafayette. A kindred chord seemed to vibrate in each heart, as for the first time they met, and exchanged their salutations. Lafayette felt an unbounded veneration, while he stood in the presence of THE MAN OF THE AGE. Washington's sympathies were drawn instantly and intensely towards the young hero, whose whole being was swayed by an impulse and purpose similar to his own. There was, in a sublime sense, a mutual *recognition;* and around the willing hearts of both was woven then, that tie of friendship which afterwards became a band, that death only could sever. It was a dinner party that opened this acquaintance. "When the company were about to separate, Washington took Lafayette aside, spoke to him very kindly, complimented him on the noble spirit he had shown, and the sacrifices he had made in favor of the American cause, and then told him, that he should be pleased if he would make the head quarters of the Commander-in-Chief his home, establish himself there whenever he thought proper, and consider himself at all times as one of his family; adding, in a tone of pleasantry, that he could not promise him the luxuries of a court, or even the conveniences which his former habits might have rendered essential to comfort; — but since he had become an American soldier, he would doubtless contrive to accommodate himself to the character he had assumed, and submit with a good grace to the customs, manners and privations of the republican army." This invitation was accepted with eagerness by the Marquis, and was never afterwards revoked by the Commander-in-Chief. Lafayette placed himself under his care and tuition, and owned himself the adopted son of Washington. With all the fire of youth, and all the enthusiasm of his nature, he attached himself to the unrivaled chieftain.

It was now a critical period in the revolutionary movement. Disasters had been numerous, and victories few; many, who at the beginning, met firmly the shock of the foe, were becoming disheartened and despairing.

Discontent in open murmurs spread through the camp, and the half-clad and famished militia, in great numbers, disbanding, returned to their homes. The brilliant success at Trenton had revived for a while the drooping courage of the nation, but it was only for a deeper depression. The British forces were mustering with renewed energy for a decisive onset, anticipating in the present campaign a consummation of their work — and, with the stripes and stars trailing in the dust, they confidently hoped to see their royal standard waving over a submissive people. The cantonments of the main body of the English host, while in winter quarters, stretched in a vast chain from the river Raritan on the North, to the banks of the Delaware on the South. Rhode Island had yielded with little opposition. A strong detachment under the savage Tryon, had overrun with a terrifically desolating march, the whole southern section of Connecticut. New York city and Long Island were conquered, and among the spoils of the exulting enemy. In addition, many distinguished citizens of Pennsylvania and the Jerseys, had made overtures for a voluntary submission. A panic consequently was felt throughout the country, and the beacon light of freedom shone with a fading and uncertain radiance upon the troubled deep of oppressed humanity. For hardly a station which the Americans occupied, from Ticonderoga to Charleston, was free from peril. But the most appalling danger was the jealousies and machinations against the Commander-in-Chief. A strong faction was forming; the envy and hate which are always cherished by little souls against the great, were burning towards him. Gates was plotting for the supreme command, and as it afterwards transpired, there were many in his interest of those who had high rank, both in the army and in the state. Of all these difficulties Lafayette gradually became aware, but looked upon them calmly and undismayed. America shall conquer, and Washington rise proudly above conspiracy, was a resolve that never wavered, amid the thickest perils with which he was afterwards environed.

No apprehensions being entertained of an immediate attack on Philadelphia, Washington took Lafayette with him to the camp. The General soon found in his young *protege* a hero of no ordinary stamina. His generous devotion, the wisdom and scope of his plans, became daily more apparent. The commission which he had received from Congress was, as yet, only an honorary one, conferring upon him no real command. This was a source of much embarrassment to Washington, as well as to the Marquis. Lafayette felt that he was young and inexperienced, and had not the boldness to ask outright to be invested with the active duties of his commission, but while stating his incapacities to Washington, he at the same time took occasion to hint that as soon as he should be deemed fit for the command of a division, he would be ready to enter upon the duties of it. Washington accordingly wrote to Congress upon the subject, but received in return the intelligence, that the commission given to the Marquis de Lafayette, was only honorary, and that he could not yet receive an appointment. He manifested no displeasure at this result, but patiently waited for the time, when he could earn his rank, and claim it by virtue of his own services.

On the 11th of September, 1777, was fought the battle of Brandywine. The British fleet under Sir William Howe, whose movements along the American coast, at one time seeming to threaten Philadelphia, and at another appearing to meditate an attack upon Charleston, had caused much apprehension and doubt, had, at last, entered the Chesapeake; and, having proceeded up the Elk river as far as it was safely navigable, landed the forces at the ferry on the 25th of August. The determination of an assault upon Philadelphia was no longer questionable. The same army had in vain attempted to reach the city by land across the Jerseys, a few months before. With eighteen thousand men, in good health and spirits, admirably supplied with all the implements of war, and led on by the ablest officers, the hopes of the invading army were high of a splendid victory. The day before Sir William Howe landed, General Washington, to inspire the citizens with confidence, paraded his troops through the streets of Philadelphia, and then proceeded boldly to the Brandywine. The popular clamor, favored by the voice of Congress, demanded a battle, and he determined to risk one, though without many probabilities on which his judgment could base a hope of success. With not over eleven thousand troops, and these miserably clothed and fed, with their spirits depressed by the recent calamities and present darkening prospects, Washington greatly apprehended that he could not successfully compete with the strength of the battalions marching against him. The wisdom of his course, when viewed in the light in which it should be regarded, is, however, unquestionable. In the present condition of affairs, defeat was better than inaction. A battle was demanded by the public feeling, and, though disastrous, would be less injurious than to suffer the enemy to advance to Philadelphia without opposition.

Washington, having halted for a few days on the banks of the Brandywine, to refresh his troops, and get a better knowledge of the face of the country and the plans of the enemy, sent forward two divisions under Greene and Stephen, who proceeded nearer to the head of the Elk, and encamped behind White Clay Creek. Three miles farther on, at Iron Hill, was stationed General Maxwell, at the head of an effective corps of light infantry, formed from a regiment of Morgan's riflemen, which had been detached to the northern army. Posting the cavalry along the lines, Washington, with the main body, crossed the Brandywine, and took up his position behind Red Clay Creek, on the road which Sir William Howe would have to traverse on his march to Philadelphia. Lafayette was with him, and watched with the liveliest interest, the preparations for the approaching contest. These were made with consummate adroitness and prudence, but Sir William Howe was no common foe; and the direction which he seemed contemplating for his vastly superior force, decided Washington that a change of his own position was necessary. A council of war was held on the night of the 9th of September, when it was determined to retire behind the Brandywine, and meet the enemy near Chadd's Ford, from the heights which ranged along upon the opposite side of the river. Lafayette says in one of his papers, that a letter from Congress had secured this position, although it had hardly been examined by the American troops. It was in many respects favorable, though the difficulty and ineligibility of undertaking to dispute the passage of a river by fronting the enemy on the opposite side, has been generally insisted upon by writers on the art of war.* Foreigners have blamed Washington for taking this ground, and engaging in battle with his small army. Their error consists not that they misapply their military tactics, but that they do not rightly judge of the circumstances under which Washington was placed. Congress required that the enemy should be fought, and the country could not have been satisfied without a conflict.

On the morning of the 11th of September, soon after day break, Lafayette sprang to his feet at the intelligence, that the whole British army was in motion, and advancing towards them on the direct road

* The Marquis de Feuquiere says: "It is impossible to guard the shores of a river when the ground to be guarded is of a great extent, because the assailant, pointing his efforts to several places, for the purpose of separating the forces of his adversary, and to draw his attention to spots very distant from each other, at length determining to make his effort at the point where he finds the least ability to resist, always prevails over the labors and vigilance of his enemy, more especially when he employs the night for the execution of his enterprise, that being most favorable for concealing the place of his principal effort."

leading over Chadd's Ford. General Maxwell had been advantageously stationed, so that he could command this road from the hills, on the south side of the river; and the first action accordingly began with him. The foe advanced in two magnificent columns, the right commanded by General Knyphausen, and the left by Lord Cornwallis. The plan of Howe was, that Knyphausen's division should occupy the attention of the Americans, by making repeated feints of attempting the passage of the ford, while Cornwallis should make a long sweep up the river, and cross it at Birmingham. Knyphausen accordingly advanced with his column, and speedily dislodging General Maxwell from his post, forced him to cross over, though with but little loss. A furious cannonading was instantly begun, and other demonstrations made, which indicated the intention of the British immediately to attempt the passage of the Ford. The day was occupied in preventing this, till eleven o'clock in the morning, when the movement of Cornwallis was first announced to Washington. A smile of delight played upon his countenance, and he immediately determined upon one of those bold, but judicious plans, for which he was remarkable. Placing himself at the head of the center and left wing of the army, he resolved to cross the river in person, and overwhelm Knyphausen before Cornwallis could be summoned back to his aid. His ranks were already formed for the passage, and his troops had answered to the proposition with deafening shouts, when a messenger arrived with the intelligence, that

Cornwallis had only made a feint of crossing the fords above, and was now actually bringing his division down the southern side of the river, to re-unite with Knyphausen. The tidings were agony to Washington; though false, they came in a form which constrained him to believe them true, and his bold project was accordingly abandoned. His troops were impatient for the encounter, but for two hours he could only give them quiet directions, while he endeavored, in distressing suspense, to gain some clue to the movements of the enemy on the opposite side. At about two o'clock in the afternoon, his uncertainty was removed, when the certain intelligence reached him, that Lord Cornwallis, after having made a circuit of nearly seventeen miles, had forded the river above its forks, and, accompanied by Sir William Howe, was advancing upon him. Close action was immediately prepared for, and all along the American lines ran the accents of welcome for the conflict. The three divisions which formed the right wing, under Generals Sullivan, Stirling, and Stephens, were detached, and, moving up the Brandywine, fronted the British column marching down the river. Selecting an advantageous piece of ground near Birmingham, with the river on their left, and, having both flanks covered by a thick wood, they hastily formed, and awaited the attack.

Lafayette, who had kept by the side of Washington during these scenes, and marked them with absorbing interest, soon saw that the divisions designed to meet Cornwallis, were to receive most of the heavy blows of that day's battle, and petitioned and obtained permission to join them. A burst of enthusiasm greeted his arrival, as he threw himself into the midst of the troops, eagerly waiting the approach of the foe. The opportunity which he sought was not wanting long. The host was visible, sweeping in grand and imposing array over the plain before them. When he saw the enemy, Lord Cornwallis formed in the finest order, and hastening forward, his first line opened a brisk fire of musketry and artillery upon them. It was about half past four when the battle began. The Americans returned the fire with great injury, but the impetuosity with which the English and Hessian troops threw themselves upon their ranks, was more than they could withstand. For a time, both parties fought with unparalleled bravery, and the carnage was terrible. Above the shrill notes of "death's music," and louder than the roar of combat, rose the wild shout of living men. The maddening exultation and the groans, terrible imprecations and shrieks of the fallen in their last anguish, were mingled in a horrid chorus, which might have made angels grieve, and the Demon of War ashamed of his work. For some time it was a doubtful struggle, but the fiery emulation which stimulated the English and Hessians, at last compelled the Americans to give way before them. The right wing first yielded, then the left, while the central division, where Lafayette was bravely fighting, was the last to breast the storm, which now concentrating its strength, spent its fury upon those devoted ranks. Firm as a rock amid the waves of ocean, they bore themselves proudly against the tide of victory, which rolled in fearfully upon them. By a skillful manœuvre, Cornwallis had managed to separate them from the two wings, when defeat became inevitable. The whole fire of the enemy was united against it, and the confusion became extreme. The troops at first wavered, then rallied, then wavered again, and at last fell into a disorderly retreat. It was in vain that Lafayette endeavored to check it. Defying danger, he stood almost single handed against the on-coming host, and endeavored to reanimate his flying comrades by his own example. It was all fruitless. A ball struck him, and as he fell, those remaining on the field gave way. Gimat, aid-de-camp to the Marquis, assisted his master in getting upon a horse, and though the blood was flowing profusely from his wound, Lafayette reluctantly turned and joined the fugitives. General Washington at this moment arrived with fresh troops, upon the field. Greene's divisions had marched four miles *in forty-two minutes,* but were too late to avert the disasters of the day. Lafayette, as soon as he saw Washington, started to join him, but loss of blood obliged him to stop and have his wound bandaged. While submitting to this, a band of soldiers came upon him so suddenly, that he had barely time to re-mount for flight, escaping as by a miracle the shower of bullets which whistled around his form.

A general rout was the order of the day. The road to Chester was crowded with the retreating.

Knyphausen had forced the passage of Chadd's Ford, notwithstanding the obstinate resistance of Generals Wayne and Maxwell, who had been left to defend it. Washington found that all that could be done was to stay the pursuit. So successful were his efforts, and those of General Greene, that as night approached, Sir William Howe called in his troops and gave over the chase. Lafayette was unwearied in his endeavors to save the army. Forgetting himself, his wound, and every thing but this one object, he exerted himself to the utmost, amid the darkness and dreadful confusion of that night, to restore order among the fleeing and despairing soldiery. At Chester Bridge, twelve miles from the scene of battle, he was in part successful. The Generals and the Commander-in-chief arrived, and Lafayette, at last fainting from loss of blood and excessive fatigue, was borne away to receive the attention which his situation demanded.

Lafayette was conveyed by water the next day to Philadelphia, while the army moved forward by land. As soon as he reached the city he sat down and wrote the following to her, who, next to liberty, was the dearest idol of his heart. Dating his letter, Philadelphia, Sept. 12th, he says :

"I must begin by telling you that I am perfectly well, because I must end by telling you that we fought seriously last night, and that we were not the stronger party on the field of battle. Our Americans, after having stood their ground for some time, ended at length by being routed. While endeavoring to rally them, the English honored me with a musket ball, which slightly wounded me in the leg, but it is a trifle, my dearest love; the ball touched neither bone nor nerve, and I have escaped with the obligation of lying upon my back for some time, which puts me much out of humor. I hope you will feel no anxiety. This event ought, on the contrary, rather to re-assure you, since I am incapacitated from appearing on the field for some time. I have resolved to take great care of myself; be convinced of this, my love. This affair will, I fear, be attended with bad consequences for America, but we will endeavor, if possible, to repair the evil. You must have received many letters from me unless the English be as ill-disposed towards my epistles as towards my legs. I have not yet received one letter, and I am most impatient to hear from you. Adieu; I am forbidden to write longer."

The news of the battle of Brandywine occasioned so much apprehension for the safety of Philadelphia, that Congress abruptly adjourned from that city to Bristol. Lafayette was also carried thither, whence he was taken to Bethlehem to remain under the care of the Moravian Society there, until his permanent recovery. Soon after his arrival at this quiet retreat, he again wrote a letter, full of interest, to his wife. It is dated October 1st, 1777, and reads as follows:

"I wrote to you, my dearest love, the 12th of September; the twelfth was the day after the eleventh, and I have a little tale to relate to you concerning that eleventh day. To render my action more meritorious, I might tell you that prudent reflections induced me to remain for some weeks in bed, safe sheltered from all danger; but I must acknowledge that I was encouraged to take this measure by a slight wound, which I met with I know not how, for I did not, in truth, expose myself to peril. It was the first conflict at which I had been present, so you see how very rare engagements are. It will be the last of this campaign, or, in all probability, at least the last great battle; and if any thing should occur you see that I could not myself be present.

"My first occupation was to write to you the day after that affair; I told you that it was a mere trifle, and I was right; all I fear is, that you may not have received my letter. As General Howe is giving, meanwhile, rather pompous details of his American exploits to the king his master, if he should write word that I am wounded, he may also write word that I am killed, which would not cost him anything; but I hope that my friends, and you especially, will not give faith to the reports of those persons who last year dared to publish that General Washington and all the general officers of his army, being in a boat together, had been upset, and every individual drowned. But let us speak about the wound; — it is only a flesh wound and has neither touched bone nor nerve. The surgeons are astonished at the rapidity with which it heals; they are in an ecstacy of joy each time they dress it, and pretend it is the finest thing in the world. For my part, I think it most disagreeable, painful, and wearisome; but tastes often differ. If a man, however, wished to be wounded for his amusement only, he should come and examine how I have been struck, that he might be struck precisely in the same manner. This, my dearest love, is what I pompously style my wound, to give myself airs and render myself interesting.

"I must now give you your lesson as wife of an American general officer. They will say to you,—'They have been beaten,'—you must answer,—'That is true; but when two armies of *equal number* meet in the field, old soldiers have naturally the advantage over new ones; — they have, besides, had the pleasure of killing a great many of the enemy, many more than they have lost?' They will afterwards add;—'All this is very well, but Philadelphia is taken, the capital of America, the rampart of liberty!' You must politely answer;—'You are all great fools! Philadelphia is a poor forlorn town, exposed on every side, whose harbor was already closed; though the residence of Congress lent it, I know not why, some degree of celebrity.' This is the famous city which, be it added, we will, sooner or later, make them yield back to us. If they continue to persecute you with questions, you may send them about their business in terms which the Viscount de Noailles will teach you, for I cannot lose time by talking to you of politics.

"Be perfectly at ease about my wound; all the faculty in America are engaged in my service. I have a friend who has spoken to them in such a manner that I am certain of being well attended to. That friend is General Washington. This excellent man, whose talents and virtues I admired, and whom I have learned to revere as I know him better, has now become my intimate friend. His affectionate interest in me instantly won my heart. I am established in his house, and we live together like two attached brothers, with mutual confidence and cordiality. This friendship renders me as happy as I can possibly be in this country. When he sent his best surgeon to me, he told him to take charge of me as if I were his son, because he loved me with the same affection. Having heard that I wished to rejoin the army too soon, he wrote me a letter, full of tenderness, in which he requested me to attend to the perfect restoration of my health. I give you these details, my dearest love, that you may feel quite certain of the care which is taken of me. Among the French officers who have all expressed the warm est interest in me, M. de Gimat, my aid-de-camp, has followed me about like my shadow, both before and since the battle, and has given me every possible proof of attachment. You may thus feel quite secure on this account, both for the present and the future.

"I am at present in the solitude of Bethlehem, which the Abbe Raynal has described so minutely. This establishment is a very interesting one; — the fraternity lead an agreeable and very tranquil life, but we will talk over all this on my return. I intend to weary those I love, yourself, of course, in the first place, by the relation of my adventures, for you know that I was always a great prattler.

"You must become a prattler also, my love, and say many things for me to Henriette — my poor little Henriette! embrace her a thousand times; — talk of me to her, but do not tell her all I deserve to suffer;—

my punishment will be, not to be recognized by her on my arrival; that is the penance Henriette will impose upon me."

At Bethlehem Lafayette remained for a number of weeks, but his anxiety for active service led him to the camp again before his wound was healed. Washington received him with open arms, but gently chided his imprudent zeal, and urged him to remain at head quarters. Irksome as this advice was, the judgment of Lafayette approved it, and for a while it was scrupulously followed. But, with returning strength, he panted again for action. Though willing to serve in any capacity, he did not conceal from Washington his wish to become invested with authority corresponding to his commission. Washington understood and felt the force of the suggestion. Detecting in the Marquis abilities adapted to the station desired, he was aware of the barrier interposed, by the jealousy against foreign officers, which was strongly felt both by Congress, and the army. He renewed his efforts, feeling increasingly solicitous because several French gentlemen, who came over under assurances of obtaining an honorable command, had recently returned disappointed to France. Congress, however, was not yet disposed to comply with the request. Lafayette, though it cannot be doubted that he was somewhat chagrined at the failure, admirably concealed his feelings, and though his wound was not yet sufficiently healed to permit him to wear a boot, he asked and obtained permission to join as a volunteer, an expedition which was then fitting out under General Greene, to operate in

New Jersey. The object of it, in part, was to give battle to Lord Cornwallis. Before reaching Billingsport, where that officer was preparing to attack Fort Mercer, Greene learned with vexation that the enemy had been recently greatly augmented, by a reinforcement from New York. This news determined him that it would not be safe to offer battle, and the intention was accordingly dismissed, though he remained in New Jersey watching for an opportunity to harass, if he dare not attack. Fort Mercer was evacuated on the 20th of November, and the British fleet had thus an uninterrupted intercourse with their troops in Philadelphia. Lord Cornwallis entrenched himself in a strong position on Gloucester Point, and Greene well knew that he could not with his present force drive him from it. Thus the main purpose of the expedition was likely to be defeated; but Lafayette was not inclined to retire without a trial of strength. With a small company, he reconnoitered the enemy's picket, and was authorized to make an attack upon it if circumstances justified. This was on the 25th of November. Having spent most of the day in examining fully as possible the situation of the enemy's camp, he was at length discovered, and a detachment of dragoons sent off to intercept him. Eluding these, he came suddenly upon a picket of four hundred Hessians, with their field pieces posted, at about two and a half miles from Gloucester. His own company numbered about three hundred men, but all being in fine spirits, the enemy was immediately attacked. So sudden was the onset, that the Hessians were forced to fly, barely firing a single shot. They were driven for more than half a mile, when detachments came to their assistance, and they turned to face their pursuers. Lafayette was not dismayed. His men had as yet met with no loss, and now fought with great impetuosity The reinforcements were first overthrown, and then the Hessians again precipitately fled. The heroic band chased them till dark, and then returned in high glee to camp with only five wounded, and having lost but one man. The loss of the British was considerable, and a number of prisoners were taken in the engagement. Lafayette was elated with the adventure and highly commended by General Greene, for the skill and bravery he displayed.

This engagement offered a fresh opportunity for Washington to press the claims of Lafayette upon the attention of Congress. That body, as if conscious of their injustice, now promptly responded to the pressing entreaties of the Commander-in-Chief. On the 1st of December, 1777, the following resolution was passed:

"RESOLVED, That General Washington be informed it is highly agreeable to Congress that the Marquis de Lafayette be appointed to the command of a division in the continental army."

This was joyful tidings both to the Marquis and to Washington. Three days after it was received Lafayette was publicly invested with his rank, and placed over the division of Virginia troops, lately led by General Stephens. He returned suitable thanks to Washington, but it should be mentioned to his honor, that he had been entirely devoted to the cause of freedom, during the time he was suffering the rebuffs of the nation for whose sake he was an exile from princely affluence and domestic joy.

It was now almost time for the campaign of 1777 to close. General Greene had been ordered to recross the Delaware, and join again the main body of the army. Sir William Howe had also recalled Lord Cornwallis, determining, if attainable, to bring on a decisive engagement between his own and the continental forces. With the avowed purpose of forcing Washington from his position, and driving him beyond the mountains, he marched out of Philadelphia, on the evening of the 4th of December, at the head of twelve thousand men, and entrenched himself upon a range of hills lying about three miles from the American encampment at Whitemarsh. The two armies were about equal in number, and Washington determined to await the assault, without giving the enemy any advantage, by acting upon the defensive. From this purpose Sir William Howe craftily endeavored to seduce him, but in vain. Several days were spent in slight skirmishes, in all of which Lafayette signally distinguished himself, but in none of them could the British general decoy from his position his wary foe. Not daring to attack him in his camp, and unable, by all his manœuvres, to draw him from it, Howe marched back to Philadelphia without having effected a battle ; thus giving, though unwillingly, "the highest testimony of the respect which he felt for the talents of his adversary, and the courage of the troops he was to encounter."

Soon after, Washington broke up his encampment, and Lafayette accompanied the army into winter quarters at Valley Forge. The details of this terrible winter are familiar to every reader of Revolutionary history. The undaunted bravery of a soldiery whose naked feet tracked with blood the frozen ground, in their march from Whitemarsh to Valley Forge, is calculated to touch a chord of admiration in a tyrant's breast. Lafayette, himself, thus describes the condition of the army after it had taken up its winter quarters: "The unfortunate soldiers were in want of every thing;—they had neither coats, hats, shirts, nor shoes;—their feet and legs froze until they became black, and it was often necessary to amputate them. From want of money they could neither obtain provisions nor any means of transport. The Colonels were often reduced to two rations and sometimes to one. The army frequently remained whole days without provisions, and the patient endurance of both soldiers and officers was a miracle, which each moment served to renew. But the sight of their misery prevented new engagements;—it was almost impossible to levy recruits;—it was easy to desert into the interior of the country. The sacred fires of liberty were not extinguished, it is true, and the majority of the citizens detested British tyranny; but the triumph of the North*

*Gates defeat of Burgoyne.

and the tranquillity of the South, had lulled to sleep two-thirds of the continent." In all these trials, Lafayette was himself uncomplaining. He sympathized with the soldiers, and cheered the officers, both by word and example. "He adopted in every respect the American dress, habits and food. He wished to be more simple, frugal, and austere, than the Americans themselves. Brought up in the lap of luxury, he suddenly changed his whole manner of living, and his constitution bent itself to privations as well as to fatigue." The British officers in their luxurious quarters at Phila delphia laughed at the privations of the "*rebels*," but even under this stern discipline, there was strengthening a spirit which could not be subdued. Through the rigors of that awful winter, the fires of patriotism burned with steady flame; and amid the tempests that howled across the snow-clad plains of Valley Forge, the tree of liberty grew, nourished, it is true, with blood and tears. It was a dark day, indeed, but there was a light in every heart among those ill-clad soldiers, which the midnight of adversity could not shroud.

From Valley Forge the Marquis writes to his father-in-law, the Duke d'Ayen, in France. His letter is dated December 16th, 1777, and we extract from it the following interesting passages :

"The loss of Philadelphia is far from being so important as it is conceived to be in Europe. If the difference of circumstances, of countries, and of proportions between the two armies, were not duly considered, the success of General Gates would appear surprising when compared with the events which have occurred

5

with us, — taking into account the superiority of General Washington over General Gates. Our General is a man formed, in truth, for this revolution, which could not have been accomplished without him. I see him more intimately than any other man, and I see that he is worthy of the adoration of his country. His tender friendship for me, and his complete confidence in me, relating to all political and military subjects, great as well as small, enable me to judge of all the interests he has to conciliate, and all the difficulties he has to conquer. I admire each day more fully the excellence of his character and the kindness of his heart. Some foreigners are displeased at not having been employed — although it did not depend on him to employ them — others, whose ambitious projects he would not serve, and some intriguing, jealous men, have endeavored to injure his reputation; but his name will be revered in every age by all true lovers of liberty and humanity. Although I may appear to be eulogizing my friend, I believe that the part he makes me act, gives me the right of avowing publicly how much I admire and respect him.

"America is most impatiently expecting us to declare for her, and France will, one day, I hope, determine to humble the pride of England. This hope, and the measures which America appears determined to pursue, give me great hopes for the glorious establishment of her independence. We are not, I confess, as strong as I expected, but we are strong enough to fight, and we shall do so, I trust, with some degree of success. With the assistance of France, we shall gain with costs the cause that I cherish, because it is the cause of justice; because it honors humanity; because it is important to my country, and because my American friends and myself are deeply engaged in it. The approaching campaign will be an interesting one. It is said that the English are sending us some Hanoverians; some time ago they threatened us with what was far worse, the arrival of some Russians. A slight menace from France would lessen the number of these reinforcements. The more I see of the English, the more thoroughly convinced I am, that it is necessary to speak to them in a loud tone.

"After having wearied you with public affairs, you must not expect to escape without being wearied also with my private affairs. It is impossible to be more agreeably situated in a foreign country than I am. I have only feelings of pleasure to express, and I have each day more reason to be satisfied with the conduct of Congress towards me; although my military occupations have allowed me to become personally acquainted with but few of its members. Those I do know, have especially loaded me with marks of kindness and attention. The new President, Mr. Laurens, one of the most respectable men of America, is my particular friend. As to the army, I have had the happiness of obtaining the friendship of every individual; not one opportunity is lost of giving me proofs of it. I passed the whole summer without accepting a division, which you know, had been my previous intention; I passed all that time at General Washington's house, where I felt as if I were with a friend of twenty years' standing. Since my return from Jersey, he has desired me to choose among several brigades, the division which may please me best. I have chosen one entirely composed of Virginians. It is weak in point of numbers, at present, just in proportion, however, to the weakness of the whole army, and almost in a state of nakedness, but I am promised cloth of which I shall make clothes and recruits, of which soldiers must be made, about the same period;— but, unfortunately, the latter is the more difficult task, even for more skillful men than I. The task I am performing here, if I had acquired sufficient experience to perform it well, would improve exceedingly my future knowledge. The Major-General replaces the Lieutenant-General and the Field Marshal in their most important functions, and I should have the power of employing to advantage both my talents and experience, if Providence and my extreme youth allowed me to boast of possessing either. I read, I study, I examine, I listen, I reflect, and the result of all is, the endeavor at forming an opinion, into which I infuse as much common sense as possible. I will not talk much for fear of saying foolish things; I will still less risk acting much for fear of doing foolish things; for I am not disposed to abuse the confidence which the Americans have so kindly placed in me. Such is the plan of conduct which I have followed until now, and which I shall continue to follow; but when some ideas occur to me, which I believe may become useful when properly rectified, I hasten to impart them to a great judge, who is good enough to say he is pleased with them. On the other hand, when my heart tells me that a favorable opportunity offers, I cannot refuse myself the pleasure of participating in the peril, but I do not think that the vanity of success ought to make us risk the safety of an army, or of any portion of it, which may not be formed or calculated for the offensive. If I could make an axiom, with the certainty of not saying a foolish thing, I should venture to add, that whatever may be our force, we must content ourselves with a completely defensive plan, with the exception, however, of the moment when we may be forced to action, because I think I have perceived that the English troops are more astonished by a brisk attack than by a firm resistance.

"This letter will be given you by the celebrated Adams, whose name must undoubtedly be known to you. As I have never allowed myself to quit the army, I have never seen him. He wished that I should give him letters of introduction to France, especially to yourself. May I hope that you will have the goodness to receive him kindly, and even to give him some information respecting the present state of affairs. I fancied you would not be sorry to converse with a man whose merit is so universally acknowledged. He desires ardently to succeed in obtaining the esteem of our nation. One of his friends himself told me so."

The tribute which Lafayette paid in this letter to General Washington, came warmly from his heart. The annals of friendship scarcely show an intenser reciprocal affection, than existed between these two individuals. Each looked upon the other as a friend, and their confidence strengthened constantly during their long intercourse together. In the present winter, Washington was made the object of a base and jealous intrigue, and an attempt was made to induce the Marquis to join the Cabal. Horatio Gates, intoxicated by his recent success against Burgoyne, assisted by a few ambitious partisans, was plotting the removal of Washington. The popularity of Gates was at this moment extreme, and many true friends of America would have hailed with applause his appointment as Commander-in-Chief. Plans, which were at first only talked of in secret whispers, at length became loudly hinted even in the National Legislature. Some of the most prominent men in the nation, Patrick Henry among them, were approached, if possible, to shake their attachment to Washington. Men of discretion repelled at once the base insinuations, and Patrick Henry took occasion to make known to him the influences which were operating against him. The most cautious but deep laid conspiracy was made to win over Lafayette to the faction. Promises of high rank and command were held out to him, and the strongest appeals made to his love of honor and renown. Motives drawn from his love of liberty and interest in the mighty struggle were also brought to bear upon him. The superiority of Gates to Washington as a military leader, was greatly enlarged upon in his presence, but these only strengthened the love with which the soul of Lafayette was bound to Washington. In a letter dated December 30th, 1777, he thus communicates his feelings to him:

"MY DEAR GENERAL,—I went yesterday morning to head-quarters, with an intention of speaking to your excellency, but you were too busy, and I shall lay down in this letter what I wished to say.

"I don't need to tell you that I am sorry for all that has happened for some time past. It is a necessary dependence of my most tender and respectful friendship for you, which affection is as true and candid as the other sentiments of my heart, and much stronger than so new an acquaintance seems to admit; but another reason to be concerned in the present circumstances is the result of my ardent and perhaps enthusiastic wishes for the happiness and liberty of this country. I see plainly that America can defend herself if proper measures are taken, and now I begin to fear lest she should be lost by herself and her own sons.

"When I was in Europe, I thought that here almost every man was a lover of liberty, and would rather die free than live a slave. You can conceive of my astonishment when I saw that toryism was as openly professed as whiggism itself; however, at that time I believed that all good Americans were united together—that the confidence of Congress in you was unbounded. Then I entertained the certitude that America would be independent in case she should not lose you. Take away for an instant that modest diffidence of yourself, (which, pardon my freedom, my dear General, is sometimes too great, and I wish you could know as well as myself what difference there is between you and any other man,) you would see very plainly that, if you were lost for America, there is nobody who could keep the army and the revolution six months. There are open dissensions in Congress ; parties who hate one another as much as the common enemy ; stupid men, who, without knowing a single word about war, undertake to judge you, to make ridiculous comparisons ; they are infatuated with Gates, without thinking of the different circumstances, and believe that attacking is the only thing necessary to conquer. These ideas are entertained in their minds by some jealous men, and perhaps secret friends to the British Government, who want to push you, in a moment of ill humor, to some rash enterprise upon the lines, or against a much stronger army. I should not take the liberty of mentioning these particulars, if I had not received a letter about this matter from a young good-natured gentleman at York, whom Conway has ruined by his cunning, but who entertains the greatest respect for you." Lafayette then goes on to recount the efforts which had been made to win himself away from Washington, and closes his letter with earnest assurances of "the most tender and profound respect," with which he still felt proud to regard him. The next day, Washington replied to this letter, thanking Lafayette for the "fresh proof of friendship and attachment which it gave him," and giving his own calm opinion about the plot concerning him. In conclusion, this illustrious man writes:—"But we must not, in so great a contest, expect to meet nothing but sunshine. I have no doubt that every thing happens for the best, that we shall triumph over all our misfortunes, and, in the end, be happy ;—when, my dear Marquis, if you will give me your company in Virginia, we will laugh at our past difficulties and the folly of others ; and I will endeavor, by every civility in my power, to show you how much, and how sincerely, I am your affectionate and obedient servant."

Notwithstanding the Cabal was destined to prove ingloriously fruitless, it nevertheless gave Washington great annoyance.

Conway, his bitter enemy and next to Gates in the guilty plot, had been appointed Inspector-General of the Army, a promotion so offensive to the officers, that it required skillful management of the Commander to restrain them from open mutiny. A new Board of War, had been instituted by Congress, designed to have a general control of military affairs. Of this Board Gates was made President, and his influence was accordingly given for measures which he knew were contrary to the views of Washington. This was done with a view of inducing him to retire in disgust from the army. Thinking to promote the design by separating from him so faithful and efficient a friend as Lafayette, and having been foiled hitherto, the conspirators brought forward a new plan. On the 22nd of January, 1778, it was resolved by Congress ;—"That an irruption be made into Canada, and that the Board of War be authorized to take every necessary measure for the execution of the business, under such general officers as Congress shall appoint." On the 23d of

January, Lafayette was appointed to the command of this expedition. It was said that the character of Lafayette as a Frenchman of illustrious rank, rendered him peculiarly qualified for the conquest of a province recently attached to the French empire. But it was also reported that, "the authors of this scheme had it principally in view, by separating Lafayette from Washington to deprive the Commander-in-Chief of the defense of so trustworthy a friend." Washington was not consulted at all respecting this movement. The first intimation which he received, was given in a letter from General Gates of the 24th of January, enclosing one of the same date to Lafayette, requiring his attendance on Congress to receive his instructions. Without noticing at all the want of confidence in himself, manifested by the action of the Board, Washington calmly handed the commission to Lafayette, and advised him to accept the appointment, which was an honorable one for the Marquis; and, as it was urged upon him, he consented, and immediately proceeded to the capital. The troops were to be furnished by the northern states, and Lafayette was instructed by the Board of War to proceed as soon as possible to Albany, where they were to rendezvous. He was further counselled, "that, considering the length of the route into that country in an inclement season, he should be particularly attentive to have his men well clothed, and so supplied with provisions, as effectually to guard against any misfortune which might happen for want of these necessary articles ; — and, in case he should fail in obtaining the forces which he might judge competent, or supplies sufficient for them, that he should carefully attend to those contingencies, and regulate his conduct according to the probability of success, without exposing his troops to any very great, or very apparent hazard." With these vague instructions Lafayette departed to join his force in Albany, taking with him the Baron De Kalb as second in command. General Conway,* who was also to accompany him, proceeded before him, and waited his arrival at Albany. The account of this campaign we cannot make more interesting than by letting the Marquis relate it, chiefly in his own words. On his route he writes to General Washington as follows :

"HEMMINGTOWN, February 9th, 1778

"DEAR GENERAL, — I cannot let go my guide with out taking this opportunity of writing to your excellency, though I have not yet public business to speak of. I go on very slowly ; — sometimes drenched in rain, and sometimes covered by snow, and not enter

---

* As General Conway was one of the chief intriguers against Washington, and as we do not propose again to refer to this infamous transaction, we will here introduce the acknowledgement which he afterwards voluntarily made to Washington. Having been wounded in a duel with General Cadwallader, and thinking his end approaching, he addressed the following letter to the man whom he had attempted grossly to injure :

"PHILADELPHIA, July 23d, 1778.

"SIR, — I find myself just able to hold the pen during a few minutes, and take this opportunity of expressing my sincere grief for having done, written, or said anything disagreeable to your excellency. My career will soon be over, therefore, justice and truth prompt me to declare my last sentiments. You are, in my eyes, the great and good man. May you long enjoy the love, veneration and esteem of these states, whose liberties you have asserted by your virtues.

"I am with the greatest respect, Sir,

"Your Excellency's most obedient humble servant,

"PHS. CONWAY."

taining many handsome thoughts about the projected incursion into Canada; if success were to be had it would surprise me in a most agreeable manner, by the very reason that I don't expect any shining ones. Lake Champlain is too cold for producing the least bit of laurel, and if I am not starved I shall be as proud as if I had gained three battles.

"Mr. Duer had given to me a rendezvous at a tavern, but nobody was to be found there. I fancy that he will be with Mr. Conway sooner than he has told me; — they will perhaps conquer Canada before my arrival, and I expect to meet them at the Governor's house in Quebec.

"Could I believe for one single instant, that this pompous command of a *northern army* will let your excellency forget a little us absent friends, then I would send the project to the place it comes from. But I dare hope that you will remember me sometimes. I wish you very heartily the greatest public and private happiness and success. It is a very melancholy idea for me that I cannot follow your fortunes as near your person as I could wish; but my heart will take, very sincerely, its part of every thing which can happen to you, and I am already thinking of the agreeable moment when I may come down to assure your excellency of the most tender affection and highest respect."

Having arrived at Albany, he wrote again to Washington:

"ALBANY, February 19th, 1778.

"DEAR GENERAL, — Why am I so far from you, and what business had the Board of War to hurry me through the ice and snow, without knowing what I should do, neither what they were going to do themselves? You have thought, perhaps, that their project would be attended with some difficulty, that some means had been neglected, that I could not obtain all the success and that immensity of laurels which they had promised me; — but I defy your excellency to conceive any idea of what I have seen since I left the place where I was quiet and near my friends, to run myself through all the blunders of madness or treachery, — God knows what, — But let me begin the journal of my fine and glorious campaign.

"According to Lord Stirling's advice, I went by Corich Ferry, to Ringo's tavern, where Mr. Duer had given me a rendezvous, but there no Duer was to be found, nor did they ever hear from him. From thence I proceeded by the state of New York and had the pleasure of seeing the friends of America as warm in their love for the Commander-in-Chief as his best friend could wish. I spoke to Governor Clinton, and was much satisfied with that gentleman. At length I reached Albany on the 17th, though I was not expected before the 25th. General Conway had been here only three days before me, and I must confess I found him very active, and looking as if he had good intentions;— but we know a great deal upon that subject. His first word has been, that the expedition is quite impossible. I was at first very diffident of the report, but I have found that he was right. Such is, at least, the idea I can form of this ill-concerted operation within these two days.

"General Schuyler, General Lincoln, and General Arnold had written before my arrival, to General Conway, in the most expressive terms, that, in our present circumstances, there was no possibility to begin, now, an enterprise into Canada. Hay, Deputy Quarter Master General; Cuyler, Deputy Commissary General; Mearsin, Deputy Clothier General, in what they call the northern department, are entirely of the same opinion. Colonel Hazen, who has been appointed to a place which interferes with the three others above mentioned, was the most desirous of going there. The reasons of such an order I think I may attribute to other motives. The same Hazen confesses we are not strong enough to think of the expedition in this moment. As to the troops, they are disgusted and (if you except some of Hazen's Canadians) reluctant, to the utmost degree to begin a winter incursion into so cold a country. I have consulted every body and every body answers me that it would be madness to undertake this operation.

"I have been deceived by the Board of War. They have, by the strongest expressions, promised to me one thousand, and—what is more to be depended upon—they have assured to me in writing, *two thousand and five hundred combatants at a low estimate.* Now, sir, I do not believe I can find *in all* twelve hundred fit for duty, and most part of those very men are naked, even for a summer's campaign. I was to find General Stark with a large body, and indeed General Gates had told me, '*General Stark will have burnt the fleet before your arrival.*' Well, the first letter I receive in

Albany is from *General Stark, who wishes to know what number of men, from whence, for what time, for what rendezvous, I wish him to raise.* Colonel Biveld who was to rise too, would have done something *had he received money.* One asks what encouragement his people will have, the other has no clothes; not one of them has received a dollar of what was due them. I have applied to every body, I have begged at every door I could these two days, and I see that I could do some thing were the expedition to be begun in five weeks. But you know that we have not an hour to lose, and indeed it is now rather too late had we every thing in readiness.

"There is a spirit of dissatisfaction prevailing among the soldiers, and even the officers, which is owing to their not being paid for some time since. This department is much indebted, and as near as I can ascertain, for so short a time, I have already discovered near eight hundred thousand dollars due to the continental troops, some militia, the quarter master's department, &c., &c., &c. It was with four hundred thousand dollars, only the half of which is arrived to day, that I was to undertake the operation, and satisfy the men under my commands. I send to Congress the account of those debts. Some clothes, by Colonel Hallen's activity, are arrived from Boston, but not enough by far, and the greater part is cut off.

"We have had intelligence from a deserter, who makes the enemy stronger than I thought. There is no such thing *as straw on board the vessels to burn them.* I have sent to Congress a full account of the matter; I hope it will open their eyes. What they will resolve upon I do not know, but I think I must wait here for their answer. I have enclosed to the president copies of the most important letters I had received. It would be tedious for your excellency, were I to undertake the minutest detail of every thing; it will be sufficient to say that the want of men, clothes, money, and the want of time, deprives me of all hopes as to this excursion. If it may begin again in the month of June by the east, I cannot venture to assure; but for the present moment, such is the idea I conceive of the famous incursion, as far as I may be informed in so short a time.

"Your excellency may judge that I am very distressed by this disappointment. My being appointed to the command of the expedition is known through the continent, it will be soon known in Europe, as I have been desired by members of Congress to write to my friends; — my being at the head of an army, people will be in great expectations, and what shal I answer?

"I am afraid it will reflect on my reputation, and I shall be laughed at. My fears upon that subject are so strong, that I would choose to become again only a volunteer, unless Congress offers the means of mending this ugly business by some glorious operation; — but I am very far from giving to them the least notice upon that matter. General Arnold seems very fond of a diversion against New York, and he is too sick to take the field before four or five months, I should be happy if something were proposed to me in that way, but I will never ask nor even seem desirous of any thing directly from Congress; — and as for you, dear General, I know very well that you will do every thing to procure me the only thing I am ambitious of — glory.

"I think your excellency will approve of my staying here till further orders, and of my taking the liberty of sending my dispatches to Congress by a very quick occasion, without going through the hands of my General ; — but I was desirous to acquaint them early of my disagreeable and ridiculous position." Four days afterwards he writes as follows :

"My Dear General, — I have an opportunity of writing to your excellency, which I will not miss by any means, even should I be afraid of becoming tedious and troublesome ; but if they have sent me far from you, I don't know for what purpose, at least I must make some little use of my pen, to prevent all communication from being cut off between your excellency and myself. I have written lately to you my distressing, ridiculous, foolish, and indeed nameless situation. I am sent with great noise, at the head of an army, for doing great things ; — the whole continent, France and Europe herself, and what is the worst, the British army, are in great expectations. How far they will be deceived, how far we shall be ridiculed, you may judge by the candid account you have got of the state of our affairs.

"There are things, I dare say, in which I am deceived — a certain Colonel is not here for nothing ; one other gentleman became very popular before I

6

went to this place — Arnold himself is very fond of him. Every part on which I turn to look I am sure a cloud is drawn before my eyes; — but there are points I cannot be deceived upon. The want of money, the dissatisfaction among the soldiers, the disinclination of every one (except the Canadians who mean to stay at home) for this expedition, are as conspicuous as possible. I am sure I shall become very ridiculous and laughed at. *My expedition* will be as famous as the *secret expedition* against Rhode Island. I confess, my dear General, that I find myself of very quick feelings whenever my reputation and glory are concerned in anything. It is very hard indeed that such a part of my happiness, without which I cannot live, should depend upon schemes which I never knew of but when there was no time to put them into execution. I assure you, my most dear and respected friend, that I am more unhappy than I ever was.

"My desire for doing something was such, that I have thought of doing it by surprise with a detachment, but this seems to me rash and quite impossible. I should be every happy if you were here to give me some advice, but I have nobody to consult with. They have sent to me more than twenty French officers, but I do not know what to do with them. I beg you will acquaint me with the line of conduct you advise me to follow on every point. I am at a loss how to act, and indeed I do not know what I am here for myself. However, as being the eldest officer, (after General Arnold has desired me to take the command,) I think it is my duty to mind the business of this part of America as well as I can. General Gates holds yet the title and power of Commander-in-Chief of the Northern Department, but as two hundred thousand dollars have arrived, I have taken upon myself to pay the most necessary part of the debts we are involved in. I am about sending provisions to Fort Schuyler; — I will go see the fort. I will try to get some clothes for the troops, to buy some articles for the next campaign. I have directed some money to be borrowed upon my credit to satisfy the troops, who are much discontented. In all I endeavor to do for the best, though I have no particular authority or instructions. I will come as near as I can to General Gates' intentions, but I want much to get an answer to my letters.

"I fancy (between us) that the actual scheme is to have me out of this part of the continent, and General Conway in chief under the immediate direction of General Gates. How they will bring it up I do not know, but you may be sure something of that kind will appear. You are nearer than myself, and every honest man in Congress is your friend; — therefore, you may foresee and and prevent, if possible, the evil, a hundred times better than I can. I would only give that idea to your excellency.

"After having written in Europe (by the desire of the members of Congress) so many fine things about my commanding an army, I shall be ashamed if nothing can be done by me in that way. I am told General Putnam is recalled; but your excellency knows better than I do what would be convenient, therefore I don't want to mind these things myself.

"Will you be so good as to present my respects

to your lady? With the most tender affection and highest respect, I have the honor to be, &c."

Washington deeply sympathized with the Marquis in his trying condition, and replied to these letters in terms of condolence and commendation. He assured him that his character stood as fair as it ever did, and that the prudence which he had displayed, and his manifest wisdom in abstaining from the expedition under the difficulties by which he was unexpectedly surrounded, would brighten rather than tarnish his reputation. With the kindness of a father, he assured the Marquis of his undiminished confidence, that the most prompt to slander could have nothing in his conduct upon which to found a story of blame. His influence was also exerted to procure an order from Congress authorizing the abandonment of the Canadian enterprise, and the return of Layfayette. On the second of March, the Board of War were directed "to instruct the Marquis de Lafayette to suspend, for the present, the intended irruption; and at the same time inform him, that Congress entertain a high sense of his prudence, activity, and zeal; and that they are fully persuaded, nothing has, or would have been wanting on his part, or on the part of the officers who accompanied him, to give the expedition the utmost possible effect." On the thirteenth of March, Washington was permitted to recall the Marquis, and in pursuance of this order, he rejoined Washington at Valley Forge; where self-denial and mutual sympathy made their attachment scarcely less beautiful than that between the Hebrew Bard and the young Prince of Israel, who fought and suffered together.

CHAPTER III.

BRIGHTENING PROSPECTS — OPENING OF THE CAMPAIGN OF 1778 — LAFAYETTE AT BARREN HILL — PERILOUS POSITION — BRILLIANT MANŒUVRE, AND SAFE RETREAT — ATTACHMENT OF THE ARMY — AFFECTING INTELLIGENCE FROM HOME — DEATH OF HIS DAUGHTER — LETTER TO HIS WIFE — EVACUATION OF PHILADELPHIA — BATTLE OF MONMOUTH — ARRIVAL OF COUNT D'ESTAING AND THE FRENCH FLEET — LAFAYETTE AT RHODE ISLAND — SULLIVAN AND D'ESTAING — D'ESTAING DETERMINES TO SAIL FOR BOSTON — REMONSTRANCE — LAFAYETTE AND THE ADMIRAL — REASONS FOR THE MEASURE — RETREAT FROM NEWPORT — EFFORTS OF LAFAYETTE — REPAIRS TO BOSTON — AGAIN AT RHODE ISLAND — RETREAT — RESOLUTIONS OF CONGRESS — CORRESPONDENCE — LAFAYETTE PREPARES TO RE-VISIT FRANCE — ACTION OF CONGRESS — DEPARTURE.

THE campaign of 1776 had closed gloomily to the friends of freedom ; and the defeated, yet not disheartened army took up their winter quarters at Valley Forge. But while the shadows were deepening, there was below the horizon the on-coming of day.

The genius of Washington was not slumbering. In the early part of 1778, he was industriously employed in forming plans for the next campaign. The regulations for the militia service were re-organized and established upon a firmer basis than before. A new spirit of discipline was infused into the regular force, and both officers and soldiers found the spring opening upon them with new courage, and brighter expectations than at any former period. The influence of the example and representations of Lafayette upon France was not unmarked. The French ministry, who had always secretly favored the Revolution, were giving decided evidence of their interest ; and at length, on the 6th of February, the independence of the United States was formally acknowledged by that nation. The treaties of amity and commerce, and of defensive alliance which were entered into between the American Commissioners at Paris and the Government, were hailed with unbounded joy throughout the land. The star of independence, which had trembled upon the verge of gathering clouds, shone brightly forth, the herald of morning glory.

Valley Forge was about twenty miles from Philadelphia, but the British, though vastly superior in numbers, had not attempted a general attack; confining their operations to predatory excursions against the inhabitants of the surrounding country. Early in the month of May the vigilance of General Washington discovered indications that they were about to evacuate the city; and at once took measures to harass them on their departure. Lafayette was detached with a picked company of two thousand men, with orders to cross the Schuylkill, and take up his post as an advance guard to the army, where he could be in readiness to annoy if practicable the rear of the enemy, should they move as expected. "You will remember," said Washington to him, "that your detachment is a very valuable one and that any accident happening to it, would be a severe blow to the army; you will therefore use every precaution for its security, and to guard against a surprise." Lafayette was specially enjoined to avoid any permanent station, as it would facilitate the execution of designs which might be concerted against him. With these instructions, the Marquis crossed the river and halted, on the 18th of May, at Barren Hill, situated about midway between the encampments at Valley Forge and Philadelphia.

Intelligence of this was instantly communicated to Sir William Howe. The Marquis had chosen his position and fortified it with great care, but the British General found means to learn the exact number of his men and immediately formed a finely devised mode of surprise. So well laid was his scheme, and so confident was he of success, that on the 19th of May he invited a large number of ladies to meet him at a banquet on the following day, promising that they should then be introduced to the captured Marquis. The same night he dispatched General Grant with Sir William Erskine at the head of five thousand select troops, who were ordered to gain the rear of Lafayette, and thus intercept the passage between his division and the main body at Valley Forge. By a forced and circuitous march, he reached his point of destination a little before sunrise; which was about a mile from the Marquis, at a place where the roads fork;—the one leading to his camp and the other to Matson's Ford, over the Schuylkill. In the course of the same night Sir William Howe sent General Gray with another strong division, which went up the Schuylkill, to a ford of the river, directly in front of the right flank of Lafayette. The main column led on by Sir William Howe, in person, then marched out of the city and took the direct road along the river to Barren Hill. So secret were the operations of the British General, that they entirely escaped the vigilance of Lafayette, and on the morning of the 20th, he found himself completely hemmed in by a powerful army; — his retreat cut off,—his advance opposed by a force far stronger than his own, — and scarcely the faintest hope of extricating himself from the difficulties with which he was surrounded. He had taken every precaution to fortify himself against surprise, and could hardly credit his senses when he heard that the militia which he had stationed to guard one of the passes, through which General Gray marched, had left it unprotected, by changing their post during the night without his order or knowledge.

The Marquis received the tidings of his perilous situation, with unshaken fortitude. A wild huzza broke out, all along the lines, as they witnessed the entire calmness with which he began to plot their deliverance from the perils out of which, apparently, they could be rescued by no human power. The three divisions of the British, were now moving simultaneously against him, able to crush him at the first onset. Still, he did not for a moment betray an emotion of dismay. A retreat was soon seen to be the only possible escape, and he accordingly resolved to re-cross the river by Matson's Ford, though he knew that Grant with five thousand men had possession of the heights, commanding the road. It was at this crisis that he executed one of those brilliant manœuvres, for which he was remarkable. With the head of his column, he advanced boldly toward Grant as if to attack him, while the rear, which was partially concealed by the woods, filed off rapidly towards the Schuylkill. Grant, naturally supposing that the whole strength of Lafayette was coming against him, instantly halted and prepared for battle. The delay was just what the hunted Marquis desired—and with unbounded joy he witnessed the hopeful result of his experiment. Preserving the most perfect order, he saw the rear of his brave regiments, gaining the point between the enemys' division and the stream ; and before Grant could prevent, or even fully comprehended the purpose, his apparently advancing column fell gradually back, and joined the retreating ranks. The whole now reached Matson's ford in safety ; though it must be confessed, that so gross negligence on the part of the British General, can scarcely be accounted for, except as an interposition of Providence. A corps of cavalry had taken possession of a hill, from whose elevation Lafayette was first discovered on his retreat through the low woody grounds which bordered the river. Even at this time, Grant might have intercepted the passage to the ford, but supposing that these were merely a detachment and that the main body still lay at Barren Hill, he persisted in his resolution of marching thither notwithstanding he was strongly opposed by Sir William Erskine, and other Generals of his staff. Barren Hill was concealed from their view by intervening trees, and not till they had fully arrived upon the ground, did they find that it was abandoned. The bird had escaped, notwithstanding the net had been so carefully set, and so warily sprung.

Still it might not be too late. A hot pursuit was instantly ordered by the foiled Commander, burning with desire to avert the dishonor which he saw would fall upon his name, if his enemy were allowed thus easily to elude his grasp. But before he reached Matson's Ford, Lafayette had crossed safely the river, and made a stand upon the heights on the opposi' side. So advantageous was his position, that General Grant did not venture to meet him; and overwhelmed with mortification, he wheeled to join the other forces, and return to head quarters, having accomplished nothing. "Finding the bird flown," says Chastelleux, "the English returned to Philadelphia, spent with fatigue and ashamed of having done nothing. The ladies did not see M. de Lafayette, and General Howe himself arrived too late for supper."

The joy with which Lafayette was greeted at Valley Forge after his escape, knew no bounds. General Washington embraced him, and complimented him in the highest terms. His danger had been seen with glasses, and he had been watched with intense interest, till it was fully known that he had passed the Ford. Loud acclamations saluted him, as his gallant troops, with inconsiderable loss, filed into the camp; and from that moment, his influence over the men he commanded became unlimited. He lived in their hearts, and few officers in the American army claimed a profounder admiration or warmer regard.

Soon after this exploit Lafayette received tidings of the death of Henriette, his eldest, and at the time he left France, his only daughter. The warm emotions of affection, which a soldier's life could not chill, are thus expressed in an extract from a letter to his wife, dated June 16th, 1778. . . "What a dreadful thing is absence! I never experienced before all the horrors of separation. My own deep sorrow is aggravated by the feeling that I am not able to share and sympathize in your anguish. The length of time that had elapsed before I heard of this event had also increased my misery. Consider, my love, what a dreadful thing it must be to weep for what I have lost, and tremble for what remains. The distance between Europe and America appears to me more enormous than ever. The loss of our poor child is almost constantly in my thoughts. This sad news followed almost immediately that of the treaty, and while my heart was torn by grief, I was obliged to receive and take part in expressions of public joy.

"If the unfortunate news had reached me sooner, I should have set out immediately to rejoin you;—but the account of the treaty, which we received the first of May, prevented me from leaving this country. The opening campaign does not allow me to retire. I have always been perfectly convinced that by serving the cause of humanity and that of America, I serve also the interests of France."

About this time dispatches reached Sir Henry Clinton, who by the resignation and departure for England of General Howe, was left Commander-in-Chief of the British forces, ordering him to evacuate Philadelphia. The assistance which France had decided to render America, and the naval force which was fitting out at

Toulon for this object, made Philadelphia a dangerous post, and induced the Ministry to withdraw the army from the Delaware. Washington was early apprised of these movements, and when on the morning of the 18th of June, the British defiled out of the city, he was prepared to act accordingly. Judging that General Clinton was expecting to reach New York by land, across the Jerseys, Washington had previously endeavored to impede his way by breaking down the principal bridges, and placing obstructions in the roads through which he would have to pass. At this crisis a council of war was held at Valley Forge, upon the propriety of hazarding a general engagement. A wide diversity of opinion prevailed. General Lee, whose opinion carried great weight, was vehement against risking either a general or partial battle. General Du Portail, a French officer of distinction, the Baron de Steuben and most of the foreign officers took the same ground, and maintained that an action ought to be carefully avoided. A majority of the American generals were influenced by their counsels; and of seventeen, in all, only Wayne and Cadwallader were decidedly in favor of attacking the enemy. Lafayette, however, was inclined to this latter opinion, but without openly avowing it; and General Greene was also disposed to venture more than the views of the greater number would sanction. Washington for weighty reasons desired an action, but the voice of the majority prevailed, though not without evident dissatisfaction to him.

Determining to follow the foe on their march, he left Valley Forge the same day that they deserted Philadelphia and crossing the river at Coryell's Ferry, made a stand at Hopewell. On the 24th of the month, another council of war was held at this place, in which, after stating the relative strength and position of the two armies, the Commander-in-Chief proposed the following questions:

"Will it be advisable for us, of choice, to hazard a general action? If it is, should we do it by immediately making a general attack upon the enemy, by attempting a partial one, or by taking such a position, if it can be done, as may oblige them to attack us? If it is not, what measures can be taken, with safety to this army, to annoy the enemy in their march? In fine, what precise line of conduct will it be advisable for us to pursue?"

In this consultation, as in the first, Lee made a strenuous opposition to a general encounter. Being next to Washington in rank, and moreover a General of great experience, his arguments and opinions had much influence over the younger officers present. It was finally decided that an attack was not advisable, but that "a detachment of fifteen hundred men be immediately sent to act, as occasion may serve, on the enemy's left flank and rear, in conjunction with the other Continental infantry and militia, who are already hanging about them, and that the main body preserve a relative position, so as to be able to act as circumstances may require." This decision was little to the taste of Washington. Lafayette had expressed his opinion precisely, when in the latter council be contended "that it would be disgraceful to the officers and humiliating for the troops, to allow the enemy to traverse the Jerseys unmolested; that without running an imprudent risk, the rear guard at least of the British might be attacked; that it was best to follow the enemy, manœuvre with prudence, and take advantage of circumstances, even to the hazard of a general battle." After the deeision, Lafayette and Wayne strongly represented to Washington the inefficiency of the designated force, and urged the appointment of additional men. As this coincided with the Commander's view, he promptly resolved to act in conformity therewith, and even to risk a conflict if unforseen circumstances should not prevent.

Washington accordingly entered upon prompt measures. General Dickenson with the Jersey militia consisting of about one thousand men, and Maxwell with his brigade already hung on the enemy's left flank towards their rear. General Cadwallader with Jackson's regiment were behind, while Colonel Morgan with his six hundred tried soldiers, was ready to harass them on their right. Fifteen hundred men ordered by the last council of war, had also been marched forward to the lines under command of Brigadier-General Scott. Firmly fixed in his purpose, to bring on an engagement if possible, Washington now sent Wayne with a further division of one thousand select troops to reinforce General Cadwallader. This swelled the continental battalions in front of the enemy to between four and five thousand; and as the simultaneous action of these was of the highest importance, Washington deemed it proper that a Major-General should be entrusted with their supreme command. This duty would naturally have fallen to Lee, but as he was totally opposed to the course taken, Lafayette went to Washington and offered himself to lead the attacking division. Washington referred him to Lee, who very readily assented to the offer of the Marquis, saying that he disapproved of the plans of the Commander-in Chief, that he was sure they would fail, and that he was willing to be relieved from any responsibility in carrying them into execution. Upon this, Washington had no hesitation in conferring the command upon Lafayette. It was an important post but the keen insight of Washington had not mistaken his man. Young as he was the Marquis had already inspired a confidence in his bravery, prudence, and skill, which was both flattering and merited. He was ordered to proceed immediately with the detachment under General Poor, and form a junction speedily as possible with the one which had just been sent forward under Scott. "You are to use," says Washington in his instructions, "the most effectual means for gaining the enemy's left flank and rear, and giving them every means of annoyance. All continental parties, that are already on the lines, will be under your command, and you will take such measures, in concert with General Dickenson, as will cause the enemy the greatest impediment and loss in their march. For these purposes you will attack them as occasion may require by detachment, and, if a proper opening should be given, by operating against them with the whole force of your command. You will naturally take such precautions as will secure you against surprise, and maintain your communication with this army." But no sooner had Lafayette left than Lee began to repent of having declined the commission. He wrote to Washington setting forth his changed views, and soliciting in the most urgent manner that he might yet be entrusted with the appointment. Here was a new difficulty. Washington had already given it to Lafayette, and he could not recall it without danger of offending him; and he could not refuse the present entreaty of Lee without giving umbrage to that General. There was, however, an obvious impropriety in withdrawing the command so soon, and this was accordingly represented to Lee. He then appealed to Lafayette. He told him of the position in which he was placed, and of the partial glance which he had bestowed on the subject, when he declined. Lee evidently saw that his reputation might be impaired when his opposition to the action would be connected with the fact that he afterwards refused to take the command of a strong division which, it was expected would meet and engage the rear of the enemy. "My fortune and honor," he wrote to Lafayette, "are placed in your hands; — you are too generous to cause the loss of both." Lafayette was pleased with the post, and was at first unwilling to relinquish it. But the repeated entreaties of Lee, and his appeals to his generosity and magnanimity, at length gained the point, and he wrote to Washington, assuring him that if it was believed necessary or useful to the good of the service and the honor of General Lee, to send him down with a couple of thousand men, or any greater force, he would cheerfully obey and serve him, not only out of duty, but out of the respect he owed to that officer's character. Upon the receipt of this letter Washington wrote to Lee offering an expedient which he deemed would be satisfactory to both. He proposed that General Lee should march at the head of two brigades to support the Marquis at Englishtown, where as senior officer, he would have the direction of the whole front section, which after he had joined it, would amount to over five thousand men. It was, however, expressly stipulated, that if any enterprise had been already formed by Lafayette, it should go forward the same as if no change were made. To this condition Lee readily acceded, and Washington thereupon wrote to Lafayette as follows : — "General Lee's uneasiness on account of yesterday's transaction, rather increasing than abating, and your politeness in wishing to ease him of it, have induced me to detach him from this army with a part of it, to reinforce, or at least cover the several detachments at present under your command. At the same time that I felt for General Lee's distress of mind, I have had an eye to your wishes, and the delicacy of your situation ; and have therefore obtained a promise from him, that, when he gives you notice of his approach and command, he will request you to prosecute any plan you may have already concerted for the purpose of attacking, or otherwise annoying the enemy. This is the only expedient I could think of to answer the views of both. General Lee seems satisfied with the measure, and I wish it may prove agreeable to you, as I am, with the warmest wishes for your honor and glory, and with the sincerest esteem and affection, yours, &c."

Sir Henry Clinton, who was not unapprised of these designs against him, had taken a strong post on the heights of Freehold, near Monmouth. Washington saw that this was unassailable, and, aware that if the British were allowed to proceed twelve miles, till they should gain the heights of Middletown, they would be perfectly secure, he gave orders to General Lee to attack the British rear as soon as it should move from its present ground.

Morning broke of the 28th of June, 1778. Washington was in his saddle at five in the morning, listening to the intelligence just received from General Dickenson, that the front of the enemy was in motion. "To arms!" was sounded along the American ranks; and the order was instantly dispatched to General Lee to advance upon the enemy, "unless there should be powerful reasons to the contrary." He was at the same time informed that Washington with the rear division of the American force, would be on the way to support him. Washington, with his usual decision, had thus prepared for combat, contrary to the opinion of Lee and that of the officers generally. The orders sent to Lee were prompt and urgent; and though his judgment demurred, now that they were given, it only remained for him to execute them. His first movements were those of ready obedience. Appearing upon the heights of Freehold soon after Lord Cornwallis had left them, he followed the enemy into the plain and made immediate disposition for the onset. Hitherto his tactics had been marked with skill and caution, but here he seemed to lose all prudence. He ordered Lafayette to a station where he was subjected to the galling fire of the English artillery without any prospect of good, while he himself, stood apparently uncertain what course to pursue. The Marquis was soon forced to retire, but nothing daunted, he waited a more favorable field for heroism. A fair opportunity seemed to offer itself, and, full of energy and enthusiasm, he rode up to Lee and solicited permission to avail himself of it. "Sir," said Lee, "you do not know British soldiers; — we cannot stand against them; — we shall certainly be driven back at first, and we must be cautious." This was far from suiting the fiery nature of the Marquis, and he answered with as much spirit as was becoming, that British soldiers had been beaten, and, it was to be presumed, they might be beaten again. At this crisis began the strangest act in that day's drama. Lee was supported by five thousand men, all panting for the conflict, and though he knew he could trust in their bravery to an unlimited extent; — that Washington who earnestly desired battle was already bringing forward the whole army to his support, yet after the slightest skirmishing, before any advantage had been gained on either side, he *ordered a retreat*. Lafayette was enraged but could not disobey. He instantly dispatched a messenger to Washington, informing him of the state of affairs, and earnestly beseeching him to hasten to the scene of retreat; who saw the condition of things at a glance, and instantly rode forward. He was not, however, prepared for the whole scene. Every where there was the appearance of disorder and confusion. General Dickenson, with his division of militia on the left flank of the British, had been utterly routed, and was flying over the plain in dismay, with no effort from Lee to check the retreat. Lafayette seemed every where present among the troops, and as he could not prevent flight, he struggled nobly to save the army from a total rout. Lee had ordered back the whole force under his command, and Washington gave utterance to a storm of indignation, when he met them fleeing before the enemy, without having made an endeavor to maintain their ground. Riding up to General Lee, he accosted that officer in tones of cutting severity and disapprobation ; and then set himself with a superhuman activity at work, to retrieve the disasters of the morning. A look at his calm, majestic figure, at this moment, sitting upon his white horse, covered with dust and foam, and casting his eagle eye over the field where almost beneath the banners of the exulting foe, the regiments were retreating, sent a thrill of returning hope, like an electric current, along the broken ranks. A new courage rose throughout the smitten host when they found the Commander-in-Chief was present to guide the terrible strife, the rest of that fatal day. "Never," said Lafayette to Marshal — "never was General Washington greater in war than in this action. His presence stopped the retreat. His dispositions fixed the victory. His fine appearance on horseback, his calm courage roused by the animation produced by the vexation of the morning, gave him the air best calculated to excite enthusiasm." The day was oppressively sultry, and the heat was at 96 deg. Fahrenheit. Not a breath of air lifted the drooping colors, or stirred the plumes around the throbbing temples of the soldiers, while the charge was sounded, and the flying companies wheeled to face the deadly sweep of their pursuers. Order began to smile upon the chaos of the continental brigades, and "*Long live Washington!*" was heard above the thunder of artillery, repeated by unnumbered lips parched with thirst, and pallid with weariness. That single man, by the quiet might of his splendid genius, turned back the tide of war upon the enemy with astonishing haste, and under a wasting fire. His white charger amid the deepening smoke of battle, was like the shining cross to the crusaders, when Jerusalem lay at their feet, and they were sinking beneath the fierce and vastly outnumbering foe. The columns pressed steadily up to the blaze of cannon; and many a brave fellow fell unpierced by the hail of death, gasping for *water*, and yet struggling to follow his leader back to the scene of carnage. The entire aspect of that field was now changed. Colonel Stewart and Lieutenant Colonel Ramsay, were sent with their regiments to an important point on the left, to sustain the shock of the advancing enemy there. Lee, with the remainder of the force, was directed to command the front, arrayed again for the furious onset, while Washington galloped away to bring his own division up to the desperate encounter. Lee, stung with the reproaches of his General, naturally extremely sensitive in regard to his honor, was fully aroused to wipe off the morning's disgrace. He could fight with unrivaled courage, if he willed, and was indeed a brave officer. He dashed into the contest with bitter determination, and though compelled to yield, he retired in fine order and with courageous resistance to the last. Washington soon appeared, and then followed the wild uproar and falling ranks of wide and sanguinary battle. Each army poured into the bosom of the other a tempest of bullets, while the batteries grew hot from rapid discharges, which opened a momentary gape through living men; and upon all beat the scorching sun of that *Sabbath day.* General Greene commanded the right wing of the first line, Lord Sterling the left, and Lafayette led on the second line. The impetuous charge forced the British back in front, and, attempting to turn on the left, were here also repulsed. Wheeling to the right, Sir Henry Clinton now bore down upon General Greene, who met the attack as a rock flings back the wave. He had sent a body of troops with artillery to a commanding elevation, which now operated with so much effect, that he not only foiled the present attempt of Clinton, but completely enfiladed the division which yet remained in front of the left wing. Sir Henry had, therefore, no resort but to withdraw behind a marshy ravine, on the ground which he had occupied before the commencement of the battle. Arrangements were immediately made for attacking him there, but the excessive heat, the fatigue of the soldiers, and the approach of night, dissuaded Washington, and he accordingly issued his orders to desist. Lafayette had been in his saddle and incessantly active since four in the morning, displaying the utmost coolness, and sharing every where in the toils and dangers of the day. Nothing could intimidate him, nothing appeared to weary him; but with a bearing ever high and heroic, he passed unscathed amid the rage of that battle-storm. "I have been charmed," said an officer under his immediate command, "with the blooming gallantry, and sagacity, of the Marquis de Lafayette, who appears to be possessed of every requisite to constitute a great General." This praise of his prudence, and skill, and courage, was universal in the army.

An incident of this battle connected with Lafayette is found in the "Historical Anecdotes of the reign of Louis XVI." It is related as follows;—"During the American War, a General officer, in the service of the United States, advanced, with a score of men, under the English batteries, to reconnoitre their position. His aid-de-camp, struck by a ball, fell at his side while the officers and orderly dragoons fled precipitately. The General, though under the fire of the cannon, approached the wounded man to see whether he had any signs of life remaining, or whether any assistance could be afforded him. Finding the wound had been mortal, he turned his eyes away with emotion, and slowly rejoined the group which had got out of the reach of the pieces. This instance of courage and humanity took place at the battle of Monmouth. General Clinton, who commanded the English troops, knew that the Marquis de Lafayette generally rode a white horse;—and it was upon a white horse that the General officer, who retired so slowly, was mounted. Sir Henry Clinton, therefore, commanded the gunners not to fire. This noble forbearance probably saved General Lafayette's life, for it was he himself. At that time he was but twenty-two years of age." Such was the battle of Monmouth.

Washington and Lafayette passed the night upon the field of strife, in the folds of the same mantle, worn by the former. In the morning when they arose, the enemy had departed. At midnight they had left their camp and fled with such secrecy that no knowledge of the fact was communicated to the Americans till day-break, by which time they were beyond the reach of their disappointed enemy. Washington, though he had hoped for a renewal of the engagement, saw the folly of pursuit, and quietly allowed his army to rest upon the field.

On the 7th of July the French force, which Lafayette had so anxiously solicited, arrived off the Capes of Delaware. It consisted of twelve ships of the line and six frigates, having on board a respectable body of land forces, and was commanded by the Count d' Estaing, a French nobleman of some distinction. He had sailed from Toulon on the 13th of April and made his point of destination the Delaware, hoping to find the British fleet in that river, and their army in Philadelphia. Adverse winds had, however, protracted his voyage across the Atlantic, till the English fleet and army, warned of his approach, had made good their escape. Upon learning this, the next plan of d' Estaing was to make an attack upon New York, but this he was induced to abandon by the representations of the pilots, that it would be impossible to pass the bar at Sandy Hook, with his heavy ships. A combined enterprise against the enemy at Rhode Island, was next planned. D'Estaing sailed for Newport, and Lafayette with two brigades was to join at Providence General Sullivan, who commanded the American forces in Rhode Island.

The prospects of the Revolutionary arms were again bright. All over the land rang the shouts of enthusiastic welcome, to the forces sent by a monarch to cheer and sustain the suffering cohort of freedom. Adulation and praise were lavished upon them from every quarter, and in many bosoms joy succeeded the sadness of deep despondency. The Count came to anchor off Newport on the 25th of July. His earnest manner of proceeding increased the universal gladness, which his arrival awakened, and he seemed inclined to throw his whole strength into the struggle, and ready to carry forward any project that energy and wisdom could suggest.

The character of Count d'Estaing has been misrepresented, and perhaps hardly understood. We shall endeavor to unfold it somewhat particularly, in our account of succeeding transactions.

On the 21st of July, Lafayette with two brigades was ordered to join General Sullivan at Providence. Before arriving there, the French fleet had appeared at Newport, and impatient of delay, d' Estaing immediately concerted with Sullivan, the course of action, without waiting for the reinforcements. The Count was all ardor, and with Gallic zeal in haste for the contest. We apprehend that the only law of his character which offers to us a satisfactory solution to the problem of his after history, is found in his ardent nature and consequent restiveness under restraint. His long passage, while it had soured his temper, had also strongly increased his desire for a signal achievement, now that he had arrived on the field of display. The delay of the expected force, though unavoidable, offered a temporary barrier to his progress, and was exceedingly displeasing to him. A plan was, however, agreed upon, which promised important results in future success. As soon as Lafayette and his division were there, its execution was immediately determined upon. The British with a force 6,000 strong, occupied Newport, and this stronghold became the grand object of the allies. Here was the arena of conflict. Towards Narragansett Bay were turned the anxious eyes of friends and foes of American liberty. Washington, at White Plains, having sent out an additional force, waited with solicitude for the issue; while the English Admiral closely followed the fleet, to that port. General Pigot, who commanded the troops in Rhode Island, was regarded as a doomed man, when the designs against him were disclosed. Completely encircled by enemies, an easy overthrow was apparent, yet he was not disposed to submit without resistance. Withdrawing the men which had been stationed on the north end of the island into the lines at Newport, he fortified himself for the expected attack.

When he heard of this, General Sullivan resolved to take immediate possession of the works which the British had just abandoned, and on the 9th of August he crossed over the Sea-connet passage, and landed on the north end of Rhode Island.* This movement though perfectly just in itself, was yet the source of much subsequent difficulty. The Count d'Estaing was a Lieutenant-General at home, and as such, held a higher rank than Sullivan, who was only a Major-General. Difficulties on subjects of mere punctilio, to avoid which, Washington advised Sullivan to take every precaution, had previously arisen between them, although neither had given intimations of resentment. His crossing over from the main land before the time agreed upon for the joint attack, and without having communicated his purpose to d' Estaing was immediately regarded disrespectful by him, who expressed his suspicion that the measure was taken with other motives than those assigned. A letter from Sullivan in vindication of himself, he refused to answer, and a day that ought to have been devoted to action, was spent in fruitless discussion and recriminations.

Towards evening of the same day, the English fleet which had been dispatched from New York for the succor of General Pigot hove in sight. A change at once came over Count d'Estaing. His imperious bearing softened, and the next morning, with favorable

*This, of course, will be understood as Rhode Island proper. The term was first given to this island upon which Newport is situated, and afterwards applied to the State.

breeze he determined to stand out to sea and give battle, at the same time assuring Sullivan that on his return, he would co-operate with him. This purpose displayed a great want of the highest qualities of a military leader. Every thing was ready for the attack upon Newport, and an energetic prosecution of it, was now only necessary for success. The British Admiral, soon as he saw the strength and position of the French fleet, despaired of rescuing the town, but dropped anchor to take advantage of any accidental circumstance which might arise. To throw away this advantage for the sake of entering upon what was at best a doubtful adventure, was the height of folly. Still, we are not inclined to blame d' Estaing to the extent many have done. It was *folly*, and not cowardice, or want of interest in the cause to which he was allied. He was enthusiastic and impatient, and that these traits blinded him is evident, from his previous and after history. He fancied, and doubtless sincerely, that he could make a brilliant *coup de main*, by dispersing the hostile fleet, and afterwards return to capture the city.

Sullivan's army amounted to ten thousand men, and a council of war was called in which an immediate battle was proposed. Notwithstanding the departure of d'Estaing, it was urged that the American force was sufficient for the emergency, which demanded the trial. Lafayette alone dissented. He admitted the favorable views expressed, but objected to the commencement of operations, before the return of d'Estaing. He urged that the Admiral had already felt himself aggrieved, and that his feeling would be revived with keener edge if they advanced upon the enemy before his return, and without his co-operation. His advice, therefore, was, that they should take a position near Newport till the Count should be ready to act with them. Time, however, was of so much importance to a body of troops organized as the continental army was, that the opposite counsels prevailed, and it was decided to open the trenches and begin the siege without delay.

Preparations, therefore, went briskly forward. Fifty rounds of ammunition were distributed to each soldier, and through all the ranks were heard the busy notes of preparation for the contest. But, suddenly, while the stirring pageant of war was moving to the measures of death's music, the moan of a coming tempest was heard above the tumult of the tented plain. The breeze increased to a gale ; the black clouds rose above the horizon, and rushed across the heavens, till twilight was the illumination of noon-day. There was a pause throughout the camp, and impatient waiting for a calm. But, hour after hour, the tempest increased in fury, the sky blackened, and the winds howled, mingling in wildest chaos the lighter materials of a military campaign ; and at length, rending the curtains of the tents, scattered them like autumnal leaves. The rain descended in sheets, deluging the men, amunition and arms. A wilder scene can scarcely be imagined. Over the wide field, were files of soldiers shelterless in the storm, around them the ruins of their white dwellings ; officers standing with drooping plumes, and their horses bracing in terror to meet the now pauseless hurricane that raged on ; while artillery and magazines were exposed to the unsparing elements, whose battle made the hero of the sanguinary conflict shrink with terror. Several perished during this tempest, which continued for three days with unexampled severity.

As soon as the storm was over, and order could be restored, the siege was opened. This was on the 15th of August ; and for several days the work was vigorously prosecuted. The two fleets had sailed out of sight, and as no news was heard from either of them, the anxiety of the Americans became intense. Their situation was, moreover, becoming critical, since, in the absence of their allies, new regiments might without interruption be thrown into Newport, and not only defeat the enterprise, but render retreat hazardous. The re-appearance of d'Estaing on the morning of the 19th, was hailed with peculiar joy. After a day or two spent in manœuvering, he was upon the point of engaging with his rival, when the same storm which had made the terrible havoc on shore, swept the shipping and instantly dispersed the vessels, leaving them at the end of forty-eight hours, totally unfit for action. The British fleet sailed back to New York. The hopes excited by the return of d'Estaing were soon to be most lamentably dispelled. He wrote to Sullivan, stating that in pursuance of the orders of his King, and the advice of all his officers, he was about to sail for Boston to repair the damage done by the tempest. His instructions were to repair to Boston if any accident should happen to his fleet, or a superior British force should appear off the coast. This design excited universal indignation in the camp. The accents of applause which had greeted the arrival of d'Estaing were at once exchanged for bitter execrations; and through the army ran the murmur of disapprobation. With the fleet, they had calculated with confidence on a brilliant termination of the expedition; without it, their efforts were useless. Sullivan was in despair, though he could hardly believe that the Count would desert them in a moment so critical, did he understand the precise nature of their situation. Generals Greene and Lafayette were accordingly dispatched with a letter, and directed to use their utmost efforts to induce him to reconsider. "They represented to him the certainty of carrying the garrison if he would co-operate with them only two days, urged the impolicy of exposing the fleet at sea, in its present condition, represented the port of Boston as equally insecure with that of Newport, and added that the expedition had been undertaken on condition that the French fleet and army should co-operate with them; — that, confiding in this co-operation, they had brought stores into the island to a great amount, and that to abandon the enterprise in the present state of things, would be a reproach and a disgrace to their arms. To be deserted at such a critical moment, would have a pernicious influence on the American people, and would furnish their domestic foes, as well as the common enemy, with the means of animadverting severely on their prospects from an alliance with those who could abandon them, under circumstances such as the present. They concluded with wishing that the utmost harmony and confidence might subsist between the two nations, and especially between their officers ; — and entreated the Admiral, if any personal indiscretions had appeared in conducting the expedition, not to permit them to prejudice the common cause." These points and others were presented and pressed with the earnestness of pleading necessity. The Marquis, especially, besought him on his honor as a Frenchman and as a man, not to abandon the cause he had espoused, in such hazardous extreme. It was, however, in vain ; the Count positively refused to listen. We cannot agree with those who represent d'Estaing as impelled to his singular course through pique at Sullivan, for acting without consultation with himself. This idea appears absurd. D'Estaing himself would have coveted the renown attending the capture of Newport, and would eagerly have joined the American forces in attempting it, had no other reason interfered. Lafayette was doubtless right in his conjecture. D'Estaing was properly a land officer, and his naval subordinates were dissatisfied with his appointment. The Marquis saw that they were his enemies and determined to thwart any plan which would give him a famous exploit. Hence, he supposes, and with great probability, that, appealing to the strict letter of the Count's instructions, they unanimously opposed deviation from them. Whatever might have been his own preference, he could not disregard both of these claims, and was consequently driven to the alternative which was taken. Nor can we doubt that his own desire was to remain. General Greene was of this opinion. Upon the return of the latter with Lafayette, Sullivan determined to make one more effort to secure the Admiral's aid. In this, his solicitude blinded his judgment. A protest containing expressions which he ought to have known would be offensive, was signed by the officers except Lafayette, and dispatched with a letter, beseeching him to change his plans. D'Estaing was, of course, highly incensed by the protest, and sailed directly for Boston.

Sullivan, now thrown upon his own resources, called a council of war and proposed an assault upon the garrison, provided five thousand men who had seen nine months' service could be obtained. The militia were, however, so discouraged by the departure of the fleet, that the number could not be procured. They had begun to desert, and in a few days the army was reduced to only five thousand. It was determined to break up their fortifications, and await the result of another en deavor to prevail upon d'Estaing to hasten back. Lafayette used all his tact and persuasion to remove the prejudice against the French alliance, caused by the desertion of d'Estaing. His unbounded popularity gave him favor every where, and words of conciliation were received from him with deference, which would have been rejected with contempt from another source. Perhaps nowhere does his devotion to the Colonies shine more purely than in these transactions. The French officers, besides him, were generally inclined to take part with their countrymen, and were incensed by the reproaches of the continental troops. Lafayette was unwearied as a peace-maker between the two.

He poured oil upon the troubled waters of discontent, soothing one party and softening the asperity of the other, in his mediation to bring union and harmony again. He was the sun shining through the angry storm, and dropping the rain-bow of peace upon its threatening brow. After the army had been drawn off to the north part of the island, Lafayette advised a farther retreat to the main land. This being delayed, he was sent to Boston, to make the desired reconciliation and co-operation with d'Estaing. Absorbed with his mission, traveling all night, he arrived just in time to see the corps of officers enter the city to attend a public dinner, which had been tendered them by the civil and military authorities there. After the festival, a council was held, in which Lafayette proposed his object, and brought all his influence to restore the friendly relations so seriously interrupted. He was eminently successful, and d'Estaing, after assuring the Marquis of the crippled condition of his fleet, offered to march in person with his troops to Newport. But before this arrangement could be made, Lafayette received intelligence that Sir Henry Clinton had arrived at Newport, and the American army was flying before the enemy. Here was *action*, and without a moment's delay, he started for the scene. He traveled the whole distance, (eighty miles,) in less than eight hours, and arrived at Howland's Ferry on the Seaconnet passage, just as the troops were crossing it. One moment was spent in a rapid survey, and then he threw himself into the arena of danger and of glory. His post was chosen when he perceived the rear guard, composed of a thousand men, still upon the island and surrounded. He placed himself at their head, and his clear voice of command rising above the roar of conflict, made the hearts of that despairing band leap with hope and courage. Sullivan had conducted the affair with great skill; and with one of his magical strokes, Lafayette turned the tide of pursuit, while his ranks poured down in regular files to the Ferry, and passed safely over amid the acclamations of their comrades upon the opposite shore. Not a man was lost. Thus closed the expedition against Newport. It was undertaken with unusual promise, and its unsuccessful close produced a proportionate chagrin. The cause of the failure was charged entirely upon d'Estaing throughout the country, and has been reiterated by succeeding historians, who have accused him of want of fidelity to the American Flag. We have endeavored to give a faithful and fair narration, from which the reader can draw his own inferences. Our own opinion is, that the accusation has no foundation whatever. Congress passed a resolution expressing their approbation of the Count's conduct, and directed the President to assure him that they entertained the highest sense of his zeal and attachment.

The conduct of Lafayette met with universal praise. He received many testimonials of approbation, but none more welcome than the following Resolution passed by Congress on the 9th of September :

"Resolved, That Mr. President be requested to inform the Marquis de Lafayette, that Congress have a due sense of the sacrifice he made of his personal feelings in undertaking a journey to Boston, with a view of promoting the interest of these States, at a time when an occasion was daily expected of his acquiring glory in the field, and that his gallantry in going on Rhode Island, when the greatest part of the army had retreated, and his good conduct in bringing off the pickets and out sentinels, deserve their particular approbation." Mr. Laurens, who was then President of Congress, accompanied this resolution with the following letter :

"PHILADELPHIA, Sept. 13, 1778.

"SIR,—I experience a high degree of satisfaction in fulfilling the instructions embraced in the enclosed act of Congress of the ninth instant, which expresses the sentiments of the representatives of the United States of America, relative to your excellent conduct during the expedition recently undertaken against Rhode Island. Receive, Sir, this testimonial on the part of Congress as a tribute of respect and gratitude, offered to you by a free people.

"I have the honor to be with very great respect and esteem, Sir, your obedient and most humble servant,

"HENRY LAURENS, *President.*"

Lafayette replied as follows :

"CAMP, Sept. 23, 1778.

"SIR,—I have just received the letter of the 13th instant with which you have favored me, and in which you communicate the honor which Congress has been pleased to confer by the adoption of its flattering resolution. Whatever sentiments of pride may be reasonably excited by such marks of approbation, I am not the less sensible of the feelings of gratitude, nor of the satisfaction of believing that my efforts have, in some measure, been considered as useful to a cause in which my heart is so deeply interested. Have the goodness, Sir, to present to Congress my unfeigned and humble thanks, springing from the bottom of my heart, and accompanied with the assurances of my sincere and perfect attachment, as the only homage worthy of being offered to the representatives of a free people.

"From the moment that I first heard the name of America, I loved her; — from the moment that I learned her struggles for liberty, I was inflamed with the desire of shedding my blood in her cause; and the moments that may be expended in her service, whenever they may occur, or in whatever part of the world I may be, shall be considered as the happiest of my existence. I feel more ardently than ever, the desire of deserving the obliging sentiments with which I am honored by the United States, and by their representatives, and the flattering confidence which they have been pleased to repose in me, has filled my heart with the liveliest gratitude and most lasting affection."

After the retreat, Lafayette was entrusted by Sullivan with the care of Warren, Bristol, and the eastern shore of Rhode Island. From the camp he writes to Washington. "I am to defend a country with a very few troops, who are not able to defend more than a single point. I cannot answer that the enemy will not go and do what they please — for I am not able to prevent them — with only a part of their army, and yet this part must not land far from me ; but I answer, that if they come with equal or not very superior forces to those I may collect, we shall flog them pretty well ; at least I hope so. My situation appears to be uncertain, for we expect soon to hear from your excellency. . . . You know Mr. Touzard, a gentleman of my family — he met with a terrible accident in the last action. With the greatest excess of bravery, he ran before all the others to take a piece of cannon in the midst of the enemy, when he was immediately covered with their shots, had his horse killed, and his right arm shattered to pieces. He was happy enough not to fall into their hands, and his life is not despaired off. Congress was going to send him a commission of Major.

"Give me joy, my dear General, I intend to have your picture. Mr. Hancock has promised me a copy of the one he has in Boston. He gave one to Count d' Estaing, and I never saw a man so glad at possessing his sweetheart's picture as the Admiral was to receive yours."

The reply of Washington is interesting and we extract the following. "The sentiments of affection and attachment which breathe so conspicuously in all your letters to me, are at once pleasing and honorable, and afford me abundant cause to rejoice at the happiness of my acquaintance with you. Your love of liberty, the just sense you entertain of this valuable blessing, and your noble and disinterested exertions in the cause of it, added to the innate goodness of your heart, conspire to render you dear to me; — and I think myself happy in being linked with you in bonds of the strictest friendship.

"The ardent zeal which you have displayed during the whole course of the campaign to the eastward, and your endeavors to cherish harmony among the officers of the allied powers, and to dispel those unfavorable impressions which had begun to take place in the minds of the unthinking, from misfortunes, which the utmost stretch of human foresight could not avert, deserved, and now receive, my particular and warmest thanks. I am sorry for Mons. Touzard's loss of an arm in the action on Rhode Island; — and offer my thanks to him, through you, for his gallant behavior on that day.

"Could I have conceived that my picture had been an object of your wishes, or in the smallest degree worthy of your attention, I should, while Mr. Peale was in the camp at Valley Forge, have got him to take the best portrait of me he could, and presented it to you; — but I really had not so good an opinion of my own worth, as to suppose that such a compliment would not have been considered as a greater instance of my vanity, than means of your gratification; and, therefore, when you requested me to sit to Monsieur Lanfang, I thought it was only to obtain the outlines and a few shades of my features, to have some prints struck from."

Lafayette's position at Bristol was ill-suited to his nature. He had, indeed, to be incessantly engaged, but it was not the kind of activity he liked. To defend himself and the surrounding country from the marauding attacks of British squadrons, was not enough for him. His force did not allow him to make a heavy blow, and skirmishes, which could give no advantage to either side, were uninviting. News reached him of important transactions in France which rekindled his flagging excitement. Advices from the Duke d' Ayen, his father-in-law, apprised him that the ministry were planning a descent upon England; and created an intense desire to revisit his country. "My great object in wishing to return," he writes d' Ayen, "is the idea of a descent upon England. I should consider myself as almost dishonored, if I were not present at such a moment. I should feel so much regret and shame, that I should be tempted to drown or hang myself according to the English mode. My greatest happiness would be to drive them from this country, and then to repair to England, serving under your command. This is a very delightful project; — God grant it may be realized." Other causes conspired to foster his intention. The difficulties here were exciting, and he feared the influence of the exaggerated reports which might reach the French court. He wished, moreover, to see the alliance placed upon a firmer basis, and believed that his influence would be conducive to this consummation. His heart too, throbbed with a gentler sympathy as he thought of his wife and child, and distant home. A hasty visit to d' Estaing at Boston, settled his purpose; for he there saw that there were weighty matters affecting the interests of both nations which he could best lay before the ministry in person. Returning to Bristol he solicited permission to visit the Commander-in-Chief at Head Quarters, to consult with him respecting his intended absence. Permission was accordingly granted, and Lafayette repaired to his revered friend at Fishkill. Washington, from motives of unfeigned friendship, as well as from a regard to his country's good, was very desirous of preserving Lafayette's connection with the army, and accordingly, while he made no objections to his departure, advised him to solicit from Congress an unlimited leave of absence, rather than to present his resignation. The following letter upon the subject was written to the President of Congress.

"HEAD QUARTERS, October 6, 1778.

"SIR,—This letter will be presented to you by Major General Lafayette. The generous motives which formerly induced him to cross the ocean, and serve in the armies of the United States, are known to Congress. The same praise-worthy reasons now urge him to return to his native country, which, under existing circumstances, has a claim to his services.

"However anxious he was to fulfill the duty which he owes to his King and country, that powerful consideration could not induce him to leave this continent, while the fate of the campaign remains undecided. He is, therefore, determined to remain until the termination of the present campaign, and takes advantage of the present cessation from hostilities to communicate his designs to Congress, so that the necessary arrangements may be made at a convenient season, while he is at hand, if occasion should offer, to distinguish himself in the army.

"At the same time, the Marquis, being desirous of preserving his connection with this country, and hoping that he may enjoy opportunities of being useful to it, as an American officer, only solicits leave of absence, for the purpose of embracing the views which have been already suggested. The pain which it costs me to separate from an officer who possesses all the military fire of youth, with a rare maturity of judgment, would lead me, if the choice depended on my wishes, to place his absence on the footing which he proposes. I shall always esteem it a pleasure to be able to give those testimonials of his service to which they are entitled, from the bravery and conduct which have distinguished him on every occasion; — and I do not doubt that Congress will, in a proper manner, express how sensibly they appreciate his merits, and how much they regret his departure. I have the honor to be, &c.

"George Washington."

Bearing this letter, Lafayette proceeded to Philadelphia, whence he addressed the following to the President of Congress:

"Philadelphia, October 13, 1778.

"Sir, — However attentive I ought to be not to employ the precious moments of Congress in the consideration of private affairs, I beg leave, with that confidence which naturally springs from affection and gratitude, to unfold to them the circumstances in which I am, at present, situated. It is impossible to speak more appropriately of the sentiments which attach me to my own country, than in the presence of citizens who have done so much for their own. So long as I have had the power of regulating my own actions, it has been my pride and pleasure to fight beneath the banners of America, in the defence of a cause, which I may dare more particularly to call *ours*, as I have shed my blood in its support.

"Now, Sir, that France is engaged in war, I am urged, both by duty and patriotism, to present myself before my sovereign, to know in what manner he may be pleased to employ my services. The most pleasing service that I can render, will be that which enables me to serve the common cause, among those whose friendships I have had the happiness to obtain, and in whose fortunes I participated, when your prospects were less bright than they now are. This motive, together with others which Congress will properly appreciate, induce me to request permission to return to my own country in the ensuing winter. So long as a hope remained of an active campaign, I never indulged the idea of leaving the army, — but the present state of peace and inaction, leads me to prefer to Congress this petition. If it should be pleased to grant my request, the arrangements for my departure shall be taken in such a manner, that the result of the campaign shall be known before they are put in execution. I enclose a letter from his Excellency, General Washington, consenting to the leave of absence which I wish to obtain. I flatter myself that you will consider me as a soldier on leave of absence, ardently wishing to rejoin his colors as well as his beloved comrades. If, when I return to the midst of my fellow citizens, it is believed that I can, in any manner, promote the prosperity of America, — if my most strenuous exertions can promise any useful results, I trust, Sir, that I shall always be considered as the man who has the prosperity of the United States most at heart, and who entertains for their representatives the most perfect love and esteem. I have the honor to be, &c.,

"LAFAYETTE."

Congress acceded promptly to this request. They not only had a too high regard for the Marquis to refuse him, but they well knew that his vast influence would be exerted at the court of Versailles wholly in their favor, and in the present state of affairs this was a consideration not to be disregarded. On the 21st, resolutions were passed by Congress, which were communicated to Lafayette by the President in the following manner:

"PHILADELPHIA, October 24, 1778.

"SIR,—I had the honor of presenting to Congress your letter, soliciting leave of absence, and I am directed by the house to express their thanks for your zeal in promoting that just cause in which they are engaged, and for the disinterested services you have rendered to the United States of America. In testimony of the high esteem and affection in which you are held by the good people of these states, as well as in acknowledgment of your gallantry and military talents, displayed on many signal occasions, their representatives in Congress assembled have ordered an elegant sword to be presented to you by the American minister at the court of Versailles.

"Enclosed within the present cover will be found an act of Congress of the 21st instant, authorizing these declarations, and granting a furlough for your return to France, to be extended at your own pleasure. I pray God to bless and protect you, Sir; to conduct you in safety to the presence of your prince, and to the re-enjoyment of your family and friends. I have the honor to be, &c.,

HENRY LAURENS, *President.*"

The resolutions referred to were as follows:

1778, IN CONGRESS, OCTOBER 21ST, RESOLVED,— That the Marquis de Lafayette, Major-General in the service of the United States, have leave to go to France, and that he return at such time as shall be most convenient to him.

"RESOLVED,—That the President write a letter to the Marquis de Lafayette, returning him the thanks of Congress for that disinterested zeal which led him to America, and for the services he has rendered to the United States, by the exertion of his courage and abilities on many signal occasions.

"RESOLVED,—That the Minister Plenipotentiary of the United States of America at the court of Versailles, be directed to cause an elegant sword, with proper devices, to be made and presented in the name of the United States to the Marquis de Lafayette.

"OCTOBER, 22D, RESOLVED,—That the following letter of recommendation of the Marquis de Lafayette be written to the King of France:

"To our great, faithful, and beloved friend and ally, Louis the Sixteenth, King of France and Navarre:

"The Marquis de Lafayette, having obtained our leave to return to his native country, we could not suffer him to depart without testifying our deep sense of his zeal, courage, and attachment. We have advanced him to the rank of Major-General in our armies, which, as well by his prudent as spirited conduct, he has manifestly merited. We recommend this young nobleman to your majesty's notice, as one whom we know to be wise in council, gallant in the field, and patient under the hardships of war. His devotion to his sovereign has led him in all things to demean himself as an American, acquiring thereby the confidence of these United States, your good and faithful friends and allies, and the affection of their citizens. We pray God to keep your Majesty in His holy protection.

"Done at Philadelphia, the 22d day of October, 1778, by the Congress of the United States of North America, your good friends and allies.

"HENRY LAURENS, *President.*"

In a becoming manner Lafayette acknowledged these testimonials, and after some days spent at Philadelphia in busy consultations upon his mission, he started for Boston on horseback, to meet the vessel fitted out for his passage. At Fishkill, which was near the American camp, a severe illness awaited him. An inflammatory fever, induced by his recent fatigues and excitement, brought him to the borders of the grave. For a time his life was despaired of, and he himself gave up the hope of recovery. No record is left us of his view of eternity, while its awful portals seemed opening before him, and we cannot learn what were his emotions, interesting as such experience would be. General

Washington watched over him with the solicitude of a father. The best medical attendance was bestowed upon him, and through a kind Providence his life was preserved. A universal gloom spread over the army during the dangerous moments of his illness, which gave place to lively demonstrations of joy at the first fair prospect of a favorable issue to the disease. A gentleman who visited him at Fishkill during his recovery, thus describes his personal appearance at that time: "Visited my friends at Fishkill, and by the request of Colonel Gibson, I waited on the Marquis de Lafayette. The Colonel furnished me with a letter of introduction, and his compliments, with inquiries respecting the Marquis' health. I was received by this nobleman in a polite and affable manner. He is just recovering from a fever, and is in his chair of convalescence. He is nearly six feet high, large, but not corpulent, being not more than twenty-one years of age. He is not very elegant in his form, his shoulders being broad and high, nor is there a perfect symmetry in his features; his forehead is remarkably high, his nose large and long, eyebrows prominent and projecting over a fine animated hazel eye. His countenance is interesting and impressive. He converses in broken English, and displays the manners and address of an accomplished gentleman. Considering him a French nobleman of distinguished character, and a great favorite of General Washington, I feel myself highly honored by this interview." As soon as he was able, Lafayette took leave of Washington, and resumed his journey early in December. Reaching Boston on the 11th of that month, he found the ship in which he was to sail, not yet ready for sea.

Meanwhile, he was sedulously employed in preliminaries bearing upon the interests of both his native and adopted land. Never was Lafayette more worthy to be called "the man of two worlds," than when, on the 11th February, 1779, he sailed from Massachusetts Bay for his beloved France, bearing upon his great heart the welfare and honor of a modern republic, and an ancient kingdom.

CHAPTER IV.

LETTER TO WASHINGTON—THE VOYAGE—STORM AND CONSPIRACY—ARRIVAL IN FRANCE—RECEPTION—POLITICAL QUARANTINE—LAFAYETTE IS ADMITTED TO THE ROYAL PRESENCE AND FAVOR—HIS POPULARITY—HIS LABORS IN BEHALF OF FRANCE AND AMERICA—LETTER TO PRESIDENT LAURENS—PRESENTATION OF THE SWORD TO LAFAYETTE—DR. FRANKLIN'S LETTER AND LAFAYETTE'S REPLY—LAFAYETTE AND THE MINISTRY—SUCCESS AT LAST—PROPOSED PLAN OF AID—LAFAYETTE SAILS FOR BOSTON—ARRIVAL AND LETTER TO GENERAL WASHINGTON—RECEPTION AT BOSTON—REPAIRS TO HEAD QUARTERS—GOES TO PHILADELPHIA—SITUATION OF THE ARMY—WASHINGTON—LETTERS—DESIGNS UPON NEW YORK—ARRIVAL OF THE FRENCH FLEET—LAFAYETTE AT NEW YORK—HEAD QUARTERS.

The Marquis wrote the following farewell to Washington.

"On board the ALLIANCE off BOSTON, Jan. 11, 1779.

"The sails are just going to be hoisted, my dear General, and I have but time to take my last leave of you. I may now be certain that Congress did not intend to send any thing more to me. The navy board and Mr. Nevil write me this morning from Boston, that the North River is passable, and that a gentleman from camp says, he did not hear of any thing like an express for me. All agree for certain that Congress think I am gone, and that the sooner I go the better.

"Farewell my dear General. I hope your French friend will ever be dear to you. I hope I shall soon see you again, and tell you myself with what emotion I now leave the coast you inhabit, and with what affection and respect I am forever, my dear General, your respectful and sincere friend,—LAFAYETTE."

The voyage was not without its incidents and its perils. It was an inclement season and they encountered a terrible storm when off the Banks of Newfoundland. The frigate, unconscious of the treasure it bore, reeled to the gale, and was tossed like a feather upon the mad waters. So violent was the tempest that as night settled down upon the vessel already half filled with water, and with the main top mast blown away, few even of the crew expected to see the morning alive. When it dawned, the ship rolled upon the heavy swells a dismantled hulk, but the heavens were calm again, and the inmates of the Alliance safe. Another danger, however, awaited the Marquis. While the bark was getting ready for sea, a great difficulty had been found in procuring sailors. D' Estaing, from whom Lafayette hoped to obtain them, had sailed from Boston before the Marquis' arrival. After much difficulty, the number required was made up by accepting several English and Irish deserters and prisoners, who had offered their services. It was a strange rough set that were thus brought together, but they were the best that could be found, and were necessarily taken. They had most of them been engaged in the war, and their sympathies were enlisted in the royal cause. The presence of Lafayette did not awe these seamen, but excited them the more. By a recent proclamation they would be entitled to the ship, could they bring it into an English port, and they had hardly recovered from the effects of the storm, when a plan was formed to murder all on board except Lafayette, and, taking the vessel to England, surrender him as a prisoner of sufficient rank to be exchanged for General Burgoyne. When the frigate had arrived within two hundred leagues of the coast of France, this plot was matured and a day and hour set for its execution. But before the time arrived the secret was discovered. It had been revealed to an American sailor who was promised the command of the ship if he would engage in it. Feigning assent for a time, he watched for a favorable opportunity, and disclosed the whole plot to the Marquis, who immediately caused thirty-one of the mutineers to be placed in irons for the rest of the voyage. The promptness and energy with which Lafayette acted upon this occasion effectually quelled all disaffection, and secured tranquillity.

Lafayette landed at Brest in February, eight days after he had so effectually checked the sedition. The gladness with which he was welcomed was exceedingly flattering. He was not yet twenty-two years of age, but his splendid career had already given him a world-wide reputation. His fame had spread into every city and hamlet of the kingdom. On the 12th of February he met his wife and family at Versailles, and, in the rapture of their re-union, the pain of their sad separation was forgotten. Proceeding to Paris, he was for more than a week forbidden the king's presence as a penance for having left the realm in disobedience to his commands. This "*political quarantine*" was soon passed, and after a gentle reproof he was admitted to the palace, and restored again to favor. He immediately busied himself in the accomplishment of magnificent plans which he had formed for the benefit of America. He was almost daily closeted with the Prime Minister, the Count de Vergennes, astonishing that old statesman by the comprehensiveness of those designs, and the vigor with which he proposed to execute them. In the descent upon England which had greatly influenced his return, he was impatient to engage, hoping that, if successful, it might close the war, and bring peace at the same time to both France and the Colonies. The expedition after being duly matured, was abruptly abandoned by the ministry, and Lafayette sought a new channel for his heroism. Although no regular authority had been delegated to him by Congress, yet he set himself assiduously at work, to solicit for their army assistance in men, money, and clothing. So intense was his zeal, that he offered to pledge his entire fortune for the present wants of the Republic. He proposed to the Count de Vergennes that four ships of the line with half of their crews should be hired for one year for the service of the United States, and that it should be done in the name of the administration; "and as for the necessary funds," says he, "the government should pledge itself *only in case that it should exceed my fortune!*" A loan which the English had been negotiating in Holland was suddenly broken off, and Lafayette immediately besought the ministry to secure it. Writing to de Vergennes, he presses it earnestly upon his attention. So remarkable were his efforts, while he was unceasingly active for the best interests of his own nation, that no one wondered at his success abroad. An extensive correspondence was all the while kept up with his friends across the Atlantic. He strove to heal the dissensions which existed between some of these, and to allay the party contests which began to embitter the national councils. The following extracts from a letter which he wrote to President Laurens, are interesting not only as showing the employment of the Marquis while at home, but as revealing the views and feelings cherished towards the land for which he had bled. The letter is dated at St. Jean d'Angely, June 12th, 1779. Alluding to the gratitude and love which he bore the Americans, he says : "So deeply are those sentiments engraven upon my heart, that I every day lament the distance which separates me from them, and that nothing was ever so warmly and passionately wished for, as to return again to that country of which I shall ever consider myself as a citizen.—There is no pleasure to be enjoyed which could equal that of finding myself among that free and liberal nation, by whose affection and confidence I am so highly honored ;—to fight again with those brother soldiers of mine to whom I am so much indebted. But Congress knows that former plans have been altered by themselves, that others have been thought impossible, as they were asked too late in the year. I will, therefore, make use of the leave of absence they were pleased to grant me, and serve the common cause among my countrymen, their allies, until happy circumstances may conduct me to the American shores, in such a way, as would make that return more useful to the United States. The affairs of America I shall ever look upon as my first business while I am in Europe.

Any confidence from the King and ministers, any popularity I may have among my own countrymen, any means in my power shall be, to the best of my skill, and to the end of my life, exerted in behalf of an interest I have so much at heart. What I have hitherto done or said relating to America I think needless to mention, as my ardent zeal for her is, I hope, well known to Congress;—but I wish to let them know that if, in my proposals, and in my repeated urgent representation for getting ships, money, and support of any kind, I have not always found the ministry so much in earnest as I was myself, they only opposed to me *natural fears* of inconveniences which might arise to both countries, or the conviction that such a thing was impossible for the present;—but I never could question their good will towards America. If Congress believe that my influence may serve them in any way, I beg they will direct such orders to me, that I may the more certainly and properly employ the knowledge which I have of this court and country for obtaining a success in which my heart is so much interested.

"The so flattering affection which Congress and the American nation are pleased to honor me with, makes me very desirous of letting them know,—if I dare speak so friendly,—how I enjoyed my private situation. Happy in the sight of my friends and family, after I was by your attentive goodness safely brought again to my native shore, I met there with such an honorable reception, with such kind sentiments as by far exceeded any wishes I durst have conceived. I am indebted for that inexpressible satisfaction which the good will of my countrymen towards me affords to my heart, to their ardent love for America, to the cause of freedom and its defenders, their new allies, and to the idea which they entertain, that I have had the happiness to serve the United States. To these motives, Sir, and to the letter Congress was pleased to write on my account, I owe the many favors the king has conferred upon me. Without delay I was appointed to the command of his own regiment of dragoons, and every thing he could have done, every thing I could have wished, I have received on account of your kind recommendations.

"I have been some days in this small town, near Rochefort harbor, where I have joined the king's regiment, and where other troops are stationed, which I for the moment command. I hope, however, to leave this place ere long, in order to play a more active part and come nearer the common enemy. Before my departure from Paris, I sent to the Minister of foreign affairs — who is one of our best friends — intelligence concerning a loan in Holland, which I want France to make or answer for in behalf of America; but I have not yet heard the result. M. le Chevalier de la Luzerne* will give you more explicit and fresher news, as he is particularly ordered to do so, and he sets out directly from Versailles.

"Wherever the interests of beloved friends are seriously concerned, candid and warm affection knows

* The Chevalier de la Luzerne was the second minister sent out by the French Government to the United States.

not how to calculate and throws away all considerations. I will frankly tell you, Sir, that nothing can more effectually hurt our interest, consequence, and reputation in Europe than to hear of disputes or divisions between the whigs. Nothing could urge my touching upon this delicate matter but the unhappy experience of every day on that head, since I can hear, myself, what is said on this side of the Atlantic ; and the arguments I have to contend with."

During the month of August, the sword which had been voted him by Congress was finished. "It was appropriately devised and splendidly executed by the best artists. The knob of the handle exhibited on one side a shield, with Lafayette's arms, a marquis' coronet, surmounted by a streamer, on which his motto, *cur non*, was inscribed. On the other side was a medallion, representing the first quarter of the moon, whose rays were shed over the sea, and the land of the American continent, which is seen in the horizon. In the foreground, was the coast of France, surrounded by a scroll on which were inscribed the words "*crescam ut prosim*," in reference to the rising liberty and subsequent prospects of the country. In the center of the handle on each side, were two oblong medallions. The first represented Lafayette with his sword drawn, and his foot upon the prostrate British lion, in the attitude of inflicting a mortal wound, but pausing, extending his hand, and inclind to spare the life of his victim. On the other medallion, America was represented under the device of a young half-clad female, seated beneath a military tent, with one hand holding up her broken fetters, and with the other presenting a laurel branch to Lafayette. Other devices, of arms, laurel crowns, &c., encircled the handle and on one side of the guard. On the other were the words — 'FROM THE AMERICAN CONGRESS TO THE MARQUIS DE LAFAYETTE, 1779.' On the curved parts of the guard were represented in medallions four memorable events of the American war, in which Lafayette acted a distinguished part. These were: 1.— THE BATTLE OF GLOUCESTER; 2.— RETREAT OF BARREN HILL; 3.— BATTLE OF MONMOUTH; 4.— RETREAT OF RHODE ISLAND."

The sword was presented to the Marquis at Havre by a grandson of Dr. Franklin, accompanied by the following letter:

"PASSY, August 24, 1779.

"SIR, — The Congress, sensible of your merit towards the United States, but *unable adequately to reward it*, determined to present you with a sword, as a small mark of their grateful acknowledgment. They directed it to be ornamented with suitable devices. Some of the principal actions of the war, in which you distinguished yourself by your bravery and conduct, are, therefore, represented upon it. These with a few emblematic figures, all admirably well executed, make its principal value. By the help of the exquisite artists France affords, I find it easy to express every thing but *the sense we have of your worth, and our obligations to you.* For this, figures, and even words are found insufficient. I, therefore, only add, that with the most perfect esteem and respect, I have the honor to be your obedient servant, B. FRANKLIN."

The reply of Lafayette is fully indicative of himself. It is as follows :

"HAVRE, August 29, 1779.

"SIR, — Whatever expectation might have been raised from the sense of past favors, the goodness of the United States to me has ever been such, that on every occasion it far surpasses any idea I could have conceived. A new proof of that flattering truth I find in the noble present which Congress has been pleased to honor me with, and which is offered in such a manner by your excellency, as will exceed any thing but the feelings of an unbounded gratitude.

"In some of the devices I cannot help finding too honorable a reward for those slight services which, in concert with my fellow soldiers, and under the god-like American hero's orders, I had the good fortune to render. The sight of those actions, where I was a witness of American bravery and patriotic spirit, I shall ever enjoy with that pleasure which becomes a heart glowing with love for the nation, and the most ardent zeal for its glory and happiness. Assurances of gratitude, which I beg leave to present to your excellency, are much too inadequate to my feelings, and nothing but such sentiments can properly acknowledge your kindness towards me. The polite manner in which Mr. Franklin was pleased to deliver that inestimable sword, lays me under great obligations to him, and demands my particular thanks. I have the honor to be, &c.

"LAFAYETTE."

The fidelity of Layfayette to the stars and stripes was conspicuous every where. The difficulties among his people were not all with which he had to contend. Influences were spreading in America, unfavorable to receiving the aid he sought. The discord between the allies had awakened a very extensive prejudice in this country, against the employment of any more foreign troops. Lafayette was not ignorant of it; for, like water to the fire, it chilled his spirit. Still his labors were not diminished. He saw the importance of enlisting France, and, though in the attempt he met with but little favor, he persevered. But the popular feeling was so strong in the colonies, that before he succeeded, there came a direct injunction from Congress, that he should not ask the aid of land forces from his government. This staggered him for a moment, but his comprehensive mind surveyed the whole subject, and he determined to proceed. He was confident that ere long Congress would view the matter in the same light that he did. With great decision he therefore continued imploring the ministry. The king at first smiled at his enthusiasm, and then began to wonder at his unflagging perseverance. "He would unfurnish the palace of Versailles to clothe the American army," said M. de Maurepas one day, and, said Lafayette, when he heard of it, "*I would!*" He solicited a naval armament, and a large supply of auxiliary troops for the service, and was inclined to take no denial. At the request of the Count de Vergennes, he submitted an important paper, containing his views respecting the proposed expedition. He states its importance to both nations, urges it as a matter of duty and policy, and then details in extended terms the plan which he would see adopted. In conclusion, he says: "For my own part, you know my sentiments, and you will never doubt that my first interest is to serve my country. I hope for the sake of the public good, that you will send troops to America. I shall be considered too young, I presume, to take the command, but I shall surely be employed. If, in the arrangement of this plan, any one, to whom my sentiments are less known than to yourself, in proposing for me either the command or some inferior commission, should assign as a reason, that I should thereby be induced to serve my country with more zeal, either in council or in action, I take the liberty,—putting aside the minister of the King,—to request M. de Vergennes to come forward as my friend, and refuse, in my name, favors bestowed from motives so inconsistent with my character."

This had a material effect upon subsequent affairs. The attack upon England, after another discussion, was entirely dismissed, and the ministry regarded more favorably Lafayette's proposal. His first suggestion was the combined power of naval and land forces; but if this could not be granted immediately, he desired them to send two or three thousand men with three hundred dragoons to Boston, to act with the army till the sea force could be got in readiness. Early in February, 1780, a plan was accepted chiefly in accordance with his own wishes. An army was to be fitted out, and dispatched early in the succeeding April, under command of Major-General le Compte Rochambeau. It was to consist of six ships of the line with the necessary transports, which were to take out six thousand men with the requisite artillery for sieges and field service. With these were to be sent large supplies of clothing, arms, and munitions of war. In view of former troubles at Rhode Island and elsewhere, Lafayette expressly stipulated that the troops now to be sent should be considered as auxiliaries; that they should be held under the command of General Washington, and subjected to the various regulations which the American officers should adopt. Lafayette had not solicited, and did not expect, a command in this expedition. With a bounding heart he received his instructions, which were "to proceed immediately to join General Washington, and communicate to him the secret, that the King, willing to give the United States a new proof of his affection and of his interest in their security, is resolved to send to their aid, at the opening of the spring, six vessels of the line and six thousand regular troops of infantry." It was a glad day for the Marquis when he received these directions. The darling wish of his heart was gratified, and he had nothing farther than speedily to return to the scene of his conflicts and renown. Taking an affectionate leave of Madame Lafayette and his family, he stepped on board the French frigate Hermione, and sailed from Rochelle on the 19th of March, 1780. His voyage was pleasant and without any special incident. The Hermione arrived at the entrance of Boston harbor on the 27th of April; and before landing, thus apprised General Washington of his approach:

"AT THE ENTRANCE OF BOSTON HARBOR,
"April 27, 1780.

"Here I am, my dear General, and, in the midst of the joy I feel in finding myself again one of your loving soldiers, I take but the time to tell you that I came from France on board a frigate which the King gave me for my passage. I have affairs of the utmost importance, which I should at first communicate to you alone. In case my letter finds you any where this side of Philadelphia, I beg you will wait for me, and do assure you a great public good may be derived from it. To-morrow we go up to the town, and the day after I shall set off in my usual way to join my beloved and respected friend and general."

The next day Lafayette landed. His reception was highly flattering. The day was made one of public rejoicing; all the bells in the city rung their merry peals over the inhabitants flocking to the shore, to receive their generous defender. Amid the roar of cannon, the enlivening strains of military music, and the loud shouts of the multitude, he was escorted to the house of Gov. Hancock, which had been arranged for his reception. The festivities there were unattractive, because his thoughts were with Washington. Leaving Boston, he hurried to headquarters, and no public reception was ever so grateful to him as the warm embrace and words of welcome from his noble friend. The army celebrated his arrival with public gratulations, but Washington's smile eclipsed all these rejoicings. The warm friendship which subsisted between these two great men is pleasing to contemplate.

There was no outward display of affection for mere effect. In the breast of each was a fountain, which, at the mention of the other's name, would overflow.

The news brought from France Lafayette disclosed to no one, till he saw Washington. The tidings were peculiarly grateful to the weary heart of the father of his country. Pressed by the burden of accumulated difficulties, the prospect which now opened before him, gave him hope of a speedy relief from them all. The proposed measures, to be adopted upon the arrival of the French fleet, were discussed by Washington and Lafayette, and then the Marquis proceeded to Philadelphia. On his arrival there he was greeted with the warmest welcome. Upon the 13th of May he offered his services in the army, to Congress, whereupon the following resolution was immediately adopted :

"RESOLVED,— That Congress consider the return of the Marquis de Lafayette to America, to resume his command, as a fresh proof of the disinterested zeal and persevering attachment which have justly recommended him to the public confidence and applause ; — and that they receive with pleasure a tender of the further services of so gallant and meritorious an officer."

The fleet was now daily expected, and the two heroes began to busy themselves upon a plan of operations. The Commander-in-Chief earnestly hoped that the present campaign might witness a termination of the war. He longed to be permitted to lay down his sword again, and now that France had promised so largely assistance, he anticipated that consummation.

Still there were many obstacles in the way. Difficulties surrounded Washington under which ordinary men would have sunk; but his great soul was unmoved. No gloom or danger ever shut out from his view the bright vision of future peace and liberty. Trials thickened, but the hope was there. New obstacles were continually to be surmounted;—new difficulties were constantly crossing his way, but his path was onward, and he trod it with an unfaltering footstep. He saw in perils only clouds hiding the sun; and though at times they were black and heavy, yet he knew that the bright orb upon which his faith rested, was rolling radiantly behind them, and would come gloriously forth from obscurity, lighting up a wondering world with its rays. Washington has received the homage of the world, and needs no other eulogy than a simple delineation of his character. Among the brave generals who fought around him, he is isolated by a serene elevation of thought and action, resembling in position the solitary grandeur of Niagara upon this continent of majestic rivers. Perhaps there never was a man who illustrated the balance of powers, a mental and moral harmony, so sublimely as himself. His entire being obeyed the laws designed to govern it, with the beautiful uniformity with which the tides rise and fall, under the attractive influence of the spheres. His patriotic ardor and active energies were always within the confines of sober reason and an enlightened conscience. His monument will adorn the capital of the Union, but a hemisphere is consecrated to his memory, and his name has reached, like a spell-word, the darkest despot and the humblest serf of remotest lands. The care of the Commander-in-Chief for his troops was proverbial. On the 20th of June, 1780, he writes to Congress, giving a melancholy account of their condition at this time. Many of them were destitute of shirts, and almost without clothing of any description. This subject he urges strongly, as he had often done before, upon the attention of Congress. "For the troops to be without clothing at any time," he says, "is highly injurious to the service, and distressing to our feelings; but the want will be more peculiarly mortifying when they come to act with those of our allies. If it be possible, I have no doubt, immediate measures will be taken to relieve their distress.

"It is also most sincerely wished that there could be some supplies of clothing furnished to the officers. There are a great many whose condition is still miserable. This is, in some instances, the case with the whole lines of the States. It would be well for their own sakes and the public good if they could be furnished. They will not be able, when our friends come to coöperate with us, to go on a common routine of duty; and if they should, they must, from their appearance, be held in low estimation."

"This picture," says Marshall, "presents in strong colors the real patriotism of the American army. One heroic effort, though it may dazzle the mind with its splendor, is an exertion most men are capable of making,—but continued patient suffering and unremitting perseverance, in a service promising no personal emolument, and exposing the officer unceasingly, not only to wants of every kind, but to those circumstances of humiliation which seem to degrade him in the eyes of others, demonstrate a fortitude of mind, a strength of virtue, and a firmness of principle, which ought never to be forgotten."

This condition of the American soldiers was also an object of solicitude to Lafayette. The ladies of Philadelphia started a subscription and made large donations in aid of the suffering, to which the Marquis, in the name of Madame Lafayette, generously added one hundred guineas. This, however, was only a temporary supply, and could not meet the real wants of the destitute troops. Private charities and individual contributions are not adequate to the necessities of a protracted revolution. The lamentable insensibility of Congress to the real condition of things, and the failure to adopt suitable measures for relief, are amazing. Numbers who composed that body, seemed to have a faint conception of the great object for which they were struggling. Hence they neglected to act promptly and nobly in its accomplishment. The paper currency of the nation was rapidly depreciating in value, and Congress was distracted by diverse counsels, and time wasted in party animosities without heeding results. The conduct of the different states was also far from what it should have been. The supplies which they agreed to furnish, they neglected to send, or would send them after so long a delay that half their benefit was lost. Washington deeply felt this, and wrote to Congress, again and again, upon the subject. About the time of the last letter above quoted, he writes thus; — "I hope the period has not yet arrived, which will convince the different states by fatal experience, that some of them have mistaken the true situation of this country. I flatter myself, however, that we may still retrieve our affairs if we have but a just sense of them, and are actuated by a spirit of liberal policy and exertion equal to the emergency. Could we once see this spirit generally prevailing, I should not despair of a prosperous issue of the campaign. But there is no time to be lost. The danger is imminent and pressing; — the obstacles to be surmounted are great and numerous; and our efforts must be instant, unreserved, and universal."

The French fleet was delayed, but a plan of action was taken which was to go into execution immediately upon its arrival. It was the wish both of Washington and Lafayette to make an attack upon New York. With a wisdom, which, had it been shown at first, might have brought the war to a close long before, Congress, instead of foolishly attempting to guide the matter, and laying the Commander-in-Chief under useless and irksome restraints, judiciously empowered him "to take such measures for carrying on the operations of the campaign as would effectually promote the purposes in view." The attack upon New York was accordingly determined upon, as soon as practicable after the French vessels were in harbor.

Preparations for the reception of the foreign forces continued through the month of June. It was not till the 10th of July that the anxiously expected aid anchored off Newport. To the disappointment of Washington, this was only a part of the promised assistance. Five thousand five hundred men were sent, leaving two thousand, with all the arms, munitions of war, and clothing promised Lafayette, to follow on in a second division of the armament. The delay of these last mentioned supplies was embarrassing. Said Washington to Lafayette on learning it, — "Unless our allies can lend us largely, we can attempt nothing. With every effort we can make, we shall fall short four or five thousand arms, and two hundred tons of powder."

The fleet had been detained in France till the 2d of May. Meanwhile the enemy against which it was to move had not been asleep; nor had the progress of affairs escaped British vigilance. Before they were half completed the English ministry understood their object, and began to take counter measures. Intelligence was sent to Sir Henry Clinton that a French armament was fitting out for the American service, and, as it was calculated that New York would be the first place of attack, he was ordered to take special means for its defense. These dispatches reached him in time to enable him to call off a heavy detachment from South Carolina, which arrived just before the French fleet reached Newport. To aid him further, an additional naval force was dispatched from England which was expected.

Soon as arrangements could be made, Lafayette left Washington for Newport, fully commissioned by the Commander-in-Chief to arrange with the Count de Rochambeau, such prospective movements as circumstances should suggest. A combined attack upon New York was the desire of both. But, before the Marquis reached Newport, news had reached the French that Sir Henry Clinton had sailed from the city, with a large naval and land force, and was now on his way to attack them. When Lafayette arrived, therefore, (July 25th,) he found the French in a state fitted for defensive rather than offensive war. The troops were disembarked and strongly fortified on shore, while the fleet stood in line, to cover them. General Clinton upon learning this did not venture an attack; and when this immediate danger was passed, Lafayette submitted to de Rochambeau the plan of a united advance upon New York. The Count entered into it with zeal, but was disposed to wait for his second division, before decisive battle. The Marquis with energy opposed these views. All the arguments which his fertile mind suggested were brought to bear upon the Count. The easy, affable and engaging way in which he presented them, had its force, but de Rochambeau was disposed to act with extreme caution. While in this attitude, he preserved harmony between the allies, determined to avoid the disgraceful difficulties in which d' Estaing had been involved. On the 31st of July Lafayette wrote to Washington; — "The French army hate the idea of staying here, and want to join you. They swear at those who speak of waiting for the second division. They are enraged to be blockaded in this harbor. As to the dispositions of the inhabitants and our troops, and the dispositions of the inhabitants and the militia for them, they are such as I may wish.

You would have been glad the other day, to have seen two hundred and fifty of our drafts, that came on from Connecticut without provisions or tents, and who were mixed in such a way with the French troops, that every French soldier and officer took an American with him, and divided their bed and their supper in the most friendly manner.

"The patience and sobriety of our militia is so much admired by the French officers, that two days ago a French Colonel called all his officers together, to desire them to take the good examples which were given to the French soldiers by the American troops. So far are they gone in their admirations, that they find a great deal to say in favor of General Varnum, and his escort of militia dragoons, who fill up all the streets of Newport. On the other hand, the French discipline is such that chickens and pigs walk between the tents without being disturbed, and that there is in the camp a corn field, from which not one leaf has been touched. The Tories don't know what to say to it."

Rochambeau still desiring to wait for his division, Washington advised Lafayette not to urge their movements. "I would not wish you," said he,. "to press the French General and Admiral to any thing to which they show a disinclination, especially to the withdrawing of their troops from Rhode Island before the second division arrives to give them a naval superiority. Should they yield to importunity, and an accident happen, either there or here, they would lay the consequences to us. Only inform them what we can do, what we are willing to undertake, and let them entirely consult their own inclination for the rest." Accordingly Lafayette ceased his importunity, and soon after news arrived that Clinton had received a fresh reinforcement, thus giving him a decided naval superiority upon the coast. A plan was thereupon formed by him of a joint operation with his land and sea forces against Newport, and six thousand troops were embarked for that purpose. Such a design could not escape the scrutiny of Washington, who lost no time in dispatching tidings of it to Newport, and in preparing for a great emergency himself. Knowing that the force which Sir Henry had taken with him must greatly weaken the garrison left in New York, Washington formed the bold design of attacking it. Without delay he caused his army to move forward towards the city ; but his high hopes of success were dispelled, when he heard that Clinton, not venturing an assault, had suddenly returned to headquarters. To continue the descent was hopeless, and Washington drew back across the Hudson, and took post near Orangetown.

Tidings soon after reached Newport that the anticipated vessels were blockaded in the port of Brest by a British squadron. This news was soon followed by the intelligence that Admiral Rodney had sailed from England for America, with eleven ships of the line and four frigates. This disconcerted all the plans of the allies, and frustrated the hopes they had cherished at the opening of the campaign. To march against New York was now out of the question, and as Lafayette could see nothing but inaction before him at Newport, he solicited and obtained permission to return to head-quarters.

Washington received the Marquis on the 7th of August, and invested him with the command of a corps of light infantry, which he had collected and organized for this purpose. It was a fine body of two thousand men, "but," said Washington, "the greater part of them are without clothing." Lafayette was much pleased with them, and made them the subjects of his customary liberality. He clothed the soldiers in uniform, and presented each of the subordinate officers of the corps with an elegant sword, at his own expense. Nothing could exceed the ardent attachment which he immediately won from them all. They became the pride of his heart, and he the idol of their affection. "The whole army indiscriminately beloved Lafayette, not only for that amiable disposition, and those charming manners which characterized him, but for his great gallantry and ardent attachment to his country. The confidence and affection of the troops were, to him, invaluable possessions and well acquired riches, of which no one could, and no one desired to deprive him; and he always expressed by his air and countenance, that he was happier in receiving his friends at their head than at his estate in Auvergne. The influence and consideration which he acquired among the political, as well as the military body were highly flattering to a young man of his mold, and it is confidently asserted that his private letters have, frequently, produced more effect in arousing the lethargy of some of the States, than the strongest exhortations of Congress. In short, he possessed in so high a degree the character of an accomplished and perfect soldier, as to gain the confidence of his superiors, the affection of his equals, and the respect and veneration of all who served under him. It is no trifling compliment to say, that next to the Commander-in-Chief and the intrepid Greene, no General stood higher in the public favor, or more constantly commanded the admiration of the army than Lafayette."

The Marquis now busied himself in arranging an interview between General Washington, Count de Rochambeau, and the Chevalier de Ternay, the Admiral of the French fleet. This was earnestly desired by the officers, who assured Lafayette that they could do more towards arranging operations in a quarter of an hour's conversation, than they could do by multiplied dispatches. "I will do all that depends upon me, gentlemen," replied the Marquis, "to prevail upon the General to meet you half way;—but from his proximity to the enemy, and from the present situation of the army, which he has never quitted since the war, I fear it will appear very difficult for him to absent himself." Washington was unwilling to leave for a day, but at length consented to the proposed interview, hoping, at least, that it might contribute to strengthen the bonds of union. The interview was agreed upon, to take place at Hartford, Conn. on the 20th of September; and three days previously, Washington, Lafayette, and Gen. Knox, attended by an imposing retinue, left the American camp for that purpose. No definite order of things was settled as the result of the interview, but it had a favorable influence in cementing personal friendly relations, and in producing harmonious views of military coöperation between the French and American commanders.

CHAPTER V.

TREASON OF ARNOLD — FATE OF ANDRE — WASHINGTON IN NEWPORT—LAFAYETTE IN MARYLAND — MANŒUVRES AND OPERATIONS THERE — DESTITUTION OF THE SOLDIERS — GENEROSITY OF THE MARQUIS — LAFAYETTE IN VIRGINIA—PHILLIPS AND THE TRAITOR — CORNWALLIS ARRIVES, AND TAKES THE SUPREME COMMAND OF THE BRITISH TROOPS—HIS CHARACTER—PURSUIT OF CORNWALLIS AND RETREAT OF THE MARQUIS—JUNCTION WITH WAYNE—THE PURSUED TURNS PURSUER — CORNWALLIS RETREATS TO PORTSMOUTH — EMBARKS FOR YORKTOWN—FORTIFIES HIMSELF AT YORKTOWN AND GLOUCESTER POINT—ARRIVAL OF THE FRENCH FLEET—ARRIVAL OF THE ALLIED ARMY—SIEGE OF YORKTOWN—SURRENDER OF CORNWALLIS—RESULTS—LAFAYETTE GOES TO FRANCE.

THE record of September, 1780, is ever memorable for the blot of Arnold's treason. The details of this foul transaction, which will hand down to remotest posterity the picture of its principal actor, painted in tints of irremediable baseness, are familiar to every reader of history. Arnold had taken the time when Washington was absent from the camp, to carry his diabolical plans into execution, and the Commander-in-Chief first learned of it as he was returning from Hartford. The following is Lafayette's announcement of the treachery to the Chevalier de la Luzerne :

"ROBINSON HOUSE, OPPOSITE W. POINT,
"Sept 26, 1780.

"When I parted from you yesterday, Sir, to come and breakfast here with General Arnold, we were far from foreseeing the event which I am now going to relate to you. You will shudder at the danger to which we wêre exposed ;—you will admire the miraculous chain of unexpected events and singular chances, which have saved us ; — but you will be still more astonished when you learn by what instrument this conspiracy has been formed. West Point was sold,— *and sold by Arnold*,— the same man who formerly acquired glory by rendering such immense services to his country. He had lately entered into a horrible compact with the enemy, and, but for the accident which brought us here at a certain hour, but for the combination of chances that threw the Adjutant-General of the British army in the hands of some peasants, beyond the limits of our stations, at West Point and on the North River, we should both at present, in all probability, be in the possession of the enemy.

"When we set out yesterday for Fishkill, we were preceded by one of my aids-de-camp, and one of General Washington's, (Colonels Hamilton and McHenry,) who found General Arnold and his wife at breakfast, and sat down at table with them. While they were together two letters were given to Arnold, which apprised him of the arrest of the spy. He ordered a horse to be saddled, went into his wife's room to tell her he was ruined, and desired his aid-de-camp to inform General Washington that he was going to West Point and would return in the course of an hour.

"On our arrival here, we crossed the river and went to examine the works. You may conceive our astonishment when we learned, on our return, that the arrested spy was Major Andre, Adjutant-General of the English army ; and when among his papers were discovered the copy of an important council of war, the state of the garrison and works, and observations upon various means of attack and defense, the whole in Arnold's own handwriting.

"The Adjutant-General wrote also to the General, avowing his name and situation. Orders were sent to arrest Arnold ; but he escaped in a boat, got on board the English frigate, the *Vulture*, and as no person suspected his flight he was not stopped at any post. Colonel Hamilton, who had gone in pursuit of him, received, soon after by a flag of truce, a letter from Arnold to the General, in which he entered into details to justify his treachery, and a letter from the English commander, Robertson, who, in a very insolent manner, demanded that the Adjutant-General should be delivered up to them, as he had only acted with the permission of General Arnold.

"The first care of the General has been to assemble at West Point the troops that, under various pretences, Arnold had dispersed. We remain here to watch over the safety of a fort, that the English may respect less as they become better acquainted with it. Continental troops have been summoned here, and, as Arnold's advice may determine Clinton to make a sudden movement, the army has received orders to be prepared to march at a moment's warning."

The character of Arnold from his boyhood is without a luminous phase, unless it be the meteoric glare of his heroism in battle. He resembled in untamed passions — destitution of manly principle — and entire recklessness of consequences, when selfish aims demanded the hazard of human well-being, a late distinguished criminal, whose doom the traitor escaped. Both of whom are a perpetual warning to the youth of this, and other lands, to beware how they venture on the declivity of moral ruin. Never in the history of our country was the hand of God more visible, than in warding off from freedom's heart the deadly stab of this modern Judas.

The fate of Andre has awakened a melancholy interest every where, though none doubt the propriety of the course taken by the American officers in the tragical result. Lafayette was one of the Board before whom the ill-fated spy appeared for trial, and from whom he received his sentence of condemnation. To the feeling and generous heart of the Marquis the performance of this sad duty occasioned severest pangs. With the other officers he felt interested in the candor, openness, and magnanimity of Andre, but, with them, he was compelled to decide that this young and highly accomplished officer, who united the polish of a court, and the refinements of education, to the heroism of a soldier, was a spy, and as such worthy of death. Gladly would he and his associates have seen the stroke of vengeance fall on the guiltier head.

The absence of something to do, did not agree with Lafayette. He had hoped with Washington that when this campaign should have closed, the war would also close; and it was depressing to see the season pass away without a signal stroke. The reinforcements which were joining the British fleet, prevented the attack upon New York, which had been proposed with so sanguine expectations. Then Lafayette projected other exploits for himself. On the 26th of October he undertook to surprise the enemy's post upon Staten Island, but was checked by the failure of those whose duty it was to provide the boats, and make other provisions for the passage of the troops. Mortified, but not disheartened, on the 30th October, he urged upon General Washington an attack upon the upper posts of the enemy at New York. Washington had before contemplated this enterprise, but both he and the Marquis were forced to relinguish it. Said Washington "we must consult our means rather than our wishes and not endeavor to better our affairs by attempting things which, for want of success, may make them worse." Abandoning this, Lafayette next petitions to join General Greene, who had lately been appointed to the command of the southern army, hoping that he might there find active service. He wrote a long letter to Greene, who, in reply, gave him a sad account of the prospect before him, in that direction. "Were you to arrive," said he, "you would find a few ragged, half-starved troops in the wilderness, destitute of every thing necessary for either the comfort or convenience of soldiers. The department is in a most deplorable condition, nor have I a prospect of its mending. The country is almost laid waste, and the inhabitants plunder one another with little less than savage fury. We live from hand to mouth, and have nothing to subsist on but what we collect with armed parties. In this situation, I believe you will agree with me that there is nothing inviting this way, especially when I assure you our whole force, fit for duty, that are properly clothed and equipped, does not amount to eight hundred men." This did not frighten Lafayette. The army at the north had now gone into winter quarters, his corps of light infantry had been disbanded, and he saw no means of occupying the time which to him was so precious except by going south. "I hate the idea," said he to Washington, "of being from you for so long a time, but I think I ought not to be idle."

Before giving him permission, Washington advised him to proceed to Philadelphia, and take charge of some transactions there. This was early in December, and Lafayette remained there during the whole of that month, communicating to Washington almost daily such intelligence as he received, and freely consulting with him respecting future plans. At length, upon a renewed suggestion, Washington gave him leave to join General Greene, should there be no call for him at the north. In one of the letters of Washington to Lafayette, written while the Marquis was in Philadelphia, is the following passage, illustrating the great embarrassment which still existed in the finances of the army. "The Chevalier de Luzerne's dispatches came in time for the post, which is the only means left me for the conveyance of letters, there not being so much money in the hands of the quarter-master-general, (I believe I might go farther and say, in those of the whole army,) as would bear the expense of an express to Rhode Island. I could not get one the other day to ride as far as Pompton !" The hardships of the troops endured so long, continued unabated. Without money and almost unclad and unfed, their situation was distressing. With a patriotism stronger than love of life, their present sufferings appeared hopeless and needless. With too much justice they began to entertain the opinion that Congress was culpably responsible for their privations, and having suffered them so long. a part of the troops determined to take redress into their hands. This was the origin of the famous mutiny at Morristown. On the night of the 1st January, 1781, the Pensylvannia line, stationed for the winter at that place, rose in an open and almost universal revolt. They stated their grievances as having been borne till they were now past endurance, and avowed their determination of marching to the seat of Congress, and forcing redress. The authority of General Wayne, their commanding officer, availed nothing for a time, in quelling the rebellion, and the mutineers, consisting of thirteen hundred men, marched towards Princeton. Congress, made to understand at last the effects of its miserable indifference, appointed commissioners to treat with the troops, and requested Lafayette with General St. Clair and Col. Laurens, to repair to Princeton, and aid in the work of pacification. By the exertions of these officers, and the judicious intervention of Wayne, the disturbance was at length subdued ; but not till its existence had awakened a new and dark apprehension in the breast of every friend of American liberty.

From Princeton Lafayette proceeded to headquarters, and rejoined Washington on the 11th of January. Here these two devoted men with courage still unwavering, watched for light upon the darkening heavens. In every direction, they saw only the blackness of despair. The dawn of the last campaign was sadly contrasted with the gloom which hung around its close. The next campaign could not be undertaken with the slighest hope of success, unless new supplies could be obtained from some source. With this view the minds of Washington and Lafayette again turned to France, and Congress was induced to appoint a new commissioner to the court of Versailles, for the purpose of making one more effort to obtain from the ministry the help which was needed. Colonel Laurens, one of Washington's aids-de-camp, was appointed, and, before leaving, received the instructions of the Commander-in-Chief, and a letter which he wrote to Franklin, detailing with great force and ability, the state and resources of the country, with its present urgent wants. Lafayette also sent by him a letter to the Count de Vergennes, expressing his own views, and pleading earnestly the cause of the country. The following extracts from this letter show that his solicitude was as earnest as ever.

"The last campaign took place without a shilling having been spent. All that credit, persuasion and force could achieve, has been done, but that can hold out no longer; that miracle of which I believe no similar example can be found, cannot be renewed, and our exertions having been made to obtain an army for the war, we must depend on you to enable us to make use of it.

"From my peculiar situation, Sir, and from what it has enabled me to know and see, I think it is my duty to call your attention to the American soldiers, and the part they must take in the operations of the next campaign. The continental troops have as much courage and real discipline as those that are opposed to them. They are more inured to privation, more patient than Europeans, who, on these two points, cannot be compared to them. They have several officers of great merit, without mentioning those who have served during the last wars, and from their own talents have acquired knowledge intuitively. They have been formed by the daily experience of several campaigns, in which, the armies being small, and the country a rugged one, all the battalions of the line were obliged to serve as advanced guards and light troops. The recruits whom we are expecting, and who only bear, in truth, the name of recruits, have frequently fought battles in the same regiments which they are now reëntering, and have seen more gunshots than three-fourths of the European soldiers. As to the militia, they are only armed peasants, who have occasionally fought, and who are not deficient in ardor and discipline, but whose services would be the most useful in the labors of a siege. This, Sir, is the faithful picture that I think myself obliged to send you, and which is not my interest to paint in glowing colors, because it would be more glorious to succeed with slighter means. The Chevalier de la Luzerne, who, having himself seen our soldiers, will give you a detailed and disinterested account of them, will doubtless tell you as I do, that you may depend upon our regular troops. The result of this digression, Sir, is to insist still more earnestly on the necessity of sending money to put the American troops in movement, and to repeat that well known truth, that a pecuniary succor and a naval superiority must be the two principal objects of the next campaign."

By the same messenger he also writes to Madame Lafayette; — "The Americans continue to testify for me the greatest kindness. There is no proof of affection and kindness which I do not receive each day from the army and nation. I experience for the American officers and soldiers that friendship which arises from having shared with them, for a length of time, dangers, sufferings, and both good and evil fortune. We began by struggling together, for our affairs have often been at the lowest possible ebb. It is gratifying to me to crown this work with them by giving the European troops a high idea of the soldiers who have been formed with us. To all these motives of interest for the cause and the army, are joined my sentiments of regard for General Washington." In the same letter he also writes: — "Embrace our children a thousand and a thousand times for me. Their father, although a wanderer, is not less tender, nor less constantly occupied with them, and not less happy at reciving news from them. My heart dwells with peculiar delight on the moment when those dear children will be presented to me by you, and when we can embrace and caress them together."

Although recent transactions had temporarily driven from Lafayette's mind his southern plans, events that were now transpiring gave him an opportunity for renewing the consideration of them, though in a different light than before. Arnold, whose villainy had heen rewarded by the commission of Brigadier-General in the British service, at the head of sixteen hundred men, was now ravaging the lower part of Virginia. His spirit burning with resentment, spent its bitterness in acts of unparalleled atrocity. Wherever he went, the fire and the sword marked his path with devastation. Gloating over the butchery of the defenceless, his demoniac heart drank joy from the cup of horror which he pressed to the lips of the helpless inhabitants in every place through which he marched. Property which could not be pillaged was destroyed; both the old and the young of either sex fell alike the victims of his fiendish barbarity. The Baron Steuben, with his small division, could do no more than occasionally check his ravages, and Washington saw the propriety and importance of detaching a larger force to that scene of warfare. As soon as he learned the position of things in Virginia, his mind formed a design for the capture of Arnold. The French fleet, which had been blockaded in Newport, was now freed by a violent storm dispersing the British fleet at Gardner's Bay with great loss. Availing himself of this release, Washington applied to the Admiral for coöperation in an expedition against Arnold. His plan was to send Lafayette with a detachment of twelve hundred men, drafted for that purpose from the lines of New England and New Jersey, to the head of the Chesapeake, where they were to embark under convoy of a French frigate, which he expected to obtain, for Virginia. To succeed, and bring the traitor to justice, was Washington's intense desire. To ensure success, he urged the enlistment of the whole fleet in the enterprize, and that a thousand men should be embarked for the service. This would doubtless have resulted in the capture of Arnold, but the French officers refused to join with so large a detachment. Contrary to the opinion of Washington, they thought a smaller force was abundantly adequate, and accordingly, on the 9th of February, a sixty-four gun ship with two frigates under Monsieur de Tilley, sailed for the Chesapeake. Arriving there, he found, as Washington had foreseen, Arnold entrenched in a position secure against any mere naval force, and without attempting to assail it, de Tilley immediately returned to Newport, having been absent only fifteen days.

The General and Admiral determined to renew the expedition, according to the suggestion of Washington, who left his camp and hastened to consult with those officers in person upon the affair. The Admiral assured him that he would proceed to coöperate with Lafayette's detachment with the entire fleet, to which Count Rochambeau promised to add 1100 men from his land forces. This was what Washington desired, and having made the important arrangement, returned to head quarters. The fleet sailed on the 8th of March. It was commanded by Admiral Destouches, who had succeeded the Chevalier de Terney, that officer having died on the 15th of December previous.

Meanwhile Lafayette, at the head of a choice detachment, arrived at the head of the Elk, on the 3d of March. From this point he embarked his troops for Annapolis, whence he proceeded to Williamsburgh, where the Baron Steuben held his head quarters. After having consulted with him, he tarried for several days, hoping to hear of the frigate which was to convey him to Virginia. From Williamsburgh, on the 23d of March, he writes to General Washington :

"On my arrival at this place, I was surprised to hear that no French fleet had appeared, but attributed it to delays and chances so frequent in naval matters. My first object was to request that nothing be taken for this expedition which could have been intended for or useful to the southern army, whose welfare appeared to me more interesting than our success. My second object has been to examine what has been prepared, to gather and forward every requisite for a vigorous coöperation, besides a number of militia, amounting to five thousand ; and I can assure your Excellency that nothing has been wanting to ensure a complete success.

"As the position of the enemy had not yet been reconnoitered, I went to General Muhlenberg's camp, near Suffolk, and after he had taken a position nearer to Portsmouth, we marched down with some troops to view the enemy's works. This brought on a trifling skirmish, during which we were able to see something, but the insufficiency of ammunition, which had been for many days expected, prevented my engaging far enough to push the enemy's outposts, and our reconnoitering was postponed to the 21st, when on the 20th, Major McPherson, an officer for whom I have the highest confidence and esteem, sent me word from Hampton, where he was stationed, that a fleet had come to anchor within the capes. So far it was probable that this fleet was that of M. Destouches, that Arnold himself appeared to be in great confusion, and his vessels, notwithstanding many signals, durst not for a long time venture down."

Lafayette had been advised of the contemplated expedition, but as part of his dispatches had failed to reach him, he was left in great uncertainty. At length he received intelligence from Washington more definitely, and was ordered to hold himself ready to unite with them upon their arrival. The fleet sailed on the 8th, but two days afterwards it was followed by the re-collected British fleet under Arbuthnot, who had orders to frustrate the efforts of the allied armies. Destouches was overtaken off the capes of Virginia, and a naval engagement ensued. The result was not decisive, the damage being about equal on both sides. The French Admiral called a council the next day, deciding that it was unadvisable to renew the action, and accordingly sailed back to Newport, leaving Lafayette to his fate, and the expedition against Arnold to prove an entire failure.

The Marquis had received with joy the tidings

which Major McPherson had given him, of the naval strength at hand, but a few hours changed it to dismal apprehension. After the French had gone, the British entered and took undisputed possession of Chesapeake Bay. It was this fleet instead of the French which McPherson had seen, and Lafayette was not long in making the discovery. Washington, as soon as he had learned the sailing of Arbuthnot, sent word, but this failed to reach the Marquis, and he was unapprised of his danger till suddenly it was before him, threatening ruin. His situation now was an exceedingly critical one. He hastened to Annapolis, where his troops were stationed, and made preparations for their return to the head of the Elk. This was now no easy matter. To return by land was perilous, and the harbor was blockaded by two of the enemy's vessels, which apparently rendered their escape by water impossible. But Lafayette was not the man to be discouraged. His spirit rose with the difficulties which surrounded him, and in the desperate game which was now before him, he determined to win the stakes, fearful as were the odds against him. He gave orders to commence a land march in ten days. At the same time he was busy in devising a passage for the troops by water. For this purpose he executed a bold and ingenious manœuvre. He mounted two guns upon a small sloop, and filling this and another vessel with men, he gave them in charge to Commodore Nicholson, ordering him to sail out boldly towards the two blockading ships, and make demonstrations as though about to board them. The result was fully successful.

The enemy, surprised at this daring, and apprehending the force of their opponents was much greater than they had suspected, weighed anchor and immediately retreated. This was what Lafayette desired, and when night came he took advantage of it. The vessels which had transported him to Annapolis, were refilled with the troops and stores, and under cover of darkness sailed out of the harbor. The Marquis in a sloop brought up the rear, and on the morning of the 8th of April, they safely moored in the Elk.

We cannot fail to admire the sagacity again displayed by this commander. We are now about to enter upon an era of his life in which his singular foresight and prudence, are exhibited in a still clearer light. The name of Lafayette, said another, was never tarnished by a single military blunder. This is the distinguishing glory of the Marquis as a military hero. He had a courage which could face danger and death unappalled, and which gave calmness amid the most terrific battles; but others have possessed this trait in an equal degree. Rarely, however, has it been combined with so much *finesse* and facility for extricating an army from perils which would have repelled veterans in the stratagem of war.

At the head of the Elk, Lafayette met a dispatch, which Washington hoped would reach him at Annapolis, ordering him to repair with his detachment to the south, and join General Greene as soon as possible. Cornwallis and Greene were operating in the Carolinas. To reinforce Arnold and make a junction with Cornwallis, as Washington supposed, Sir Henry Clinton had sent out General Phillips with two thousand men to Virginia, and their arrival changed the destination of Lafayette. He was ordered "to proceed to Virginia, to take the command of the troops collected and collecting for its protection, and to prevent if possible the meditated descent of Phillips or his junction with Cornwallis." He accordingly took up his line of march, and started for Baltimore. But before proceeding far, he encountered trouble unknown before. The troops under his command began to express their open dissatisfaction at the hardships they endured. Their trials were severe. "Without tents,—for many, even of the officers, slept in the open air;—their shoes worn out,—their hats lost in their repeated voyages;—in a state—as the Marquis expresses it—'of shocking nakedness,'—not the least particle of baggage attending their march,—no provision made for a protracted absence from their wives and families, many of whom had joined them and been left at their winter quarters;—murmuring at being thus hurried off without notice to prepare for the service;—reasonably fearing that their destination was to serve in a climate which they dreaded, and supported by the general pity which their case excited;—such was the temper of his army, that many of the officers assured the Marquis, that it would speedily be reduced to one-half by desertion." Lafayette himself, while on his way to Baltimore, communicates to Washington this condition of things, and after stating the distress of the soldiers adds:—"While I was writing this, accounts have been brought to me, that a great desertion had taken place last night; nine of the Rhode Island company, and the best men they had, who have made many campaigns, and never were suspected; These men say they like better a hundred lashes than a journey southward. As long as they had an expedition in view, they were very well satisfied, but the idea of *remaining* in the Southern States, appears to them intolerable, and they are amazingly averse to the people and the climate. I shall do my best, but if this disposition lasts, I am afraid we shall be reduced lower than I dare express."

To render the prospect still more hopeless, advices were received from the Board of War, that they were utterly unable to remedy the wretchedness of the troops. Thus thrown entirely upon himself, Lafayette issued an order, in which, after sympathizing with their hardships, he told them he was about to enter upon an enterprise of great difficulty and danger, in which he was confident his soldiers would readily join him. He assured them, however, that if any were unwilling to accompany him, a free permit should be given them to rejoin their corps in the north, and that by making an application to him they could thus be saved from the crime and disgrace of desertion. The success of this plan was marked and immediate. Desertion ceased at once. A new spirit instantly spread through the troops. Lafayette assured Marshall that such was the enthusiasm of the moment, that a lame sergeant hired a place in a cart to keep up with the army. On reaching Baltimore, Lafayette added to this measure another with yet greater effect. From the merchants of this city he borrowed upon his own credit ten thousand dollars, which he did not hesitate in appropriating to the supply of the necessary wants of his soldiers. In a letter to General Greene he says, — "As our brave and excellent men (for this detachment is exceedingly good) are shockingly destitute of linen, I have borrowed from the merchants of Baltimore a sum on my credit, which will amount to about two thousand pounds, and will procure a few hats, some shoes, some blankets, and a pair of linen overalls, to each man. I hope to set the Baltimore ladies* at work upon the shirts, which will be sent after me, and the overalls will be made by our tailors. I will use my influence to have the money added to the loan which the French court have made to the United States, and in case I cannot succeed, bind myself to the merchants for payment with interest, in two years." The President of the Baltimore Board of War also wrote to General Greene upon the same subject. "While I admire your policy," said he, "I have more than once pitied the Marquis' situation. His troops passed here yesterday, discontented almost to general desertion; — destitute of shirts, and proper equipments, and in most respects, unprovided for a march. *You know the Marquis.* He has been with us but two days, but in this time he adopted an expedient to conciliate them to a degree, which no one but himself would have thought of. To day, April 16th, 1781, he signs a contract, binding himself to certain mer-

* This was done. Every fair hand in Baltimore promptly aided in preparing his purchases for immediate use.

chants of this place, for above *two thousand guineas*, to be disposed of in shirts, overalls, and hats, for the detachment. Without these the army could not proceed; and with these he has managed to reconcile them to the service. He is also bent upon trying the power of novelty on their minds, by giving to the march the air of a frolic. His troops will ride in wagons and carts, from Elkbridge landing to the limits of this state, and how much further he will continue this mode of movement depends upon Virginia."

Lafayette now proceeded onward in fine spirits towards Virginia. Phillips and the Traitor were carrying on their work of devastation and pillage in this state almost without interruption. Ten thousand hogsheads of tobacco were destroyed by the doughty Phillips in his predatory excursions. Baron Steuben was unable to check him, and as Lafayette learned that the British were ascending the James River, he judged that their destination was Richmond and directed his own course thither. The chief proportion of the military stores of the state were collected at this place, a fact that both Lafayette and the British General well understood. Phillips and Arnold having separated their forces for the purpose of carrying on their lawless work against defenceless women and tobacco warehouses, re-united their divisions on the 29th of April at Manchester, a small village on the south side of James River, but within sight of the metropolis. Their plans were laid for an attack upon Richmond the next day. But in this they reckoned without their host. Lafayette, with the celerity which usually attended his movements, arrived at the city, and took possession of it the same day that his enemies on the opposite side of the River, were planning its destruction for the morrow's pastime.

The 30th of April dawned, and Lafayette, upon enumerating his forces, knew the enemy could not drive him from his position. He was here joined by Baron Steuben, with his corps of regular troops, and by General Nelson with a division of the Virginia militia, making in all about a thousand regulars, two thousand militia and sixty dragoons now under his command. The British force exceeded this, but he did not doubt his ability to maintain his ground. Preparations were making by General Phillips to cross over and ravage the place, when upon reconnoitering he found to his surprise and anger that Lafayette was already in possession of the city. The rage of the British General upon discovering this, knew no bounds. With passionate vehemence he swore that he would have vengeance. Attempting to cross over the river with a body of his men, he was repulsed and forced to bear his disappointment, making a precipitate retreat.

The events which occurred subsequently to these transactions are best related by Lafayette himself, and we quote accordingly from him. Writing to General Washington under date of May 18th, he thus gives a statement of events up to that time:

"When General Phillips retreated from Richmond, his project was to stop at Williamsburg, there to collect contributions which he had imposed. This induced me to take a position between Pamunkey and Chiccahomony rivers, which equally covered Richmond and some other interesting parts of the state, and from where I detached General Nelson with some militia towards Williamsburg.

"Having got as low down as that place, General Phillips seemed to discover an intention to make a landing, but upon advices received by a vessel from Portsmouth, the enemy weighed anchor, and, with all the sail they could crowd, hastened up the river. This intelligence made me apprehensive that the enemy intended to manœuvre me out of Richmond, where I returned immediately, and again collected our small force. Intelligence was the same day received that Lord Cornwallis — who I had been assured to have embarked at Wilmington — was marching through North Carolina. This was confirmed by the landing of General Phillips at Brandon, south side of James River. Apprehending that both armies would meet at a central point, I marched towards Petersburg and intended to have established a communication over Appamatox and James Rivers; — but on the 9th General Phillips took possession of Petersburg, a place where his right flank being covered by James River, his front by Appamatox on which the brigades had been destroyed in the first part of the invasion, and his left not being attackable but by a long circuit through fords, that at this season are very uncertain, I could not — even with an equal force — have got any chance of fighting him, unless I had given up this side of James River, and the country from which reinforcements are expected. It being the enemy's choice to force us to an action, while their own position ensured them against our enterprises, I thought it proper to shift this situation, and marched the greater part of our troops to this place,* about ten miles below Richmond. Letters from General Nash, General Jones and General Sumner are positive as to the arrival of Colonel Tarleton, and announce that of Lord Cornwallis at Halifax. Having received a request from North Carolina for ammunition, I made a detachment of five hundred men under General Muhlenburg, to escort twenty thousand cartridges over Appamatox, and, to divert the enemy's attention, Colonel Gimat, with his battalion, and four field pieces, commanded their position from this side of the river. I hope our ammunition will arrive safe, as before General Muhlenburg returned he put it in a safe road, with proper directions. On the 13th General Phillips died, and the command devolved on General Arnold. General Wayne's detachment has not yet been heard from. Before he arrives, it becomes very dangerous to risk an engagement, where — as the British armies are vastly superior to us — we shall certainly be beaten, and by the loss of arms, the dispersion of militia, and the difficulty of a junction with General Wayne, we may lose a less dangerous chance of resistance."

Lafayette, with an eye open to the full nature of his situation, improved the time in his present camp to the best advantage. In a number of ways he exerted himself to increase the strength of his army. He fostered their pride and their patriotism, gave them new proofs

* Welton, on the north side of James River.

of his kindness, and thus increased their attachment to him, and kept alive in their breasts detestation of the gross outrages which the foe was daily committing upon their unoffending countrymen. He established order after the most rigid system through the several departments of his corps, and prepared them to act with efficiency and celerity at a moment's warning. Before the death of General Phillips, a correspondence was commenced between him and the Marquis relative to the exchange of prisoners, and after the death of that officer, Arnold desired to continue the negotiations. The soul of the high-minded Lafayette shrunk as from a viper, when a letter from him was sent, under cover of a flag of truce, to his camp. He did not touch the communication, but while he positively assured the bearer that he would hold no correspondence with its author, he signified to him that "in case any other English officer should honor him with a letter, he would always be happy to give the officers every testimony of esteem." General Washington highly approved of this refusal. "Your conduct," writes he to Lafayette, "upon every occasion meets my approbation, but in none more than in your refusing to hold correspondence with Arnold."

The Traitor did not long continue in the supreme command. Lord Cornwallis arrived in Virginia, and formed a junction with Arnold at Petersburg on the 20th of May. His plan was the conquest of that colony, and he immediately began his offensive movements against Lafayette. Cornwallis was no ordinary man. After Sir William Howe had returned to England, he was left the most accomplished General of the British service in America. As a man, he was high-minded and honorable ; as a soldier, he was brave and courageous ; as an officer, he united singular sagacity to an energy which the severest difficulties failed to subdue, and a skill which often turned a seeming overthrow into a victory, winning a proud triumph from the very jaws of a disgraceful defeat. In battle he was always cool and collected, guiding the contest, himself above the fury of the elements, which yielded to his control, though they disturbed not his tranquillity. No ravage or pillage like that which had just dishonored the British arms in Virginia, was allowed under his command. He came to fight with soldiers, and not to lay the sword against defenseless women, weak old men, and children. An outrage committed by some of his troops on his march from Wilmington to Petersburg, such an one as Phillips and Arnold had often instigated and gloated over, was at once punished by Cornwallis, who caused the immediate execution of the chief offenders. Had Sir Henry Clinton possessed a tithe of his talents, Cornwallis would never have met with his fate at Yorktown. Clinton, weak-minded and short-sighted, fell into a snare into which all the wisdom of Washington could not have entrapped Cornwallis.

The superiority of Cornwallis to Lafayette in the number of his troops was immense. His field force was not less than eight thousand men, while that of Lafayette did not exceed four thousand. To add to the advantage of the British General, he had four hundred dragoons, and nearly twice that number of mounted infantry, while fully three-fourths of Lafayette's men were raw militia. All this, while it increased to a certainty Cornwallis' anticipations of capturing Lafayette, did not dismay his foe. He had before escaped, and believed he should now. The efforts of Cornwallis were immediate and active. On the 24th of May he crossed the James River at the head of all his troops, and made his first direct advance upon Lafayette. The Marquis had retreated to Richmond, but he was there totally unable to meet the enemy. "Were I any ways equal to the enemy," he writes to Washington, "I should be extremely happy ; but I am not strong enough even to get beaten. The Government in this State has no energy, and the laws have no force ; but I hope the present Assembly will put matters on a better footing. I had a great deal of trouble to put things in a tolerable train ; our expenses were enormous, and yet we can get nothing. Arrangements for the present would seem to put on a better face, but for this superiority of the enemy, which will chase us wherever they please. They can overrun the country, and, until the Pennsylvanians arrive, we are next to nothing in point of opposition to so large a force. This country begins to be as familiar to me as Tappan and Bergen. Our soldiers are hitherto very healthy. I have turned doctor, and regulate their diet."

Cornwallis passed the James River at Westover, and the same day Lafayette abandoned Richmond.

Removing the most valuable military stores of that town to a place of safety, he fell behind the Chicca-homony River, and took the road towards Fredericksburg. His main object now was to avoid the enemy, and keep open his communication with the north, till he could form a junction with the Pennsylvania line under General Wayne, which was now marching down to his aid. At Westover Cornwallis received a re-inforcement from New York, and from this place he started in pursuit of the Marquis, all confident of success. "*The boy cannot escape me*," he wrote in an intercepted letter, and few in the country when they learned the condition of the two parties, thought otherwise. The "*boy*," all at once, become the center of the deepest interest. The news of his slender force together with the ability and strength of Cornwallis, awakened an intense apprehension wherever hearts were found which desired his success.

All eyes were now turned towards Virginia; and Lafayette, in proud consciousness of the interest he was exciting, the more resolutely determined to triumph. No excitement can be traced in any of his letters during this period. He seems coolly to have extricated himself from his various difficulties as fast as they arose, and as calmly to have narrated them. Witness the following, addressed to General Greene, dated at his camp, June 3d:

"Lord Cornwallis had at first a project to cross above Richmond, but desisted from it and landed at Westover. He then proposed to turn our left flank, but before it was executed we moved by the left to the forks of Chiccahomony. The enemy advanced twelve miles, and we retreated in the same proportion. They crossed Chiccahomony and advanced on the road to Fredericksburg, while we marched in a parallel with them, keeping the upper part of the country. Our position at Mattapony church would have much exposed the enemy's flank on their way to Fredericksburg, but they stopped at Cook's ford on the North Anna River, where they are for the present. General Wayne having announced to me his departure on the 23d, I expected before this time to have made a junction with him. We have moved back some distance, and are cautious not to indulge Lord Cornwallis with an action with our present force.

"The intentions of the enemy are not as yet well explained. Fredericksburg appeared to be their object, the more so as a greater number of troops are said to have gone down than is necessary for the garrison of Portsmouth. The public stores have been as well as possible removed, and every part of Hunter's works that could be, taken out of the way. It is possible they mean to make a stroke towark Charlotteville, and this I would not have been uneasy for, had my repeated directions been executed. But instead of removing stores from there to Albemarle old Court House, where Baron de Steuben has collected six hundred regulars, and where I ordered the militia south of James River to rendezvous,—it appears from a letter I received this evening, that state stores have been, contrary to my directions, collected there, lest they should mix with the continentals; — but my former letters were so positive, and my late precautions are so multiplied, that I hope the precious part of the stores will have been removed to a safer place. I had also some stores removed from Orange Court House. Dispatches from the Governor to me have fallen into the enemy's hands;—of which I gave him and the Baron immediate notice.

"The enemy must have five hundred men mounted, and their cavalry increases daily. It is impossible in this country to take horses out of their way, and the neglect of the inhabitants, dispersion of houses, and robberies of negroes,—should even the most vigorous measures have been taken by the civil authorities,—would have yet put many horses into their hands. Under this cloud of light troops it is difficult to reconnoitre, as well as counteract any rapid movements they choose to make."

It was not long before Cornwallis with great chagrin saw that the "boy" was successfully eluding his grasp. The distance between them daily increased, notwithstanding all the efforts made by the British General to overtake his foe. With a rapidity only equalled by his caution, Lafayette had passed the Pamunkey before the British army had reached the Chiccahomony, and Cornwallis, after marching some distance up the northern side of Northanora, found that the Marquis would make his junction with Wayne in spite of him, and gave over the heat of his pursuit while he turned his attention to other objects which were more attainable. Lafayette, however, did not relax his vigilance. A close watch of his adversary enabled him to foresee and thereby frustrate some of his most important plans. Cornwallis found himself harassed and frequently outwitted, exceedingly to his mortification. He dispatched Tarleton to capture the Assembly of Virginia, which was then in Session at Charlotteville ; but before Tarleton could get there, Lafayette had contrived to forward the information, and when the British arrived,—*the birds had flown.* Colonel Simcoe was sent against Baron Steuben, who defended the military stores at the Point of Fork, but before his arrival, the Baron had removed the stores to another place, and saved himself by a hasty retreat. Lafayette watching every attempt like these, endeavored to defeat them, while, having crossed the Rapidan, he awaited the junction with Wayne.

General Wayne, with the Pennsylvannia line, consisting of about eight hundred men, at length joined him. Though this addition left the force of Lafayette still feeble, in comparison with that of Cornwallis, it was yet sufficient to determine him upon a new course of action. The Pursued would become the Pursuer. He had fled long enough, too long to suit his own temper, and now, emboldened by his reinforcement, he recrossed the Rapidan, and moved forward upon the enemy. Upon his retreat from Richmond, he had removed the valuable military stores from that place up the river, and deposited them principally at Albemarle old Court House. In order to capture these, Lord Cornwallis was directing his march towards this place, when Lafayette, far in his rear, crossed the Rapidan. So quick were the evolutions of the Marquis, that he came and encamped within a few miles of the British army, while they were yet a full day's march from Albemarle. To gain this place before Cornwallis could reach it, was now the bold scheme of the Marquis, but the game was a difficult one. Cornwallis, whose army occupied and fully commanded the road leading to that place, smiled at the eagerness of his youthful foe, and laid an easy plan to entrap him. Being at no loss to understand what the design of Lafayette must be, he drew off the main body of his troops, and encamped at Elk Island, while he advanced his light troops to a position upon the road through which he presumed his enemy must pass. This was on the fourteenth of June, and never was a fowler after having carefully spread his net, surer of his prey, than Cornwallis as he laid down to rest that night. His mortification and disappointment, therefore, knew no bounds when he arose the next morning and found his young but gallant adversary in front of him, on the direct road to Albemarle, from which he would not be tempted, and could not be easily forced to leave. Cornwallis, in this, was mistaken, as when he predicted the certain capture of the youthful commander; who had in this instance proved himself fairly a match for the man. The dexterity of Lafayette had completely baffled the calculations of Cornwallis. His vigilance had discovered a shorter road, which, as it had long been disused, had hitherto escaped observation. Lafayette opened this road on the same night that Cornwallis had planned his capture, and with cautious haste marched his troops over it, crossed the Rivanna, and halted securely behind Mechunck's creek, on the direct route from the British camp to Albemarle. The whole records of the war scarcely show a more masterly movement than this. Cornwallis himself, despite his mortification, could not repress a thrill of admiration at this exploit of his gallant foe. He never afterward called him *a boy*.

Lafayette though elated was never vain from his successes. The self-complacency so often seen in military men, and the bombastic parade shown in the recital of their own exploits, never appeared in him. The reader must have noticed in his letters already quoted, the quiet unconcern with which he mentions his own performances, as if unconscious of their greatness. With singular modesty he thus relates his last mentioned achievement: "In the mean time the British army was moving to the Point of Fork, intending to strike our magazines at Albamarle old Court House. Our force was not equal to their defense, and a delay of our junction would have answered the views of the enemy. But on the arrival of the Pennsylvanians, we made forced marches toward James River, and on our gaining the South Anna, we found Lord Cornwallis encamped some miles below the camp of Fork. A stolen march, through a difficult road, gave us a position upon Mechunck creek, between that of the enemy and our stores, where, agreeably to previous appointment, we were joined by a body of riflemen."

Lord Cornwallis, over-estimating the force of the enemy, but chiefly in accordance with instructions from Sir Henry Clinton, now abandoned his designs against Albemarle and began to retreat. On the fifteenth of June he proceeded to Westham and was closely followed by the Marquis. Cornwallis did not venture a single retrograde action, but proceeded carefully forward to Richmond, which he entered the subsequent day. As he seemed disposed to halt here for a time, Lafayette took up his position on Allen's creek, about twenty-two miles from his lordship, where he quietly watched his foe. On the 18th, Cornwallis moved towards him, but again retired into the town without venturing an attack. On the 19th the Marquis was joined by the Baron Steuben, and on the following night Richmond was evacuated, and Cornwallis pursued his retreat. Lafayette at once broke up his encampment and started after them. "Having followed the enemy," says he, "our light parties fell in with them near New Kent Court House. The army was still at a distance, and Lord Cornwallis continued his route towards Williamsburg, his rear and right flank being covered by a large corps commanded by Colonel Simcoe. I pushed forward a detachment under Colonel Butler, but notwithstanding a fatiguing march, the Colonel reports that he could not have overtaken them, had not Major McPherson mounted fifty light infantry behind an equal number of dragoons, which, coming, up with the enemy, charged them within six miles of Williamsburg. Such of the advanced corps as could arrive to their support, composed of riflemen, under Major Call and Major Willis, began a smart action. Enclosed is the return of our loss.* That of the enemy is about sixty killed and one hundred wounded, including several officers, a disproportion which the skill of our riflemen easily explains. I am under great obligations to Colonel Butler and the officers and men of the detachment, for their ardor in the pursuit, and their conduct in the action. General Wayne, who had marched to the support of Butler, sent down some troops under Major Hamilton. The whole British army came out to save Simcoe, and on the arrival of our army upon this ground, returned to Williamsburg. The post they occupy at present is strong, and under protection of their shipping, but upwards of one hundred miles from the Point of Fork."

Cornwallis was mortified at the result of this skirmish, but would have felt it more keenly had he understood the real inferiority of force which Lafayette possessed, and which was greatly exaggerated to Cornwallis by his skillful marches. His lordship's estimate while he was pursuing, was nearly correct, but he could not reconcile the great prudence which Lafayette had displayed in his flight, with the boldness he now manifested, except by supposing that he had received large reinforcements to his troops. "It has been a great secret," Lafayette afterwards writes to Washington, "that our army was not superior, and was most generally inferior to the enemy's numbers.

* This was as follows: — two captains, two lieutenants, one sergeant, ten privates, wounded; two lieutenants, one sergeant, six privates, killed; one sergeant taken; and one lieutenant and twelve privates whose fate was unknown.

Our returns were swelled up, as militia returns generally are ; but we had very few under arms, particularly lately, and to conceal the lessening of our numbers, I was obliged to push on as one who heartily wished a general engagement. Our regulars did not exceed one thousand five hundred ; while the enemy had four thousand regulars, four hundred of whom were mounted. They thought we had eight thousand men. I never encamped in line, and there was thus greater difficulty to come at our numbers." "General Greene," he says in another letter, "only demanded of me to hold my ground in Virginia ; but the movements of Lord Cornwallis may answer better purposes than that in the political line."

Cornwallis now established himself at Williamsburg, and Lafayette about twenty miles above, with the Chiccahomony between himself and his adversary. Neither party, however, remained in this position long. Sir Henry Clinton suspecting that a combined attempt was about to be made by the allied forces against New York, and deeming himself too weak to resist it, ordered Cornwallis to send him a detachment of the troops under his command in Virginia. After complying with this requisition, Cornwallis thought himself not strong enough to remain at Williamsburg, and resolved to retire to Portsmouth. Accordingly, on the fourth of July, he marched from Williamsburg, and determining to cross the river at James' City Island, he encamped that day favorably for the passage. But before he was ready to move, his foe was near him. Lafayette left his camp on the fifth, crossed the Chiccahomony the same day, and pushed his best troops within eight miles of the British camp. He learned that Cornwallis was expecting to pass the river, and he at once formed the design of attacking his rear after the main body should have gone over to Jamestown. Cornwallis, however, suspected this. He knew that the ardor of Lafayette would not allow such an opportunity to escape him, and as soon as he found that the Marquis was so near, he resolved to make one more trial of stratagem upon him. He took every measure to encourage his advance, but instead of passing the river, he waited an attack. At the same time he took measures to induce the belief, that he had crossed with the main body of his army. His light parties were all drawn in, his troops were held compact, and made to cover as little ground as possible, and his piquets, which lay close to the encampment, were ordered to yield at the first attack, and exhibit an appearance of disorder and alarm. To add to the deception, the intelligence was spread, that the greater part of the British had reached the island, and a few troops were stationed there, with orders to make such demonstrations as would corroborate this news.

Lafayette was fully deceived. The plans of Cornwallis were so complete, and were carried out so accurately, that he could not perceive the snare. Every thing looked as he had anticipated; after personally reconnoitering the scene, and receiving all the intelligence he could meet, Lafayette, on the 6th of July, began his attack. A few riflemen were detached to harass the outposts of the enemy, while he advanced at the head of the continental troops to support the onset. Every thing was conducted precisely as Cornwallis had planned. His piquets fell back in disorder, and thus drew on the Americans, emboldened by their success, in a rapid pursuit. The main body of Cornwallis' army was concealed by woods, and General Wayne, who was first in advance, soon discovered it moving out in order of battle against him. Retreat was impossible, and that brave officer, with a boldness almost without parallel, rode gallantly forward, with his eight hundred men, and made a furious attack upon the British line. The action was kept up with spirit for some time, while the British army was winding its fold like a serpent round the little band. Lafayette soon came up, and saw at a glance the crisis. The plan of Cornwallis was evident in a moment, and perceiving that Wayne was outflanked right and left, and fast becoming surrounded, he ordered his retreat. A line of light infantry was drawn up about half a mile in his rear, and by a skillful movement Wayne was enabled to join these without serious loss. Here they remained for some hours, but the British army did not pursue. Cornwallis, who greatly overrated Lafayette's numbers, judged that his retreat was a stratagem to draw him into an ambuscade, and accordingly did not improve the advantage he had gained. The loss of Lafayette in this action was one hundred and eighteen men, most of whom belonged to General Wayne's detachment. The conduct of this latter officer during the day was worthy of all praise. "It is enough," says Lafayette, "for the glory of

General Wayne, and the officers and men he commanded, to have attacked the whole British army, with a reconnoitering party only, close to their encampment, and by this severe skirmish, hastened their retreat over the river."

During the night succeeding the action, the British proceeded to Jamestown, and soon after to the mouth of James river, Cornwallis encamping at Portsmouth. Lafayette followed, and halted in the vicinity, on Mal van Hill, where he allowed his harassed army some repose. Although, says Marshall, no brilliant service was performed during this campaign, yet it greatly enhanced Lafayette's military reputation, and raised him in the general esteem. That with so decided an inferiority of effective force, and especially of cavalry, he had been able to keep the field in an open country, and to preserve a considerable proportion of his military stores, as well as his army, was believed to furnish unequivocal evidence of the prudence and vigor of his conduct.

Active warfare seemed now suspended. Cornwallis was safely entrenched at Portsmouth, and Lafayette had little else to do than to watch him, and prevent any excursion which he might design to make. In this he was unceasingly busy. Lest the enemy should be inclined to retreat to North Carolina, he ordered the militia to guard the passes, and took every precaution to cut him off in that direction. To keep his own line of communication open with Philadelphia was also an object of his strictest attention. His spies surrounded Cornwallis everywhere. They were in his camp and very apartment, and entirely unsuspected, were communicating to Lafayette his daily history and plans. One of Cornwallis' own trusted spies was all the while faithful to Lafayette. "When Cornwallis," says Mr. Sparks, "had retired before Lafayette, and was near Williamsburg, as the former had a superior force, Lafayette did not choose to bring him to a general action; but he wished at the same time to impress upon him the idea of the largeness of his numbers, in order that Cornwallis might not be induced to turn upon him, and thus compel him again to retreat. He had taken into his service a very shrewd negro man, whom he had instructed to go into the enemy's camp, and pretend to give himself up to them. This task the man performed with so much cunning, that he was actually employed by Lord Cornwallis as a spy, at the time he was acting in the same capacity for the other side. But he was true to his first employer. Lafayette wrote a fictitious order to General Morgan, requiring him to take his station at a certain post in conjunction with the army. The paper was then torn and given to the negro, with directions how to proceed. He returned to Cornwallis, who asked him what news he brought from the American camp. He said there was no news, that he saw no changes, but every thing appeared as it was the day before. Holding the tattered paper in his hand, he was asked what it was, and replied that he had picked it up in the American camp, but, as he could not read, he did not know that it was of any importance. The General took it, and was surprised to find such an order. He had not heard of Morgan's having joined the army, or of his being expected. It made him cautious, however, for a day or two before he was undeceived, and the object of Lafayette was gained.

Rumors now began to reach Lafayette that his own favorite project of a combined attack upon New York by the American and French forces was soon to be attempted, and he desired earnestly to be present and engage in it.

On the 20th July, he writes to Washington :

"When I went to the southward, you know I had some private objections ;—but I became sensible of the necessity there was for the detachment to go, and I knew that had I returned there was no one who could lead them on against their inclination. My entering this state was happily marked by a service to the capital. Virginia became the grand object of the enemy, as it was the point to which the ministry tended. I had the honor to command an army and oppose Lord Cornwallis. When incomparably inferior to him, fortune was pleased to preserve us ;—when equal in numbers, though not in quality of troops, we have also been pretty lucky. Cornwallis had the disgrace of a retreat, and this state being recovered, government is properly reëstablished. The enemy are under the protection of their works at Portsmouth. It appears an embarcation is taking place, probably destined to New York. The war in the state would then become a plundering one, and great manœuvres be out of the question. A prudent officer would do our business here, and the Baron

Steuben is prudent to the utmost. Would it be possible, my dear General, in case a part of the British troops go to New York, I may be allowed to join the combined armies?" In another letter he says,

"I am entirely a stranger to every thing that passes out of Virginia, and Virginia operations being for the present in a state of languor, I have more time to think of my solitude. In a word, my dear General, I am home-sick, and if I cannot go to head quarters wish at least to hear from thence. I am anxious to know your opinion concerning the Virginia campaign. That the subjugation of this state was the great object of the ministry is an indisputable fact. I think your diversion has been of more use to the state than my manœuvres, but the latter have been much directed by political views. So long as my lord wished for an action, not one gun has been fired, but the moment he declined it, we began skirmishing, though I took care never to commit the army. His naval superiority, his superiority of horse, of regulars;—his thousand advantages over us are such that I am lucky to have come off safe. I had an eye upon European negotiations, and made it a point to give his lordship the disgrace of a retreat.

"From every account it appears that a part of the army will embark. The light infantry, the guards, the 80th regiment and Queen's Rangers, are, it is said, destined for New York. Lord Cornwallis, I am told, is much disappointed in his hopes of command. Should he go to England, we are, I think, to rejoice for it. He is a cold and active man, two dangerous qualities in this southern war.

"The clothing you long ago sent to the light infantry has not yet arrived. I have been obliged to send for it, and expect it in a few days. These three battalions are the best troops that ever took the field. My confidence in them is unbounded. They are far superior to any British troops and none will ever venture to meet them in equal numbers. What a pity these men are not employed along with the French grenadiers;—they would do eternal honor to our arms. But their presence here, I must confess, has saved this state, and, indeed, the southern part of the continent."

The intelligence which Lafayette communicated in these letters was the subject of Washington's profoundest consideration. They suggested to him a new plan, which, if successful, might bring a decisive triumph. Never was more wisdom displayed in war than now. He determined that the united attack upon New York should be brought to bear upon Cornwallis. With the new reinforcements which Sir Henry Clinton had received, he doubted of success against the city, but this same fact assured him of victory over Cornwallis. His preparations for the southern movement were necessarily secret. For a time he dared not communicate his plans to Lafayette lest his letters might be intercepted by the enemy. He requested him to stay in Virginia till matters should be reduced to a greater certainty than at present. "You will not regret this," said he, "especially when I tell you, that from the change of circumstance with which the removal of part of the enemy's force from Virginia to New York will be attended, it is more than probable we shall also entirely change our plan of operations." Such hints as these were sufficient, and he wrote to Washington accordingly. "For the present," he says, "I am of the opinion, with you, that I had better remain in Virginia;—the more so, as Lord Cornwallis does not choose to leave us, and circumstances may happen that will furnish me agreeable operations in the command of the Virginia army. I have pretty well understood you, my dear General, but would be happy in a more minute detail, which, I am sensible, cannot be intrusted to letters."

Count Rochambeau was from the first in favor of an expedition south, against Cornwallis, and, now that it had met with Washington's approbation, he readily assented to it. The French had left Newport and completed a junction with Washington upon the Highlands, the 6th of July, and the allied army was now ready for any movement to which they might be directed. Cheering news had been received from France. The French Government had agreed to furnish the United States with six millions of livres, and were also negotiating for an additional loan of ten millions from Holland. The Count de Grasse, with a large naval force, had sailed for the West Indies, with permission to spend the summer upon the American coast, in coöperation with Washington and De Rochambeau. The latter officer had advised him of a probable enterprise in the Chesapeake Bay agains Cornwallis, leaving it for him to sail there at his own discretion.

The most cautious management was now necessary to keep Sir Henry Clinton in ignorance of the proposed campaign. Knowing that the British General was expecting an attack upon New York, Washington kept up all the outward preparations, while he secretly directed every thing towards his new design. Letters to the Governor of Virginia, to Lafayette and others, detailing the vast plans which Washington was making for the enterprise upon New York, and recounting the importance of that measure to the American cause were sent, and according to his intentions were intercepted and carried to Sir Henry Clinton. The British General was entirely imposed upon, and with greater vigor than ever arranged for the defense of New York. In one of these letters which Washington had written only for Clinton's eye, he stated that an attack upon New York, and the overthrow of General Clinton, was now of the first importance and must soon be attempted;—for that he was much alarmed at the success of a general, whom, from experience, he knew to be so fertile in resources, so vigorous in decision, and so prompt and expeditious in improving every advantage! Still further to encourage the deception, Washington in person, with his engineers and chief officers, closely reconnoitred the defenses of New York and took plans of all the works, under the fire of their batteries. By all these means Sir Henry Clinton was fully deceived, and Washington, as soon as he heard that the Count de Grasse was to have sailed from Cape Francis for the Chesapeake on the 3d of August, was ready for his movement.

Meanwhile General Washington had sent a confidential officer to communicate to the Marquis his proposed undertaking, and advise him to make preparations accordingly. Lafayette received the news with joy, and determined that the enemy should not escape. Every movement of Cornwallis which would indicate a desire to retreat to North Carolina was carefully observed, and guarded against. On the 26th of July he learned from a servant of Cornwallis, who constantly kept him informed of his master's movements, that the army was preparing to leave Portsmouth, though he did not know their destination. Lafayette suspected that it might be starting for New York and longed for a French fleet to come into Hampton Roads, just then, and secure the prey. Instead, however, of proceeding to New York, Cornwallis passed up the Bay, entered York River, and landed his forces at York and Gloucester. At Gloucester Point he began his entrenchments, but was here, as he had been at Portsmouth, every moment under the careful surveillance of his vigilant foe. After a time his forts at Troy, Kemp's Landing, Great Bridge and Portsmouth, were abandoned, and his vessels and baggage with all the troops that had been left for garrison, went round to York. The cannon left at Portsmouth were spiked, and Cornwallis began to erect heavy fortifications at York and at Gloucester, so as

9

to command the River and effectually protect himselt. At first his works went slowly forward, as if he himself were uncertain what to do, but afterwards began to progress with greater rapidity. A dispatch from Sir Henry Clinton had reached him, stating that he had just received from Europe a reinforcement of three thousand Hessians, and that consequently he would not need the detachment from Cornwallis which he had previously ordered. These orders were therefore countermanded and his lordship was directed to take a strong position on the Chesapeake, from which, as soon as the storm which threatened New York should blow over, he might prosecute the meditated designs of the ministry against the states lying on that Bay.

Lafayette held his position on James River. He received, as we have said, the plan of Washington, but that it might be in no danger of being divulged to the enemy, he did not disclose it to a single individual. Under different pretexts he made his various dispositions against Cornwallis, so that even his own officers mistook their precise nature. Whether Cornwallis fathomed them or not, he soon saw that Lafayette was cutting off his retreat to the Carolinas, though he could not yet see the threatening elements which were gathering against him in the distance. On the 19th of August the whole American army was put in motion, and crossing the Hudson, began their march for Virginia. General Clinton, completely outwitted, considered their departure merely as a feint to cover their design upon New York, and does not seem for a moment to have apprehended the terrible danger which threatened Cornwallis. Washington, in communicating to Lafayette their departure, enjoins upon the Marquis the closest and most careful efforts to prevent the escape of the enemy before the allied armies should arrive. "As it will be of great importance," said he, "towards the success of our present enterprise, that the enemy, on the arrival of the fleet, should not have it in their power to effect their retreat, I cannot omit to repreat to you my most earnest wish that the land and naval forces, which you will have with you, may so combine their operations, that the British army may not be able to escape. The particular mode of doing this, I shall not, at this distance, attempt to dictate. Your own knowledge of the country, from your long continuance in it, and the various and extensive movements which you have made, have given you great opportunities for observation; of which I am persuaded your military genius and judgment will lead you to make the best improvement. You will, my dear Marquis, keep me constantly advised of every important event respecting the enemy or yourself." Lafayette, as we have seen, had anticipated these injunctions. By his untiring vigilance and skillful manœuvres, he had driven the enemy to a position most favorable to his plans, and it was no part of his designs that he should now escape.

Cornwallis soon began to discern the terrible foreshadowing of his doom. On the 30th of August, the Count de Grasse, with twenty-eight ships of the line, several frigates and convoys, arrived in the Chesapeake. Lafayette at once sent him an officer to commu nicate the intelligence of his own situation and that of Cornwallis. Learning this, the Count immediately detached four ships of the line to block up York River and then proceeded to land for Lafayette's reinforcement, the Marquis de St. Simon with a body of troops amounting to three thousand two hundred men. These formed a junction with Lafayette at Williamsburg, on the 5th of September. He united himself with Wayne, who had been stationed on the south side of James River, and so quick were his movements, that Cornwallis saw, as if by magic, that he was suddenly blockaded by sea and by land, with hardly a possibility of escape. Perilous as was his situation, he determined upon one desperate effort to free himself from it. He carefully reconnoitred Lafayette's position at Williamsburg, and though strong, he determined to pass it and retreat to the South. Lafayette discovered this, but soon found also that the plan was abandoned. Cornwallis sending an earnest request to Sir Henry Clinton for succor determined to await its arrival. Meanwhile he labored day and night on his defenses.

The Count de Grasse, who had permission to serve on the American coast only till the middle of October, was anxious to commence operations immediately. Together with the Marquis St. Simon, he urged upon Lafayette the propriety of making an immediate attack upon the enemy. It is right, said they to Lafayette, that you who have had all the difficulties of this campaign should now be rewarded with the glory of its successful termination. They argued that the works of Cornwallis were yet in an incomplete state, and that he could not resist a sudden attack made by the forces which he could then command. All these were powerful reasons with the young and ardent Marquis, but yet he determined to await the arrival of the northern armies. The attempt upon Cornwallis in his present condition, he saw would be attended with great bloodshed, even if successful, and he was unwilling, unnecessarily, to risk the lives of the brave men who had followed his fortunes, for personal glory. He therefore used every precaution to prevent the escape of Cornwallis, and patiently awaited the arrival of Washington and de Rochambeau.

Having made arrangement for the transportation of his army down the Chesapeake, Washington, accompanied by the Count and the Chevalier de Chastelleux, proceeded directly to Virginia; and on the 14th of September, Lafayette joyfully welcomed them to his camp at Williamsburg. Thence they proceeded to Hampton, where, on board the *Ville de Paris*, the plan for the siege of Yorktown was concerted with the Count de Grasse. Everything was managed to the satisfaction of both parties, and Washington, as he surveyed with high approbation the dispositions which Lafayette had made, felt certain of a brilliant success when his troops should arrive. But a dark cloud suddenly overshadowed the clear sky of his hopes. Information reached the French Admiral that the British fleet in New York had received an important addition to its strength, and de Grasse supposed by this that they would be induced to venture every thing for the relief of Cornwallis. Expecting therefore, that they would sail directly against him, and as his present condition was unfavorable for a naval combat, he determined to sail out of the Bay with his fleet and meet the enemy on the open sea. He communicated this intention to Washington, proposing to leave a few frigates to block up the mouths of York and James Rivers, while he went in quest of the enemy. Washington received this proposition with dismay. The moment de Grasse should leave, the vision of certain success would fade. A temporary naval superiority might be acquired by the British in the Bay, and the army of Cornwallis would then be placed in perfect security. He must not leave, said Washington. Writing a letter to de Grasse, he sent Lafayette with it on board the vessel, and requested the Marquis to use his personal influence with the Admiral, to dissuade him from executing his dangerous designs. Lafayette felt the emergency and acted with efficiency. He stated the crisis, and plead with the Count to remain. He appealed by turns to his honor, his pride, and his patriotism. He represented that the capture of Cornwallis would probably seal the triumph of America, while his escape would greatly protract the war, and result disgracefully to the allied arms. His appeals were successful, and the Admiral at last consented to forego plans his thirst for military glory had suggested, and continue his post.

The troops now began to arrive, and on the 25th of September the last division debarked near Williamsburg. With high hope and courage, each division swept into the ranks, and on the 28th moving forward in four columns towards Yorktown, halted about two miles in front of the enemy. THE SIEGE OF YORKTOWN* now commenced. De Rochambeau, with the French corps, took advantage of the woods, the rideaux, and the marshy creeks, so as to confine the enemy to within pistol shot of their works. The left wing of the French battalions rested upon the river above the town, and their right extended to a low ravine, where it was met by the left wing of the Americans, whose right rested upon the stream below the town. The investment was as complete and as close as possible. Mr. de Choisy, with a body of troops, then passed over to Gloucester on the opposite side. Cornwallis looked out upon the vast array which now encircled him, as the fabled draco its victim, but his great heart was still firm. He had informed Sir Henry Clinton of his peril, and had no doubt that succors would soon arrive. With unbroken fortitude he determined to face the tremendous array till he should receive aid, and reap victory.

Till the 6th of October the besieging army was employed in disembarking and bringing upon the ground the ordnance and other requisite implements for the onset. As soon as this was done, the work went for-

---

* "York is a small village on the south side of the river which bears that name, where the long peninsula between the York and the James, is only eight miles wide. On the opposire shore, is Gloucester Point, a piece of land projecting deep into the river, and narrowing it, at that place, to the space of one mile. Both these points were occupied by Lord Cornwallis. The communication between them was commanded by his batteries, and by some ships of war which lay under his guns."—[Marshall.

ward with vigor, but the strength of the English army and the character of the General who commanded it, obliged Washington to act with precision and precaution. On the night of the 6th of October, with profound silence, a trench, six or seven hundred toises in extent, and flanked by four redoubts, was opened by the Americans on the right, within six hundred yards of the British lines. At the same time a similar one was completed by the French on the left. So silently was this done, that the garrison was wholly unapprised of it till day light, by which time the embankments were so far advanced as to cover the men. Batteries and redoubts were speedily completed along the fosse, from which a tremendous fire was poured upon the enemy. So resistless was the blaze of artillery, that it tore in pieces most of their batteries, and on the eleventh they were forced to withdraw their cannon from the embrasures, and scarcely returned a shot. Kindling a spirit of emulation between the French and Americans, Washington was able to prosecute the assault with great rapidity. On the same night he opened his second parallel within three hundred yards of the lines. This was commenced noiselessly as the first, and on the morning of the next day Cornwallis first discovered it. The three succeeding days were occupied in completing the trench. The progress now was seriously harassed by two redoubts of the foe in front of their entrenchments, and which kept up a galling fire. Washington determined to silence these with the bayonet. The attack of one was given to the Americans, and of the other to the

French. Lafayette led the former and the Baron de Viomesnil the latter. Says de Rochambeau, "Four hundred grenadiers debouched at the head of this attack, under the command of Count William de Deux Ponts, and of M. de l' Estrapade, Lieutenant-Colonel of the regiment of Gatinais. M. M. de Viomesnil and Lafayette made so impetuous an attack that the redoubts were carried, sword in hand, at the same moment. The greater part of the men in them were killed, wounded, or taken prisoners. A lodgement was made by joining these redoubts by a communication to the right of our second parallel, the ground on which they stood affording means of erecting new batteries, which completed the blockade of Cornwallis, and threw balls a ricochet into the whole of the interior of the place, at a distance which could not fail to do much damage." This difficult onset was carried on and finished with a bravery highly gratifying to Washington. In the orders for the succeeding day, he complimented both Lafayette and Viomesnil, for their judicious dispositions and gallant conduct during the attack. "The General reflects," he concluded, "with the highest degree of pleasure, on the confidence which the troops of the two nations must hereafter have in each other. Assured of mutual support, he is convinced there is no danger which they will not cheerfully encounter, — no difficulty which they will not bravely overcome."

The two redoubts which had been taken were at once included in the second parallel, and in a few hours some howitzers were mounted upon them, which added their destructive vollies. Cornwallis saw that with this fire the town would be untenable, and his situation hopeless. Unable to believe that Sir Henry Clinton would leave him long without help, he thought to gain time by a bold movement. On the night of the fifteenth of October, he sent out Lieutenant-Colonel Abercrombie at the head of 800 chosen men, who made a desperate sortie against two batteries which appeared to be in the greatest forwardness. So valiant was the the charge, that they gained possession, and spiked four guns ; but were hastily repelled by the Chevalier de Chastelleux, who made a deadly assault with his reserve. The cannon were rendered serviceable again six hours afterwards, by the care of General d' Abouville, commanding the French artillery. The tremendous fire-sheet which now blazed upon Cornwallis, soon dismounted or broke his ordnance, his walls were fast crumbling into the ditches, and nearly all his defenses were razed. Unwilling to submit, and unable to remain longer with any show of resistance, he formed the daring design of crossing over in the night with such troops as were not disabled, to Gloucester Point, and with forced march hasten to rejoin the army in New York. Boats were prepared, and so secretly were the arrangements, that no tidings escaped to the opposit encampment. On the night of the 16th of October, a division was embarked and passed over unperceived. But before the boats could return, a violent storm arose, and continued till dawn, drifting them down the river, and preventing all farther execution of the plan.

The next morning, the troops which had crossed were brought back again, and re-landed on the southern shore with little loss.

On the morning of the 17th, Cornwallis, reduced to the last extremity, beat a parley, and offered to capitulate. On the 19th, formal articles of capitulation were signed, by which Lord Cornwallis and his magnificent army were made prisoners of war. The Americans and French took possession at noon of two bastions, and the garrison defiled between the armies at two o'clock in the P. M., with drums beating, carrying their arms, which they afterwards piled, with twenty pair of colors. Lord Cornwallis feigned sickness to avoid surrendering before his soldiers, and General O' Hara accordingly appeared at the head of the garrison. "When he came up," says Rochambeau," "he presented his sword to me. I pointed to General Washington, who was opposite me at the head of the American army, and told him that the French army being auxiliaries on the continent, it was the American General who was to signify his orders to him." As the result of this capitulation 8,000 prisoners, of whom 7,000 were regular troops and 1,000 sailors ; 214 pieces of cannon, of which 75 were brass, and 22 pair of colors, passed into the hands of the allies. The men, artillery, arms, military chest, and public stores of every denomination, were surrendered to Washington, the ships and seamen to the Count de Grasse.

The news of the surrender at Yorktown sped on the wings of the wind all over the land. Bon-fires were lighted on almost every hill top, and the bells of every hamlet in the country rung their glad acclamations. The names of Washington,—Rochambeau,—de Grasse,—Lafayette, resounded every where. Every association of note, political or literary, voted them their congratulations. With profound gratitude to the Supreme Disposer of all events, Congress repaired in solemn procession to the Dutch Lutheran Church, to return thanks for the victory to the Divine Providence which had granted it. Washington also ordered that suitable religious service be performed in the camp in grateful testimony of the auspicious event.

To follow up the advantages thus gained, the Commander-in-Chief desired to make an expedition against Charleston. De Grasse was solicited to lend his aid, and Lafayette was deputed by Washington to overcome any scruples which the Admiral might have against reëngaging in the enterprise. The Marquis repaired on board the Ville de Paris, but solicitations were unavailing. De Grasse replied that "the orders of his court, ulterior projects, and his engagements with the Spaniards, rendered it impossible for him to remain on the coast during the time which would be required for the operation." This enterprise failing, and also another against Wilmington, which was also proposed, military action for the season seemed to be at an end. The army went into winter quarters, and Lafayette was once more left to a repose ever irksome to him. Desiring again to revisit his native land, and thinking that he might be serviceable to the cause of his heart, he determined to return to France.

This determination was not opposed, as it was felt both by Washington and Congress that his powerful coöperation would be needed in the negotiations for an honorable peace, which it was hoped would now open. Previous to his departure, he received the highest testimonials of affection and respect, not only from his beloved Commander and Congress, but also from the King and Ministry of France. He sailed from Boston in the frigate Alliance, on the 22d December, 1781.

It is not strange that Lafayette was next to freedom in the magnanimous heart of Washington. From the devotion of himself and fortune, while amid the luxuries of an ancestral domain, to the doubtful struggle of despised "rebels;"—his unselfish adherence to their cause when repulsed—his untiring energy and reliable wisdom in the camp and conflict—his fidelity in neglect, under fearful discouragements, and in the palace of his sovereign; have probably no parallel in the annals of greatness which has its throne within a disinterested human bosom. We follow his youthful form through the bloody scenes of the Revolution, with a personal affection and admiration peculiar and unrivaled, because he fought on foreign soil, and was ready to die for STRANGERS. We *know* America could not have spared Washington, and we *feel* that Washington could not have spared LAFAYETTE!

CHAPTER VI.

LAFAYETTE'S RECEPTION IN PARIS — AT HOME — EFFORTS FOR AMERICA — PREPARATIONS OF FRANCE AND SPAIN — LAFAYETTE AT CADIZ — NEGOTIATIONS FOR PEACE — TREATY OF PEACE RATIFIED — LAFAYETTE AT MADRID — CONTINUED ENDEAVORS — FREE PORTS — DUTIES ON OIL — DESIRES TO RETURN TO AMERICA — EMBARKS AT HAVRE — ARRIVAL AT NEW YORK — ENTHUSIASTIC WELCOME — VISITS WASHINGTON AT MOUNT VERNON — TREATY WITH THE INDIANS — KAYEWLA — VISITS BOSTON — RECEPTION THERE — PROCEEDS TO VIRGINIA — MEETS WASHINGTON AT RICHMOND — RETURNS NORTH — TAKES LEAVE OF CONGRESS — RETURNS TO FRANCE — VISITS FREDERIC THE GREAT — INCIDENTS — PLANS FOR AFRICAN EMANCIPATION — INTERPOSES IN BEHALF OF PERSECURED PROTESTANTS.

Lafayette was greeted warmly by his countrymen. His name had gone back to the realm of his birth like an echo of liberty. The most flattering salutations met him at court, and demonstrations of applause were made wherever he went. But the silver notes of fame were not so sweet as the familiar accents of love in the bosom of his family ; the delights of *home*. In the social circle, his hours flew pleasantly, yet he did not forget America. Every ship brought him answers to the many letters which he was constantly transmitting to Washington and friends in the new world. He thus kept himself familiar with American affairs, while at the same time he did not forget to interest himself actively in their behalf. He urged upon the ministry the necessity of forcing peace from England, by more imposing display in favor of the colonies. So forcible were his representations, that a grand armament was prepared by France and Spain, to encounter the British power in the West Indies and North America. A part consisting of sixty vessels and twenty-four thousand men, began to assemble at Cadiz. Lafayette was appointed chief of the staff of the united armies, and himself took the lead of eight thousand troops marching from Brest to the place of rendezvous. So vast preparations as these, were looked upon by the English government with apprehension, and quickened their negotiations for peace. Commissioners were appointed by the United States and Great Britain, who held their conferences in Paris. In November 1782, the preliminary articles for a peace were agreed upon, and on the 20th of January, 1783, the final treaty was signed. Lafayette heard this news with bounding heart and longed to bear the glad tidings to a rescued nation. But though the King of Spain had signed the treaty which acknowledged the independence of the States, he refused to receive in his diplomatic relation, Mr. Carmichael, who had been appointed Chargé d' Affaires to court of Madrid. Lafayette was then at Cadiz preparing to sail for America, when Mr. Carmichael wrote to him requesting his aid. Forgetting himself, he instantly resolved to forego his anticipated pleasure. The Count d' Estaing granted him *The Triumph*, a fast sailing vessel, which the Marquis dispatched with a letter to the President of Congress, communicating the tidings of peace, while he hastened to Madrid to secure the interests of his adopted country there. Arriving, he had an interview with the monarch and his minister, and soon had the satisfaction of seeing every difficulty removed, in the full recognition of Mr. Carmichael in his official character.

The Triumph arrived at Philadelphia on the 23d of March, 1783, bearing the first intelligence of peace. Congress passed suitable testimonials to the Marquis for this fresh service, and Washington, in a letter to him dated April 5th, thus expresses his approbation;—"It is easier for you to conceive, than for me to express, the sensibility of my heart at the communication of your letter of the 5th of February from Cadiz. It is to these communications we are indebted for the only account yet received of a general pacification. My mind, upon the receipt of this intelligence, was instantly assailed by a thousand ideas, all of them contending for preëminence;—but, believe me, my dear friend, none could supplant, or ever will eradicate that gratitude, which has arisen from a lively sense of the conduct of your nation, and to my obligations to many of its illustrious characters, (of whom, without flattery, I place you at the head,) and from my admiration of the virtues of your august Sovereign, who, at the same time that he stands confessed the father of his own people, and defender of American rights, has given the most exalted example of moderation in treating with his enemies.

"The armament which was preparing at Cadiz, and in which you were to have acted a distinguished part, would have carried such conviction with it, that it is not to be wondered at, that Great Britain should have been impressed with the force of such reasoning. To this cause, I am persuaded, the peace is to be ascribed. Your going to Madrid from thence, instead of coming immediately to this country, is another instance, my dear Marquis, of your zeal for the American cause, and lays a fresh claim to the gratitude of her sons, who will at all times receive you with open arms."

The independence of the United States being established, and peace once more restored to Europe, Lafayette began to apply himself intensely to the commercial relations of France and America. The subject was one foreign to his former habits of thought, and one upon which merely military men would have entered with reluctance; but Lafayette brought to it an energy and insight into all its details, which astonished his friends. By his exertions the ports of Dunkirk and Marseilles, of L'Orient and Bayonne, were granted to the United States as free ports* by the King of France. The minister of commerce, impressed by the representations of the Marquis, assured him that the United States should be as much favored in France in commercial affairs as any other nation. "The complaints," said he to Lafayette, "which they may make to you, or which Mr. Franklin, and the other American ministers, which I would be very glad to see, may transmit to me on their behalf, shall be examined with great attention, and government will not suffer them to experience any kind of vexation." A considerable

* A free port is "a place to which all merchandises, as well foreign as domestic, may be imported, and from which they may be freely exported."—De Vergennes.

portion of the American people were interested more or less in the whale fishery, and Layfayette did not overlook the fact. He urged France to repeal the duties on whale oil; but as the ministry were just then beginning to encourage the fishery, this was refused. He then took another method, and at last gained a total exemption of duties for sixteen thousand quintals of oil, to be furnished by merchants of Boston to the Contractor-General for lighting the cities of Paris and Versailles. "I worked very hard," he says, "to bring even as much as this about, and am happy at having, at last, obtained a point which may be agreeable to New England and the people of Boston. I wish they may, at large know, I did not neglect their affairs; and although this is a kind of private bargain, yet as it amounts to a value of about eight hundred thousand French livres, and government have been prevailed upon to take off all duties, it can be considered as a matter of importance." The Marquis' name was spoken with praise on both continents, and he was constantly receiving testimonials of grateful approbation. "The unexampled attention to every American interest," writes Mr. Morris, the superintendent of American finance, to the President of Congress, "which the Marquis de Lafayette has exhibited, cannot fail to excite the strongest emotions in his favor, and we must, at the same time, admire the judgment which he has shown in the manner of his applications, as well as the industry in selecting proper materials." The tokens of gratitude received, together with the kind entreaties by which they were accompanied, to return to America, determined him again to re-visit the theater of his toils and glory. He longed to embrace his old comrades in arms, and especially to sit at Washington's feet, and learn lessons of peace from those lips which had been so wise in war. The great man having become divested of the cares of public employment, and the responsibilities of office, was enjoying the quiet of domestic life in his villa at Mount Vernon. Inviting the Marquis to visit him, he thus describes his pleasant situation; "at length I have become a private citizen on the banks of the Potomac; and under the shadow of my own vine, and my own fig tree, free from the bustle of the camp, and the busy scenes of public life, I am solacing myself with those tranquil enjoyments, of which the soldier who is ever in pursuit of fame,—the statesman whose watchful days and sleepless nights are spent in devising schemes to promote the welfare of his own, perhaps the ruin of other countries, as if this globe was insufficient for us all,—and the courtier, who is always watching the countenance of his prince, in the hope of catching a gracious smile,—can have very little conception. I have not only retired from all public employments, but am retiring within myself, and shall be able to view the solitary walk, and tread the paths of private life, with heart-felt satisfaction. Envious of none, I am determined to be pleased with all; and this, my dear friend, being the order of my march, I will move gently down the stream of life, until I sleep with my fathers."

This invitation Lafayette could not resist. It was

attended also with a polite request that the Marchioness should also visit Mt. Vernon; but this she could not accept. The Marquis embarked alone. He sailed from Havre on the 1st of July, and arrived at New York on the 4th of August. Nothing could exceed the cordiality of his reception there. It was the first time he had entered the city, and as soon as it was known that he had arrived, all ranks of the citizens left their usual occupations, and hastened to welcome him to their shores. A splendid entertainment was given him the day after his arrival, when the officers, whom he had fought with in the Revolution, appeared in their uniforms, which had been long cast aside, but were now resumed in honor of the occasion. From New York he proceeded to Philadelphia, where the happy news of his arrival from Europe had preceded him. Before he reached the city a numerous escort came out to meet him with the most enthusiastic tokens of welcome. He entered the city amid the ringing of bells and the thunder of cannon. The streets through which he passed were thronged with spectators; every door and window presenting happy faces which beamed with delight upon the distinguished guest. The corps of officers from the Pennsylvania line deputed Generals Wayne, St. Clair, and Irwin, to congratulate him upon his arrival, and to welcome him to the scenes of his former toils and fame. The legislature of Pennsylvania voted him a flattering address, and all classes were engaged in a generous rivalry to do him honor.

But, meanwhile, the subject of all these demonstrations was impatient to behold again his illustrious patron and friend. Tearing himself away from scenes of festivity, he left Philadelphia on the 14th of August, and after stopping at Baltimore, arrived on the 19th at Mt. Vernon, beneath the roof hallowed by the presence and the virtues of Washington. "When we reflect upon the principal events in the lives of these two illustrious men;— the difference in their ages and countries;— the distance which separated them from each other;— the circumstances which brought them together; — the importance of the scenes through which they had passed;— the glorious success of their courageous efforts;— their mutual anxiety again to embrace each other;—the tender and truly paternal esteem of the one, and the respect, admiration, and filial attachment of the other;—when we reflect upon all this, we find that everything contributed to stamp this interesting interview with a sublimity of character, which had no prototype in the annals of man."

Twelve blissful days were spent at Mount Vernon, at the close of which he returned to the north. Negotiations with the allied tribes of Indians were now in progress, and his influence over them being widely extended, he was invited to join the commissioners of peace, and assist them in their "talk" with the Indians. Fort Schuyler was the place of meeting, and crowds assembled to witness the ceremony. In sullen silence the Indians ranged themselves to listen to the words of Kayewla, as they termed Lafayette. They had been leagued in hostility against the whites, and it was feared that they would still refuse all propositions of peace. Lafayette had frequently been called to treat with them during the war and possessed a strong hold over their rude minds. He now addressed them, pointing out the advantages of peace, and the inevitable destruction which awaited them, if they persisted in ravaging the frontiers. The lordly denizens of the forest heard him with a confidence which they would not have given any other white man, and as he closed his speech, his point was gained. "Father," said one of the chiefs in reply, "we have heard thy voice, and we rejoice that thou hast visited thy children, to give to them good and necessary advice. Thou hast said that we have done wrong in opening our ears to wicked men, and closing our hearts to thy counsels. Father! it is all true; — we have left the good path; we have wandered away from it, and been enveloped in a black cloud. We have now returned, that thou mayest find in us, good and faithful children. Father! we rejoice to hear thy voice among us; — it seems that the Great Spirit has directed thy footsteps to this council of friendship, to smoke the calumet of peace and fellowship, with thy long lost children."

After making presents to the chiefs, he left them with the treaty fully ratified, and proceeded on his way amid the acclamations and public rejoicings of every community through which he passed. Pressing invitations were now crowding upon him to visit Boston, and he accordingly directed his journey towards that cradle of liberty,— the metropolis of New England. On his way, enthusiastic demonstrations of welcome were given him at Hartford and Worcester, as well as at the smaller towns through which his road lay. But it was for Boston to crown his ovation with the richest triumph. Before he reached the city a magnificent military procession, bearing the flags of America and France, came out to escort him thither. A salute of thirteen guns greeted him as he came in sight, which was also the signal for a vast number of citizens to join the cavalcade. With great pomp, led on by martial music, and, over all, the renewed pealing of bells, he was ushered into the metropolis. Every street through which he passed, as well as the doors, windows, and roofs of the houses, was filled with spectators, who made the air ring with their unceasing acclamations. As he passed up State street, another salute of thirteen guns was fired. With these rejoicings he was conducted to his lodgings, and on the evening of this memorable day, the municipal authorities ordered the lamps of the city to be re-lighted for the first time since the conclusion of the war. Fire works and illuminations were the order of the night. The state government also united with that of the city in their enthusiastic expressions of regard. On the 19th of October, the anniversary of the capitulation of Cornwallis,— the governor of the state — the president of the senate — the speaker of the house of representatives — the executive council, and the members of the two houses — assembled in the great hall of audience, to offer their congratulations to Lafayette on his happy arrival in America. "When the Marquis was introduced, the governor, in eloquent and impressive-terms, testified the high esteem and gratitude entertained for him by the state of Massachusetts, the remembrance of which could never be effaced.—The report of this ceremony having spread itself over the city, all the neighboring streets were completely crowded with people, and it was with great difficulty that a lane was formed, by the military through the multitude, to the City Hotel. When this was effected, Lafayette appeared, accompanied by the governor, the members of the legislature, the old continental officers, the clergymen of different sects, and the principal citizens, who escorted him into the great saloon of the the hotel, where an entertainment had been prepared for five hundred persons. Thirteen arcades were thrown across the bottom of the saloon, emblematical of the thirteen states of the Union. Lafayette was seated beneath the center arch, from which a fleur de lis was suspended. After dinner, thirteen patriotic toasts were drunk, and each one celebrated by thirteen guns stationed in the market place. When the health of WASHINGTON was pronounced, a curtain, placed behind Lafayette, immediately fell, and disclosed the portrait of that great man, encircled with laurels, and decorated with the flags of America and France. Lafayette arose and steadfastly regarded it with a mixture of tenderness, pleasure and surprise. For a few moments he gazed in silent admiration, when a voice exclaimed, — 'LONG LIVE WASHINGTON!' — the effect was electrical; — the name of the gallant chieftain of liberty resounded from all parts of the room, and the shouts of 'LONG LIVE WASHINGTON!' were drowned amid peals of applause and enthusiastic accla mations. On the same evening Mrs. Hayley gave a grand ball, accompanied with splendid fireworks in honor of Lafayette, and her house was brilliantly illuminated. The legislative assembly granted him the privilege of assisting in their sittings, which he frequently made use of during his stay in Boston."

The scenes through which he now passed were a continual triumph. The magnificent welcome which Bonaparte afterwards received, when his negotiations at Bayonne had added the Spanish crown to the French domain, did not exceed that which Lafayette now enjoyed. The triumph of the Emperor, while it displayed the most enthusiastic admiration on the part of his people, manifested but little love; while that of the Marquis mingled the highest admiration with the warmest affection. From Boston he visited the towns of Salem, Cape Ann, Marblehead, Beverly, Newburyport, Portsmouth, N. H., and then returning to Boston he proceeded to Providence and the scenes of his active labors in Rhode Island. Returning once more to Boston he embarked in the royal frigate La Nymphe and sailed for the theater of his greatest military glory, — the mouth of York River in Chesapeake Bay. He landed at Yorktown, but it was with no ordinary emotions that he set his foot upon shore and looked over the scenes, consecrated by the triumphant issue of the struggle for American freedom. Before him was Virginia and here was Yorktown where he had baffled the manœuvres, restricted the operations and involved in inextricable toils one of the bravest and most accomplished generals of Europe. A thrill of rapture rioted in his breast, as he reflected on the part he had been allowed to play in the great struggle and its successful issue. He knew that his efforts had been important, and it is not strange that he felt this, more than he had ever done before, as he now entered Yorktown. Talk about the modesty of genius, ye who will; true greatness is, and should be, conscious of itself. We have no sympathy with that mawkish feeling which denies to the man possessed of any thing true and noble all knowledge of its worth. The great soul looks upon itself with the same calm eye with which it measures the pigmies around it, and it cannot but see the difference between it and them. This feeling is, however, diverse as the poles from the puffed up vanity belonging to some minds. A vain mind must necessarily be in some respects a little mind and utterly ignorant of the conscious dignity which belongs to greatness. True greatness knows and feels its own nature and rises to a sublime elevation when contemplating, as Lafayette now did, the scenes wherein it has manifested itself.

From Yorktown the Marquis proceeded to Williamsburg whose inhabitants came out and received their gallant defender with indescribable marks of enthusiasm and love. From this city he proceeded to Richmond, which he entered on the 18th of November, meeting with a reception transcending, if possible, all former display. Washington was waiting for him here, and after the gallant Marquis had received the congratulations of the city and the legislature of the state, then in session at Richmond, he accompanied his revered friend once more to the shades of Mount Vernon. For about a week he remained, enjoying the hospitality of the Father of his country and then the two friends proceeded together to Annapolis. At this city and at Alexandria they remained for some time, honoring with their presence the brilliant festivals given them there. The legislatures of both Virginia and Maryland voted flattering addresses and conferred upon him and his male heirs the rights of citizenship in each of these states. The honors accorded to the Marquis in this, the theater of his hardest toil and brightest glory, fell gratefully upon his heart and lay there like sunbeams brightening and warming some of the dark and cold scenes through which he was afterwards to pass.

But, however pleasant these festivities to the hero, different duties awaited him. He could not bring himself to trespass too long upon the generous hospitality of the people whom his own arm had sped forward to freedom. He was still young, and he was not satisfied to allow the life before him to be spent in inactivity. His name, written upon the baptismal register of America, he would have also ineffaceably inscribed upon the records of Europe. His reception here had been more flattering than he had dreamed of, and met with his overflowing thankfulness, but the time which he had assigned for his visit was now drawing to a close, and he prepared to return to France. At Annapolis he parted, for the last time, with his revered friend. It was a mournful separation to both, for they seemed to have a premonition that they should see each other's face no more. This presentiment saddened the buoyant spirit of Lafayette, while it deepened the natural gravity of Washington, as each gave to the other his parting adieux. "In the moment of our separation," writes Washington afterwards to him, "and every hour since, I have felt all that love, respect and attachment for you, with which length of years, close connection, and your merits have inspired me. I often asked myself, as our carriages separated, whether that was the last sight I should ever have of you, — and though I wished to say, *No;* my fears answered, *Yes.* I called to mind the days of my youth, and found they had fled to return no more; — that I was now descending the hill I had been fifty years climbing, and that, though I was blest with a good constitution, I was of a short lived family, and might soon expect to be en tombed in the mansion of my fathers. These thoughts darkened the shades and gave a gloom to the picture, and, consequently, to my prospect of seeing you again."

Journeying northward, the Marquis took leave of Congress, which was then in session at Trenton. Appropriate marks of consideration were awarded him by that body, who appointed a committee, consisting of one member from each state, to receive and take leave of him in their name. They instructed the committee to assure Lafayette "that Congress continue to entertain the same high sense of his abilities and zeal to promote the welfare of America, both here and in Europe, which they have frequently expressed and manifested on former occasions, and which the recent marks of his attention to their commercial and other interests, have perfectly confirmed. That, as his uniform and unceasing attachment to this country has resembled that of a patriotic citizen, the United States regard him with particular affection, and will not cease to feel an interest in whatever may concern his honor and prosperity; — and that their best and kindest wishes will always attend him." Mr. Jay, as chairman of the committee, communicated to the Marquis these instructions, and received a reply, every syllable of which came warmly from a heart still beating with affection for the new born Republic. It concluded as follows: "In unbounded wishes to America, Sir, I am happy to observe the prevailing disposition of the people to strengthen the confederation, preserve public faith, regulate trade, and, in a proper guard over continental magazines and frontier posts, in a general system of militia, in foreseeing attention to the navy, to ensure every kind of safety. MAY THIS IMMENSE TEMPLE OF FREEDOM EVER STAND A LESSON TO OPPRESSORS, AN EXAMPLE TO THE OPPRESSED, AND A SANCTUARY FOR THE RIGHTS OF MANKIND! and may these happy United States attain that complete splendor and prosperity which will illustrate the blessings of their government, and for ages to come, rejoice the departed souls of its founders." MAY IT STAND! Perish the hand that would dare to pluck a stone from this majestic temple, after this prayer for its perpetuity from the lips of one in whose blood was laid its corner stone. Patriotism now re-utters the invocation of Lafayette, and prays that age after age may only strengthen the foundations of this edifice, and that each revolving cycle of time may find it indeed to be,

> "monumentum ære perennius
> Regalique situ, pyramidum altius."—*Horace.*

With the blessing of every one resting upon him, Lafayette proceeded on to New York and embarked again for France. On the 25th of December, 1784, he sailed from America for the third time, and after a prosperous voyage on board the La Nymphe Frigate, he arrived in Paris on the 25th of January, 1785.

Again in Europe, the mind of Lafayette became incessantly active on the interesting and important field which opened before him. He now entered the theater of European politics for the first time, though his connection with American history did not yet wholly cease. He still interested himself in the welfare of the new Republic, whose commercial interests with Europe, and particularly with France, he spared no pains to establish. That his services were appreciated, is seen in a letter from Washington to him, dated Sept. 1st, 1785, in which he assured the Marquis that his constant attention, and unwearied endeavors to serve the interests of the United States could not fail to keep alive in them a grateful sensibility, and preserve for him the affectionate regard of all their citizens.

During the year 1785 the Marquis visited his estates in Tourraine and afterwards visited the courts of many of the German princes, where were added extraordinary tokens of the admiration which his military and political conduct had diffused over Europe. But at no time did he disguise the love for freedom which was the master passion of his being. The flattering distinction with which he was greeted by the different crowned heads whom he visited could not extinguish this. The attention which he every where received, even in the midst of the most rigid aristocracy and monarchy, showed how much THE MAN could make himself felt, simply by the force of his own character and innate worth. In September of this year, he attended at Pottsdam the grand reviews of Frederic the Great, and greatly enriched his own experience by the sight of fifty thousand men going through the varied evolutions of battles, sieges and storms, under the personal direction of the most accomplished General of his age. When Frederic was advised of the presence of Lafayette, he sent an aid de camp and invited him to Sans Soucie without delay. Frederic was a tyrant, but in many respects he had a great soul, and on the present occasion he did not conceal from Lafayette the admiration which he felt for his character and that of Washington. With a nobleness which few despots possess, he treated with marked attention the still youthful hero whose heart was beating to an impulse which would crush his despotism and hurl him from his throne. The tyrant and the defender of liberty held long and interesting conversations together, in which the American Revolution and the progress of free principles were the prominent topics. In one of these conversations Frederic expressed the opinion that America would not long continue a republic. "By and by," said he, "she will return to the good old system." Lafayette replied with warmth and enthusiasm, "Never, Sire, never," said he, "neither monarchy, nor aristocracy, can ever exist in America." "Sir," said Frederic, with one of those penetrating looks which he knew so well how to command, "Sir, I knew a young man, who, after having visited countries where liberty and equality reigned, conceived the idea of establishing the same system in his own country. Do you know what happened to him?" "No, Sire." "He was hanged," said the King. Lafayette looked up with a calm smile which neither betrayed fear, nor indicated in the least, to the anxious Frederic, what were his secret thoughts. A cloud, rather than a smile, would have rested upon the countenance of both King and Marquis, could they have foreseen the events of the next ten years. This unwritten history was to be full of moment to them both. Lafayette remained for some days enjoying the hospitality and kindness of the King, and when the time came for them to part, it was with mutual regard. Upon taking his leave, Frederic presented the Marquis with his miniature set in diamonds, and with sincere affection expressed the hope that this memento might often recall his image to his thoughts.

Lafayette's love of liberty and hatred of oppression were sincere and unfeigned. His great heart would have swept the world from tyranny of every shape, and have sent the glad rills of freedom flowing through every nation, and murmuring around every hearthstone their joyous music. His sympathy was all alive for the oppressed African race. He was not one of that class so prevalent in our own time, who make their long and loud discourse about the blessings of liberty, while, at the same time, they are busily engaged in forging more strongly the chains of slavery. He had none of that mockery which would sing of freedom to the clank of the slave's fetters, and the music of his groans. His heart bled, as every great and philanthropic heart must do, over the woes of negro slavery. As Madame de Stael truly remarks, wherever a certain depth of thought exists, throughout the world, there is not to be found an enemy to freedom. From one end of the world to the other, the friends of freedom maintain communication by knowledge, as religious men by sentiments ;—or, rather, knowledge and sentiment unite in the love of freedom, as in that of the Supreme Being. The principles of liberty must live in every great soul, and make every generous heart palpitate, like love and friendship. One connected series of virtues and ideas, found in every true-hearted man, seems to form that golden chain, described by Homer, which, in binding man to Heaven, delivers him from all the fetters of tyranny. Lafayette formed one, and that, too, a conspicuous link, in the chain which binds together the brotherhood of great men. He hated slavery because he was a great man, and as such could not do otherwise. Soon after the completion of the American war, he wrote to Washington upon the subject. "Permit me, my dear General," said he, "new that you are about to enjoy some repose, to propose a plan for elevating the African race. Let us unite in purchasing a small estate, where we may try the experiment to free the negroes, and use them only as tenants. Such an example as yours, would render the practice general, and if we should succeed in America, I will cheerfully devote a part of my time to render the plan fashionable in the West Indies. If it be a wild scheme, I would rather be mad in that way, than be thought wise on the other tack." This plan, Lafayette now began to put in execution. He purchased a plantation in Cayenne, with a large number of slaves, and, proposing their gradual emancipation, he began to fit them for a proper enjoyment of their freedom, by a thorough course of education. In this he was guided only by the purest benevolence, and had the satisfaction of finding that his efforts were not in vain. He had the pleasure of a cordial sympathy with his views from distinguished American patriots, who had not learned to despise the *inalienable rights of man*, for which they had so long striven. Washington, Adams, Franklin, Jefferson, Madison, Patrick Henry and others, gave him their cheerful aid. Washington wrote to him, May 10th, 1786, in which he thus alludes to his scheme :—"Your late purchase in Cayenne, with a view of emancipating your slaves, is a generous and noble proof of your humanity. Would to God a like spirit might diffuse itself generally into the minds of the people of this country. But I despair of seeing it. Some petitions were presented to the Virginia Assembly, at its last session, for the abolition of slavery, but they could scarcely obtain a hearing. To set the slaves afloat at once, would, I really believe, be productive of much inconvenience and mischief;—but, by degrees, it certainly might, and assuredly ought, to be effected, and that, too, by legislative authority." It might be well if the sentiments of Washington and Lafayette actuated the councils of the nation which they labored effectually to bless with the boon of freedom.

This period was also distinguised by the efforts of Lafayette in behalf of the persecuted French Protestants. Though himself belonging to the Romish Church, he had none of the bigotry or intolerance so generally seen in that body, but hated the tyranny of a priesthood as intensely as that of a king. He made a visit to the Protestants who chiefly resided in the south of France, and having carefully inquired into their grievances, returned to Paris and applied his energies to their removal. Despotism was made to stay its hand before his efforts, bigotry relaxed its stern grasp, "and justice gave back to the oppressed the invaluable, inalienable, right to worship God in their own way—to obey Him rather than man."

CHAPTER VII.

A NEW ERA IN LAFAYETTE'S HISTORY — CAUSES WHICH LED TO THE FRENCH REVOLUTION — MISTAKEN VIEWS CONCERNING IT — CHARACTER OF LOUIS XVI — STATE OF THE NATION — THE WHEEL OF REVOLUTION BEGINS TO MOVE — ASSEMBLY OF NOTABLES — LAFAYETTE A MEMBER — THE STATES GENERAL — THE TIERS ETAT AND THE NOBLES — UNION OF THE THREE ESTATES — LAFAYETTE'S ORATORY — THE BILL OF RIGHTS — OUTBREAK OF THE PEOPLE — DESTRUCTION OF THE BASTILE — LAFAYETTE COMMANDS THE NATIONAL GUARDS — MURDER OF FOULON—REFUTATION OF SLANDERS AGAINST LAFAYETTE — MOB OF WOMEN — JUDICIOUS COURSE OF LAFAYETTE — THE ROYAL FAMILY LEAVE VERSAILLES FOR PARIS — RECONCILIATION AGAIN — CELEBRATION OF THE FOURTEENTH OF JULY — MAGNIFICENT FESTIVAL — LAFAYETTE REFUSES THE COMMAND OF ALL THE NATIONAL GUARDS OF FRANCE — HIS TRUE NOBILITY OF SOUL.

Though we are still to contemplate Lafayette as the same exalted character, we shall now view him in a different theater, and an actor in widely different scenes. Having accomplished his sublime mission upon a foreign soil, the mighty question now before his thought was, Why may not France be as free as America? While on his visit to Frederic the Great, said he—"Do you believe that I went to America to obtain military reputation?—It was for liberty I went there. He who loves liberty can only remain quiet after having established it in his own country." These remarkable words indicated fully what was the desire of his heart towards France, and what would be his course of action whenever a favorable opportunity should arise. He was ready for any sacrifice, and his wakeful discernment could not fail to perceive that the time was coming when one would have to be made. Clouds, dark and heavy, were gathered around the political horizon, in whose threatening aspect he clearly read the foreboded storm. What if it be a tempest, he asked of himself, which shall overthrow every tower of despotism, and leave only the ruins upon which may be erected the more glorious edifice of freedom! His heart answered calmly—Thus let it be.

Before bearing the reader to the French Revolution, *in medias res*, it will be necessary briefly to sketch the causes which gave rise to that remarkable period in history. The atrocities to which it led, have hung a pall of gloom and terror around it, which makes the mind associate with it only the idea of anarchy and reckless ferocity. We do not wish to palliate at all these features in this Revolution, and only set the matter in its true light when we say that, its beginning did not at all contemplate such an end. Its origin lay in the progress of the democratic principle which had advanced to decisive action, in the revolutionary struggles of both Britain and her revolted colonies. France had been ripening long for such an outbreak. The English struggle in the seventeenth century, would have awakened, at the same time, a corresponding one in France, had the reins of the French Government been then held by a tyrant as weak-minded and inefficient as Charles. Louis XIV. ruled his people with a rod of iron, but his dazzling genius commanded their respect, and the height of glory to which he was raising France, won from them shouts of admiration, even amid the groans of their oppression. During his reign it was, that absolute monarchy was definitely established. The crown arrogated the right to dispose alike of person and of property, without the slightest regard to law or equity. Parliament had no longer any will of its own, the noblesse were reduced to a state of perfect dependence, and at the close of the life of the greatest king she had known since the days of Charlemagne, France lay manacled in every limb. Still, outwardly, all was fair. The clear sky did not reveal the sleeping thunder. Commerce was flourishing ;—science and art were shedding their mild glories over the nation ;—letters were cultivated, and the military reputation of France was known and respected throughout Europe ; but underneath this fair exterior, were kindled the slow fires of an earthquake, destined to rock half a continent in its march, and crumble the throne of an ancient and powerful monarchy.

A reaction ensued immediately upon the death of Louis XIV., but the ascendency which the crown had gained during his reign, enabled his successor to maintain his prerogatives against the encroachments of parliament, while he perceived that the struggle between king and people was fast hastening to the unequal contest. Louis XVI. took the scepter in 1774, a prince weak-minded, but amiable, and willing to do all in his power to lessen the burdens under which his people were groaning. He had a good heart but a poor head; and while he did every thing with the best intentions, it was his misfortune to succeed in nothing. It was suicidal for him to encourage and aid the American Revolution as he did, for this was, without doubt, accessory to that which occurred in France. Says a historian of this event,—"It is difficult to suppose that so many thousand officers and soldiers had visited and fought in behalf of the rights of America, without being imbued with something of a kindred spirit. There, they beheld a new and happy nation, among whom the pride of birth and the distinctions of rank were alike unknown; there they, for the first time, saw virtue, and talents, and courage, rewarded; there they viewed, with surprise, a sovereign people fighting, not for a master, but themselves, and haranguing, deliberating, dispensing justice, and administering the laws, by representatives of their own free choice. On their return, the contrast was odious and intolerable;—they beheld family preferred to merit, influence to justice, wealth to worth;—they began to examine into a constitution, in which the monarch, whom they were now accustomed to consider as only the first magistrate, was everything, and the people, the fountain of all power, merely cyphers;—and they may well be supposed to have wished, and even languished, for a change.

"In fine, the people being left entirely destitute of redress or protection, the royal authority paramount and unbounded;—the laws venal, the peasantry oppressed; agriculture in a languishing state, commerce considered as degrading; the public revenues farmed out to greedy financiers; the public money consumed by a court wallowing in luxury; and every institution at variance with justice, policy, and reason;—a change became inevitable in the ordinary course of human events ; and, like all sudden alterations in corrupt states, was accompanied with temporary evils and crimes, that made many good men look back on the ancient despotism with a sigh." No revolution can be accomplished without some temporary evils, and the fact that these were manifold in France does not affect the purity of the motives which moved the authors of rebellion. But it was not alone the influence, of the officers and soldiers fresh from the field of American liberty, nor the hand of despotism upon the exasperated masses, which gave the greatest shock to the tottering dynasty of the Bourbons. The most fatal blow was given by the derangement of the public finances which already elicited loud murmurs throughout the kingdom. The annual deficit amounted to millions, and after having exhausted every resource to supply it, Louis and his ministers beheld the fearful gulf, from which they could only recoil by a step almost as disastrous as ruin itself. The forcible and illegal exactions, which, in the seventeenth century, had proved destructive to Charles in England, the King dared not avail himself of, for, in his weakness, he knew that it would involve him in complete overthrow. After long vacillation, at one time under the control of the ministry, at another blindly influenced by the queen ;— now ready to make any concessions to Parliament and his people, and again sternly refusing to yield at all, the King placed M. de Calonne at the head of his cabinet and tacitly committed his fortunes into his hands. At this point the wheel of Revolution began to move.

De Calonne saw at a glance the true position of affairs. He perceived that the finances of the kingdom could never be successfully arranged, except by a reform which would strike a blow at the very root of the evil, as it lay in the French constitution itself. To accomplish this was more than King or Parliament could do, and the mind of the minister turned towards the States-General, the true and legitimate Assembly of the nation, believing that hope could rise from no other source. This Body had not met since the year 1614, and when de Calonne proposed that it again be convened, the mind of the Sovereign revolted from it with terror. The States-General would be composed of representative from every class in his kingdom, and Louis shrunk with instinctive apprehension from a meeting which would submit his affairs to the closest scrutiny of those whom he knew were suffering the weight of his exactions. Another assembly had been occasionally substituted instead of this, and as it consisted only of those who were nominated by the King himself, Louis determined to invoke it. This was called the *Assembly of Notables*, and on the 29th of December, 1786, the royal proclamation was issued summoning them to meet and take into consideration the state of the realm.

Lafayette was chosen a member, and on the 22d of February, 1787, he took his seat with his associates, prepared for a bold endeavor in the removal of grievances past endurance. His own loved France was dearer than ever to his heart, now that he saw her struggling under the weight of an oppression which made every feeling of his soul burn with indignation.

The enormous deficit of over a hundred millions of livres, could not be kept secret, and when made known, Lafayette, and other members of the Assembly, saw that something more was necessary than merely to supply this present need. The investigation into the public matters, urgently demanded by the Assembly, and at last reluctantly granted by the King, showed a monstrous growth of evil and corruption which could not with safety again be concealed. The festering wound had been already allowed to prey too long in secret upon the body politic, and now that it had once been opened, it could not be outwardly closed till it was internally healed.

Lafayette, as usual, busied himself in the work of reform. The enormous peculation which existed in every department;—the shameful manner in which the administration of justice was conducted;—the illegal taxes which had been levied upon the people;—the violent subversion of right, and the long train of abuses which royal authority had sanctioned, and ministerial influence executed, revealed to him wrongs which his mind, though partially prepared for a disclosure, had yet never dreamed to exist. The abyss of corruption, as it was fully displayed, startled for a moment but did not appal him. He calmly surveyed its depth, and with the same spirit which had borne him fearlessly amid the onset of battle prepared for the crisis before him. He rose from his seat, and with dignified firmness, uttered his protest against the prevailing evils, and demanded redress. With stern rebuke he condemned the system which had been so fatally practiced by the government, and with a courage not at all intimidated by the fact that a younger brother of the King was President of the Council, he exhibited the disorder to which this had led in all the public departments. "I repeat," he concluded, "with renewed confidence, the remark, that the millions which are dissipated, are collected by taxation, and that taxation can only be justified by the real wants of the state;—that the millions abandoned to peculation or avarice, are the fruits of the labor, the tears, and perhaps the blood, of the people;—and that the computation of unfortunate individuals, which has been made for the purpose of realizing sums so heedlessly squandered, affords a frightful subject of consideration for the justice and goodness which, we feel convinced, are the natural sentiments of his majesty."

The reforms which Lafayette urged were too momentous, and involved principles too novel, to immediately enlist in their execution, men who had grown gray in the dream that France could never be otherwise than she had been; but he was unmoved by his comparative isolation. He knew that in the seed he was scattering there, was a vital energy which would at length develope itself and bring forth fruit in its maturity. The free principles which he, and a few other kindred souls, uttered in the Assembly, sent a strange thrill to the breasts of the old aristocracy, and smote the heart of the monarch with strange foreboding, but though apparently overborne by the tide of opposition, Lafayette was confident that they could not perish. They will rise again, was his unfaltering language, and their notes will be heard above the cry of oppression, and will ring in the ear of tyranny till *its* voice shall be mute forever.

Before the Assembly closed its session, Lafayette saw clear indications that he had not spoken in vain. The accents of truth had been heard, and with interest and delight he watched the energy of their quiet might. He did not, for a moment, relax his efforts. With an eye that never quailed, he looked upon the scowling minions of despotism around him, and heard without misgiving, threats which came to him in no ambiguous form. It was proposed to the King, that he be sent to the Bastile, but the Marquis only smiled at the menace, and toiled on in his work. Favors could not bribe, frowns could not force, him from his purpose. He discerned from the first a radical error in attempting to originate all the necessary reforms in a body, constituted as was the Assembly of Notables. It was the common people who were burdened, and these had no representation there. Every attempt in behalf of these, would fail unless they themselves could send a delegation which should bring their own wants and sufferings before those who held the power of relief. Lafayette felt that the Notables should give way for the States-General, and this conviction he openly expressed to the former. The known hostility of the King to this measure, and the fact that if adopted would greatly abridge the privileges of the nobility, interposed no barrier to Lafayette. He offered to the Assembly a memorial for the King, in which, after having, in a masterly manner, recounted the existing evils, he entreated his majesty to convoke a *National* Assembly, which might accomplish the regeneration of France. When this was offered, the President of the Council started from his seat in amazement, "What, sir," said he, "do you ask for the convocation of the States-General?"

"Yes, my lord, and even more than that," was the calm reply.

"You wish me, then, to write, and to carry to the King, that the Marquis de Lafayette moves to convoke the States-General?"

"Yes, my lord."

The proposition, which met with but little favor when first uttered in the Assembly, was hailed with acclamation by the public. The notables, appalled by the increasing difficulties before them, at length yielded to the public clamor, and the King, borne on against his will, issued the royal edict, and commanded the States-General to meet. This was the first act of a tragedy, in which he was to be the slain victim; and although he did not discern the prophetic present, others read, clearly as if a handwriting were tracing characters of fire on the palace-walls, the fearful announcement of his doom!

The first Assembly was convoked by Philippe le Bel, in 1303, and had since been convened at irregular periods, and at times of peculiar exigency to the kingdom. It was composed of the three estates of the kingdom, the nobles, the clergy, and the *tiers état*, or common people, in such numbers and proportions as the King, or some council which he should choose to consult, should determine. Here arose the first difficulty in the construction of the new States, General. Louis shrunk from allowing the common people a prominent representation, and they would not be satisfied without it. It was contended that the *tiers état* comprised the great body of the nation, and though owning but a small portion of the land it *tilled* the whole, and was entitled in reason and justice, to a number of deputies, equal at least, to that of the two other orders. Louis hesitated to decide the matter either for or against the people, and referred the whole subject to the notables. Free principles had been gaining ground with them, but not to the extent which would prevent a struggle, while justice and liberty attained the ascendant. A stormy debate arose in which the friends of freedom encountered the bitter hostility to right, sanctioned by ancient custom, and fostered by hoary prejudice. Lafayette, of course, espoused the cause of the masses, and lifted his voice earnestly in their behalf, but it was in vain; and the decision was at length given against the measure.

Neither the King nor the Assembly, was prepared for the storm that ensued. An outcry was heard throughout the realm, from the down trodden classes, declaring that they would submit to injustice no longer. A host of writers appeared, whose burning language fed the flame of excitement and kindled the fiercest resentment in every quarter of France. "Give us the States-General!" was the shout which came like the sound of many waters on every breeze to the ears of the King, and rolled unceasingly over Paris. From the Alps, the Pyrennees, the plains of Flanders, the borders of the Channel, and the shores of the Mediterranean and the Atlantic, the wild cry of determination was uttered. The King, unable to resist the tempest took the wisest course, and bowed before its might. A royal proclamation was issued ordaining that the total number of deputies for the States-General, should be at least a thousand, conceding the grand point that the representation of the *tiers état* should be equal to that of the other two orders united.

This body, whose strange history so far as connected with the subject of our narration, we now proceed to unfold, assembled on the 5th of May, 1789. The republicans in principle, congratulated themselves on the prospect before them, and believed that the time for the regeneration of France was at hand. Lafayette was chosen a deputy without opposition, by the nobility of Auvergne, and took his seat, supported in his views by the deepest feeling in the nation. The Assembly was opened with great pomp. A solemn procession of extraordinary magnificence took place, in which the King, the three orders, and all the great dignitaries of state, repaired to the church of Notre Dame, and invoked the blessing of Heaven to crown the deliberations about to commence. It was a splendid spectacle, and greeted with the most joyous acclamations. Says one who formed a part of the procession, — "The streets were hung with tapestry belonging to the crown ;— the regiments of the French and Swiss guards formed a line from Notre Dame to Saint Louis ;— an immense concourse of people looked on, as we passed, in respectful silence ;— the balconies were adorned with costly stuffs, the windows filled with spectators of all ages and both sexes ; — every face bespoke kindly emotions, every eye sparkled with joy ; — the clapping of hands, expressions of the warmest interest, the looks that met us and that still followed after we were out of sight, formed a rapturous, enchanting scene, to which I should vainly strive to do justice. Bands of music, placed at intervals, rent the air with melodious sounds, military marches, the rolling of drums, the clang of trumpets, the noble chants of the priests, alternately heard, without discordance, without confusion, enlivened this triumphal procession to the temple of the Almighty."

At the first meeting of the Assembly for the transaction of business, the three orders convened in separate departments. The great Hall of the States was assigned to the *tiers état*, and the first step of this body was to send up a proposition that the three estates should assemble together for the purpose of examining and verifying in common the credentials of the members. This was rejected by the nobles and the clergy, but persisted in by the *tiers état*, who refused to organize till the point was yielded. Lafayette advocated the proposed method of verification, but it was too humiliating for the aristocracy to allow their credentials to be inquired into by the populace, and they resolutely refused to meet them. After a long contest, the

States-General found themselves, at the end of five weeks, in the same inactive state as at first. Nothing had been done except proposals for union by the one party, and obstinate rejection of them by the other.

This course seemed likely to continue till the patience of those who had anticipated so much from the Assembly should be wholly exhausted. It was at this juncture that the *tiers état* resolved upon action fraught with most momentous consequences to the subsequent history of the revolution. They made a last attempt at union, and finding this to fail, they resolved themselves into a legislative body under the name of the National Assembly, and on the memorable 17th of June, 1789, made the announcement to the public, expressing their intention to accomplish their work of political reform. It was entirely unexpected, and received with consternation by the court and privileged classes. It was in vain, however, for them to oppose. The King attempted to interpose his prerogative, and the nobility asserted its rights, but neither could shake the decision, and both Louis and his advisers were at length forced to comply with its conditions. Lafayette strenuously advocated the union, and with a noble minority of forty-seven members, embracing distinguished citizens, he opposed the proceedings of the court. He warned the nobles to beware lest their resistance to the measure should only destroy themselves. He told them that they were clinging to a tottering fabric, whose crumbling foundations would at last fail and bring upon them a general destruction — that persisting in their present position, they were taking a course of folly and madness, like the shipwrecked sailor in the midst of the ocean and the storm, throwing away the only plank which could save him, and buffeting alone the billows. But they saw no danger, and urged the King to interfere for the protection of his crown and their ancestral honors. Louis, jealous of his own sovereignty, undertook the work, and proposed by his own presence to awe, as he termed them, his rebellious subjects into submission. Before, however, appearing in their meeting, he chose to make a display of his authority, by closing the doors and stationing a guard over the Hall where the *soi-disant* National Assembly was accustomed to hold its sittings. Such interposition, guided by the blindest infatuation, was only adding oil to the flames, which were burning full fiercely enough before. The deputies, gathering to the morning session on the 20th of June, were told by the police of soldiers, that the King had adjourned their sitting until the 22d. Astonishment was the first emotion, which soon gave way to one of exasperation and sternest purpose. Their former place of meeting was denied them, and they proceeded to another, where they calmly deliberated upon the darkening future. The Rubicon was passed, and there now went up accents more startling and more united, than had ever been heard in France. They fell like a death knell upon the ear of monarchy, and made the throne of despotism rock upon its heavy base. It demanded a CONSTITUTION FOR THE FRENCH PEOPLE, which should embrace in its provisions, governor and governed alike, making both strictly amenable to its sanctions. And in full view of the indignity which had that day been offered to them by the crown, and through them to the people, they solemnly resolved, under an oath administered to them in open assembly, to which all but one of the deputies subscribed, "never to separate, and to assemble whenever circumstances should require, till the constitution of the kingdom should be established and founded on a solid basis." The Assembly of the *tiers état* in their Hall, was farther postponed by the King, till the 23d, and upon assembling on the morning of that day, they found a guard still in attendance. For a long time they were denied entrance, and when this was granted, they found their seats already occupied by the higher classes. In sullen silence they ranged themselves about the Hall, each one determining for the present to hear and not to speak. The bayonet glittered there and the parade of royalty, but none were moved by either. The King addressed them, not with words of conciliation to win them back, but with haughty arrogance, well adapted to increase resistance. He annulled all the previous proceedings of the *tiers état* and energetically reproved them for assuming to themselves the liberty to act, without the union or consent of the higher orders. He reproached them for taking the title of National Assembly and bade them abandon it. He told them that he was the sole representative of the people, and that if he met with fresh obstacles from the Assembly, he would take the matter into his own hands, and singly establish the welfare of France. The King concluded his address, and ordered the Assembly to separate immediately. He left the Hall, followed by the nobility and part of the clergy, while the majority of the ecclesiastics and the commons remained. For a time no one spoke. The echoes of the retiring footsteps of Louis had died away, the last shouts of *vive le Roi* were lost in the distance, and still the profoundest silence reigned in the chamber, where the parade of authority, and the pomp of power, had been so lately seen. At length there was a movement, and a man of middle stature, with a sullen countenance disfigured by the marks of the small pox, with eyes small, but now twinkling with star-like brightness, his hair thick and uncombed, flowing down over his shoulders,—rose and addressed the assembly. It was Mirabeau. "Gentlemen," said he, "I grant that it may be for the present peace and quiet of the country, that we should give heed to the instructions we have just received. But the presence of despotism here is fraught with infinite danger! To devise good for the nation we must deliberate, and to deliberate we must be free. What means this insulting dictation?—this threatening display of arms?—this flagrant violation of the national temple? Who is it that dictates to you the way in which you shall be happy? He who acts by your commission. Who is it that gives you imperious laws? He who acts by your commission,—the minister, who by your appointment is vested with the execution of the laws,—of laws which we only have a right to make. Ours is an inviolable political priesthood. To us twenty-five millions of people are looking to guard from further desecration the sacred ark of liberty, to release them from the burdensome yoke which has so long crushed them, and to give them back their own inalienable right to peace, liberty and happiness. Gentlemen, the freedom of your deliberations is attempted to be destroyed. The iron chain of despotic prescription is laid upon you. A military force surrounds your Assembly. Where are the enemies of France? Is Cataline at our gates? Gentlemen! I demand that, clothing yourselves in your dignity and your legislative authority, you remain firm in the sacredness of your oath, which does not permit us to separate till we have framed a constitution;—till we have given a *magna charta* to France." Then turning to the grand master of ceremonies, who at this time interposed and reminded the assembly of the peremptory orders of the King—"Go," he exclaimed, "and tell your master that we are here by the order of the people, and that we shall depart only at the point of the bayonet."

The Assembly proceeded to business, and without a dissenting voice re-affirmed its rule securing inviolability to the members, declaring that any one who should offer violence to them, should be considered as a traitor and guilty of a capital crime. Day after day the sessions continued, and received constantly indications that their course was entirely the echo of the public will. Addresses were received approving in the highest terms the course they had taken, and assuring them of the coöperation of the people.

Lafayette and the few that were with him, who had pressed the expediency and the right of uniting without delay with the commons, finding argument a failure, resolved upon example. With the forty-seven who had stood by his side in his struggles, he left the nobility and took his seat in the "National Assembly," whither a majority of the clergy had already preceded him. The remaining part of the deputies continued their separate sittings for a few days longer; but their obstinacy at length gave way before the popular excitement. On the 27th of June the three orders met together and commenced their deliberations.

Lafayette was now watched narrowly by all classes. He often spoke in the Assembly, and as ever he had done, for freedom. He was not gifted with the fiery eloquence of Mirabeau, which swept every thing before it like a whirlwind; his style, though gentle, was witty and keen, passing over the audience like the pleasant breeze, yet leaving a deep and permanent impression upon the mind.

On the 11th of July he brought forward for adoption his famous Declaration of Rights; an instrument which would confer imperishable fame, though he had no other claim to immortality. It reads as follows:—

"Nature has made all men free and equal; the distinctions which are necessary for social order are founded alone on the public good.

"Man is born with inalienable and imprescriptable rights, such as the unshackled liberty of opinion, the care of his honor and life, the right of property, the complete control over his person, his industry and all his faculties; the free expression of his opinion in every possible manner; the worship of the Almighty, and resistance against oppression.

"The exercise of natural rights has no other limits than those which are necessary to secure their enjoyments to every member of society.

"No man can be made subject to laws which he has not sanctioned, either himself, or through his representatives, and which have not been properly promulgated and legally executed.

"The principle of all sovereignty rests in the people. No body nor individual can possess any authority which does not expressly emanate from the nation.

"The sole end of all government is the public good. That good demands that the legislative, executive and judicial powers should be distinct and defined, and that their organization should secure the free representation of the citizens, the responsibility of their deputies, and the impartiality of the judges.

"The laws ought to be clear, precise and uniform, in their operation toward every class of citizens.

"Subsidies ought to be liberally granted, and the taxes proportionally distributed.

"And, as the introduction of abuses, and the rights of succeeding generations will require the revisions of all human institutions, the nation ought to possess the power, in certain cases, to summon an extraordinary assembly of deputies, whose sole object shall be to examine and correct, if it be necessary, the faults of the constitution?"

A long debate ensued. It was boldly supported by republicans, and as decidedly condemned by the adherents of despotism. But an argument which the former had not sought and which the latter could not avoid, soon turned the balance for humanity. A lawless mob, feared alike by the friends and foes of the Declaration, raised the cry of anarchy and rebellion. It was only the first gust of the approaching gale, but it shook Paris to its center. The volcanic elements which had long been smothered by soothing assurances and delusive hopes, broke forth and raged with unrestrained fury. The resistless tide of insurgents, spreading terror, raged through the city, and swept down before it, and scattered in ruins, the Bastile, which had been for centuries the bulwark of tyranny, the exponent of despotic cruelty. The people had begun to understand their rights; and both King and legislature felt that they could not safely refuse to concede them. A reconciliation between the opposing interests was effected; the King went in person and unattended to the Assembly, and threw himself confidingly upon the attachment of his people —the mob were made to believe that the King wished no infringement upon their rights, and hushed the tumult. The Declaration was adopted and outward peace reigned again in the capital.

During the tumult so briefly sketched, Lafayette drew the attention and hopes of the nation to himself

Every one, his enemies even, was compelled to believe in his unsullied honesty and great capacity. The key of the demolished Bastile was given to him, as the most worthy to receive this memorial of the hideous Golgotha of oppression. The National Guards, a new order of troops composed of citizens instead of mercenary soldiers, for the purpose of protecting the people, was formed, and the command was entrusted to Lafayette by the municipality of Paris. The appellation of THE PEOPLE'S FRIEND was given to him all over the kingdom, and while the masses exalted him to the rank of a demi-god, the aristocracy admired his devotion to the mandate of duty. Says Toulongeon, "Lafayette, whose name and reputation acquired in America, were associated with liberty itself, was at the head of the Parisian National Guard. He enjoyed at once that entire confidence and public esteem which are due to great qualities. The faculty of raising the spirits, or rather of infusing fresh courage into the heart, was natural to him. His external appearance was youthful and bold, which is always pleasing to the multitude. His manners were simple, popular and engaging. He possessed every thing which is wanting to commence and terminate a revolution — the brilliant qualities of military activity, and the calm confidence of courage in times of public commotion. Lafayette was equal to every thing, if every thing had been done fairly and openly ; but he was unacquainted with the dark and narrow road of intrigue."

At the head of the Guard, he exerted himself to

prevent farther outbreak of violence, but could not always restrain the fury of the populace. The fact that they did sometimes refuse to obey his counsels, has given occasion for the basest slander which British bigotry could invent. It is asserted by English writers, that he was the direct instigator of some of the very atrocities he desired to prevent. It is especially affirmed that he was guilty of the murder of the minister Foulon. Foulon was a member of the court especially obnoxious to the people, on account his many odious acts in supporting monarchy. He was seized by the crowd, who, with a mock show of justice, hurried him before the Assembly, and then clamored loudly for revenge. No trial could proceed amid the uproar, and when the unfortunate Foulon was about to be sacrificed on the spot, loud acclamations announced the arrival of Lafayette. Placing himself by the side of the President, he waved his hand with an air of majesty over the multitude, and when they were hushed to silence, he made an appeal in behalf of the minister, which should forever efface from history the calumny thrown upon him in connection with this transaction. "I am known to you all," said he, "you have appointed me your commander; a station which, while it confers honor, imposes upon me the duty of speaking to you with that liberty and candor which form the basis of my character. You wish, without a trial, to put to death the man who is before you: such an act of injustice would dishonor you;—it would disgrace me, and were I weak enough to permit it, it would blast all the efforts which I have made in favor of liberty. I will not permit it. I am far from pretending to save him, if he be guilty, I only desire that the orders of the Assembly should be carried into execution, and that this man be conducted to prison, to be judged by a legal tribunal. I wish the law to be respected; —law, without which there can be no liberty;—law, without whose aid I would never have contributed to the revolution of the new world, and without which I will not contribute to the revolution which is preparing here. What I advance in favor of the forms of law, ought not to be interpreted in favor M. Foulon. I am free from suspicion as it regards him;—and perhaps the manner in which, on several occasions, I have expressed myself with relation to his conduct, would alone deprive me of the right of judging. But the greater the presumption of his guilt is, the more important is it that the usual formalities should be observed in his case, so as to render his punishment more striking, and, by legal examinations, to discover his accomplices. I, therefore, command that he be conducted to the prison of L'Abbaye St. Germain."

These remarks were hailed with applause by those within hearing; who consented that the minister should be conducted to prison. This sentiment, however, did not extend to those without, and in the extremity of the hall, who, as soon as Lafayette had concluded, sent up their furious call for vengeance upon Foulon. Three times the Marquis harangued them; but, just as the unfortunate object of the outcry began to hope, a shout, more terrible than before, blanched his cheek with the foreshadowing of his doom. From the square of the Hotel de Ville, and from the extreme part of the chamber, a frightful yell arose, announcing that the throngs from the Palais-Royal, and the faubourg St. Antoine, were coming to carry off the prisoner. A roar in the distance, which sounded like the surgings of the angry sea, became more distinct, till it was heard in frantic tones through the passages of the Hotel de Ville, demanding the prisoner for execution. A fresh mob broke in upon that which already filled the hall, and guided by that electric impulse which seems to pervade such a body of men, the whole mass rushed impetuously forward, and, without regarding the loud intercessions of Lafayette, snatched Foulon from his chair and bore him triumphantly from the array. The miserable victim, despite his piteous supplication, could receive no mercy from the hands of those to whom he had shown none, and with shouts of infernal exultation, he was hung to a lamp iron in front of the Hotel de Ville.

This deed has been charged upon Lafayette. With his life before us, showing his character to be unsoiled by a stain of inconsistency, we could not for a moment entertain the detraction, if we had nothing positive with which to repel it in the very transaction itself. And yet, with a jealous bigotry better befitting a horde of savages, men have stood up in the British Parliament and boldly endeavored to attach the crime to his name. If any hing more than his attempts to prevent the murder, necessary to show his abhorrence of it, we have it abundantly in the incidents which ensued. Filled with horror, and exasperated at the lawlessness of the populace, he determined to resign his office as Commander-in-Chief of the National Guards. This he did in the following letter to the Mayor of Paris, which, as it fully discloses his feelings at the time, we here insert. It is the best comment we can present upon the slanderous charge made against him:

"SIR:—Summoned by the confidence of its citizens to the military command of the capital, I have uniformly declared, that in the actual state of affairs, it was necessary, to be useful, that confidence should be full and universal. I have steadily declared to the people, that, although devoted to their interest to my last breath, yet I was incapable of purchasing their favor by unjustly yielding to their wishes. You are aware, sir, that one of the individuals* who perished yesterday was placed under a guard, and that the other was under the escort of our troops, both being sentenced by the civil power to undergo a regular trial. Such were the proper means to satisfy justice, to discover their accomplices, and to fulfill the solemn engagements of every citizen toward the National Assembly and the King.

"The people would not hearken to my advice;—

* The two individuals alluded to here, were Foulon and his son-in-law, Berthier, and it is a matter worthy of note by those who so unceremoniously call Lafayette a "*horrid ruffian,*" that during his command these were the only fatal excesses which a mob of lawless violence displayed.

and the moment when the confidence which they promised, and reposed in me, is lost, it becomes my duty, as I have before stated, to abandon a post in which I can be no longer useful. I am, with respect, &c.,

"LAFAYETTE."

The estimation in which Lafayette was regarded at this time, is fully disclosed by the effect which his letter produced. M. Bailly, the mayor of the city, laid it before the municipality, who, with one voice immediately, and earnestly, solicited its recall. The National Assembly received it with universal consternation. The National Guards flocked around him as if to compel him again to take the command. The news spread rapidly over the city, and was received every where with lamentation. The mayor and council waited upon him in a body, at midnight, and solicited him, by every possible motive, to retract his resignation. The result was ineffectual, and the next day he appeared before them, and thus, in public, declared his sentiments:

"GENTLEMEN:—I come to acknowledge the last testimonies of your kindness, with all the warmth of a heart whose first desire, after that of serving the people, is to be loved by them, and to express my astonishment at the importance they deign to attach to an individual, in a free country, where nothing should be of real importance except law. If my conduct on this occasion, could be regulated by my sentiments of gratitude and affection, I should only reply to the regrets with which you and the National Guards had honored me, by yielding obedience to your entreaties;—but, as I was guided by no feeling of private interest when I formed that resolution, so also, in the midst of the various causes for agitation that surround us, I cannot allow myself to be governed by my private affections. * * *

"Gentlemen, when I received such touching proofs of affection, too much was done for me and too little for the *law*, I am convinced how well my comrades love *me*, but I am still ignorant to what degree they cherish the principles on which liberty is founded. Deign to make known to the National Guards this sincere avowal of my sentiments. To command them, it is necessary that I should feel certain that they unanimously believe that the fate of the constitution is suspended upon the execution of law, the only sovereign of a free people;—that individual liberty, the security of each man's home, religious liberty, and respect for legitimate authority, are duties as sacred to them as to myself. We require not only courage and vigilance, but unanimity in these principles; and I thought, and still think, that the constitution will be better served by my resignation, on the grounds I have given, than by my acquiescence in the request with which you have deigned to honor me."

Was this the conduct and the language of a "horrid ruffian," or of one "ambitious of command." Does all this look as if "he used his power to promote anarchy and foster a spirit of discord in Paris?" The whole charge would be too ridiculous to merit a moment's attention, did not the source in which it originates entitle it to a passing consideration. In this circumstance, which has been so foully perverted by his enemies, the true reader of history will find a fresh laurel to add to the brow of Lafayette.

The National Guards were assembled awaiting his decision, and immediately upon receiving it, they passed the following resolution:—"The National Assembly has decreed that public force should be obedient, and a portion of the Parisian army has shown itself essentially disobedient. General Lafayette has only ceased to command that army because they have ceased to obey law. He requires a complete submission to the law, not a servile attachment to his person. Let the battalions assemble. Let each citizen-soldier swear on his word and honor to obey the law. Let those who refuse be excluded from the National Guards. Let the wish of the army, thus regenerated, be carried to General Lafayette, and he will conceive it his duty to resume the command."

Lafayette hesitated, but finally yielded to the wish so universally expressed. Thanks were offered him by public bodies and private citizens. During the time he occupied this post, he manifested the disinterestedness apparent whenever a sacrifice was needed. He forgot himself, in his care for the public good. When urged by the municipality of Paris to accept some remuneration for his services, he refused with a generosity unparalleled. "My private fortune," said he to them, "secures me from want. It has outlasted two revolutions; and should it survive a third, through the complaisance of the people, it shall belong to them alone." In this Revolution, as in the

American, Lafayette won the hearts of all observers. The great minds of the kingdom looked to him as a leading spirit among themselves. "There is one man in the state," said Mirabeau, "who, from his position, is exposed to the hazard of all events;—to whom successes can offer no compensation for reverses; and who is, in some manner, answerable for the repose, we may even say the safety, of the public,—and that man is Lafayette."

Revolutions never go backward. They are the development of a germ whose vitality must exhibit itself in growth from the action of its own inherent law. They have a progress which no human power can hold in abeyance. The French Revolution had begun its fearful course, and no arm of man could arrest it, or long retard its consummation. Day by day witnessed its slow but sure advance; the mighty wheel which a baby-hand might have set in motion, soon acquired a momentum which the strength of a giant could not meet. A force sublimer, it would seem, than any at that time understood, was working underneath the current, preparing for an awful manifestation. Unconscious of it all, the King, believing that every thing was settled and himself secure, fell back upon his advisers, and forgot that he had a people to care for, who were suffering from neglect and starvation. Famine was staring thousands in the face, but ignorant or careless of it, he increased his own luxuries and extravagance. In the midst of the hunger and wretchedness which reigned around him, he spread his banquet board and gave royal entertainments, as though to mock the misery which he would not heal. Royal arrogance looked proudly down upon its minions and fancied all was peace, because secluded from the scenes of wo. But while the saloons of Versailles rung with revelry, a sword suspended by a hair, glittered over the head of the King; yet he saw it not. "*Quem Deus vult perdere prius dementat.*"

On the first and third of October magnificent banquets were held at court, and were soon followed by an unexpected response, which told Louis and his cabinet the suicidal game they had played. On the morning of the fifth of October, a young woman rushed into a guard-house, seized a drum and then ran with it along the street, beating it hurriedly, and crying, "*Bread! Bread!*" It was the signal for a general outbreak. Her shriek woke up a thousand desolate hearts. Every *faubourg* through which she sped poured forth its crowds, chiefly of women, and soon a mighty host were flocking after her and joining in her despairing prayer for "*bread! bread!*" From the markets and public halls; from dismal and secret lurking places, where misery and vice were wont to shrink away from the sunlight; from hearth-stones where hopeless penury had urged to crime, they rushed forth and seizing such weapons as fell in their way, hurried on; while over them all went up to the unanswering heavens, that mad chorus, "*bread! bread!*" They came to the Hotel de Ville where the representatives of the commune were accustomed to assemble, and their fury knew no bounds when they found that the hour for the morning meeting had not yet arrived. They rushed upon a battalion of the National Guards which was drawn up before the hall, and drove it back by a volley of stones. They broke open the door leading to the great bell and sounded the tocsin, whose notes were a peal of alarm to every part of the city. All Paris was instantly in motion. The earthquake which had slumbered long, was on the march. As though by a magic impulse, Paris was in a state of complete insurrection. Suddenly the tide set towards Versailles and the multitude like the ocean, lashed into billows, rolled in dark waves towards the royal palace. Lafayette with the first news of the riot placed himself at the head of the Guard before the Hotel de Ville, but the immense assemblage which still continued to blockade him there, prevented his learning for some time the tumultuous departure for Versailles. "As soon as the tidings reached me," to use his own language, "I instantly perceived that whatever might be the consequence of this movement the public safety required that I should take part in it, and after having received from the Hotel de Ville an order and two commissaries, I hastily provided for the security of Paris and took the road to Versailles at the head of several battalions." Fearing that the Guard themselves might be induced to join in the revolt he halted on the way and made each one renew his oath of obedience to the law, and fidelity to the King. He arrived at Versailles about midnight, and sent word to the President of the Assembly that the army had promised to do its duty and that nothing should be done contrary to law. He then repaired to the palace, and with every demonstration of respect, assured Louis of his own attachment and that of his army. The King appeared satisfied with the precautions which had been taken and desired him to place a guard on the outposts of the palace. The inner guard was refused him, but, without a murmur, the Marquis left the royal presence and made every possible arrangement for safety. He secured the hotel of the life guards sent out numerous patrols in different directions, saw that sufficient protection was thrown around the palace, and then made additional arrangements for the quiet of Paris. Not till five o'clock in the morning, after more than twenty hours unremitting exertion, did he allow his almost exhausted nature to take the least repose.

In the immediate vicinity of the royal residence all was tranquil, but farther away the aspect of the populace presaged another tempest. "Large groups of savage men and intoxicated women were seated around the watch-fires in all the streets of Versailles, and relieved the tedium of a rainy night by singing revolutionary songs. In one of these circles their exasperation was such, that, seated on the corpse of one of the body guard, they devoured the flesh of his horse, half-roasted in the flames, while a ring of frantic cannibals danced round the group. At six o'clock a furious mob rushed towards the palace, and finding a gate open,* speedily filled the staircases and vestibules

* This gate, so carelessly left open, had been entrusted to the life-

of the royal apartments. The assasins rushed into the Queen's room a few minutes after she had left it, and, enraged at finding their victim escaped, pierced her bed with their bayonets. They then dragged the bodies of two of the body guard who had been massacred, below the windows of the King, beheaded them, and carried the bloody heads in triumph upon the points of their pikes through the streets of Versailles."

Lafayette had not yet fallen asleep, and springing up at the sound of the tumult, he leaped upon a horse and regardless of danger, galloped fearlessly into the midst of the fray. The insurgents had taken several of the life guards from the palace, and with shouts of savage vengeance were on the point of slaughtering them, when Lafayette appeared among them and sternly bade them cease. Having succeeded in liberating the captives, he sent them back with the troops which had escorted him, while, with a courage which always rose with peril, he remained alone, to stay the living tide. Foiled in their object, with their prey wrested from their grasp, the wrath of the multitude turned upon Lafayette. One of them aimed a musket at his head, but observing the act, though without changing his position, he cooly commanded the spectators to bring the man to him. The ferocity of the tiger was in a moment changed. Lafayette as

---

guards in preference to giving the charge of it to Lafayette. All the arrangements of the Marquis were perfect, and not a post which he had been entrusted with was found unguarded.

the people's friend was there, and seizing the culprit who had dared to lift his arm against his benefactor, they dashed out his brains upon the pavement, while the welkin rung with "*Vive Lafayette.*" Having calmed the excited throngs, the Marquis hastened to the palace and was hailed by the acclamations of the life guard, "*Lafayette for ever!*" His grenadiers flocked around him and received his mandate to protect the monarch with the warmest demonstrations of loyalty. The court saw and acknowledged their indebtedness to him for life, and gave particular testimonies of their gratitude. Madame Adelaide, the King's aunt, ran up to him and clasped him in her arms, saying, "General, you have saved us. I owe you more than my life, I owe you that of the King, my poor nephew."

Danger was not yet over, for peace had been only temporarily restored. The people began to collect again. They crowded into the marble hall, and expressed their designs with frightful howlings. "To Paris! to Paris, with the King!" was the fierce call which came from men and women without, and fell with startling emphasis upon the ear of beleagured royalty. A council was held, and Louis determined to present himself before his enraged subjects. With mild dignity he came out upon the balcony, respectfully attended by Lafayette, and calmly stood in the presence of those who, a moment before, burned with hostility towards him. This was regarded as a pledge from Louis that he would go to Paris, and inquire into the distresses of his people, and united with his kingly dignity, gave another interlude to the tragical scenes. Fickle as the wind, they now shouted, "Long live the King!" as earnestly as they had hurled their anathemas upon his head.

But while these acclamations were rising, threatening voices were heard against the Queen. Marie Antoinette had never been a favorite with the French, for many, with too much justice, believed that she was mainly instrumental in leading Louis to neglect the interests of his people. As Lafayette caught the imprecations, he stepped back into her saloon and respectfully inquired if it was her intention to accompany the King to Paris. "Yes," she replied, "although I know the danger." "Madame," said he, "are you resolved?"—"I am."—"Condescend, then, to appear in the balcony, and permit me to accompany you," said Lafayette. "What," said the Queen,—"without the King?—Have you observed the threats?" "Yes, madame," was the reply, "but venture to confide in me." With a courage well worthy of a daughter of the Cæsars, she suffered herself to be conducted, by Lafayette, to the balcony. She was dressed in white, her head was bare and adorned with beautiful fair locks, and with firmness, but great grace and dignity, she glided forward and stood motionless before the crowd. It was a delicate and dangerous step;—but Lafayette well knew that the danger was less than it would be, were the Queen to depart for Paris without being reconciled to the people. Threats were still made, and amid the tumult, it was necessary to speak to the eyes rather than to the ears of the multitude. Stepping forward gallantly, he stooped and raised the hand of the Queen to his lips in respectful homage. The act was a simple one, but it showed how well Lafayette knew to move the popular current. Frenchmen were transported at the sight, and the silence which it had at first caused, was soon broken by — "*Long live the Queen!*" "*Long live Lafayette!*" The King looked on as if in a dream. His palace had been kept from ruin, and his life, with that of his family, had been preserved solely through the efforts of a man whom he once had serious thoughts of consigning to the Bastile. He was compelled to ask at his hands still another favor. His body guards had fired upon the crowd, and the cry for vengeance upon these was deepening. Louis perceived this, and believing that his own safety depended upon that of his guards, besought Lafayette to interfere in their behalf. Beckoning one of them to his side, the Marquis led him forward before the people, and in the midst of curses, he unbuckled his own shoulder belt, placed it around the guard, and then clasped him affectionally in his arms. The effect was as before. The populace hesitated a moment, and then the air resounded with their plaudits as they thus ratified this new reconciliation. The work was not yet done. It was not enough to hush to a momentary quietude the human surges sweeping around the palace of Versailles. All that mortal man could do, was done by Lafayette. The whole direction of every thing was surrendered into his hands, and the King, with the reliance which a weaker nature places, in times of adversity, upon the strong, submitted, like a child, to his guidance. Louis had agreed to depart for Paris, and with this assurance Lafayette endeavored to appease the people. He used commands, entreaties, and every resource which his rare ingenuity could suggest, to induce them to disperse; and though he succeeded with many, yet a ferocious rabble remained, declaring it to be their purpose to act as an escort to the royal cavalcade on its way to the capital. Having used his utmost endeavor to pacify them, and, after taking every precaution to ensure a quiet reception in Paris, he arranged the King's departure, aware that every minute's delay was fraught with innumerable dangers. Surrounded by the rabble, and compelled to listen to their yells of defiance and threatening, the royal family set out from Versailles, closely escorted by Lafayette and his guards. The whole scene is thus described by Lavellette, an eye witness of it :—" At twelve o'clock, the frightful procession set off. I hope such a scene will never be witnessed again! I have often asked myself, how the metropolis of a nation so celebrated for urbanity and elegance of manners,—how the brilliant city of Paris, could contain the savage hordes I that day beheld, and who so long reigned over it! In walking through the streets of Paris, it seems to me, the features even of the lowest and most miserable class of people, do not present to the eye any thing like ferociousness or the meanest passions in all their hideous energy. Can those passions alter the features so as to deprive them of all likeness to humanity? Or, does the terror inspired by the sight of a guilty wretch, give him the semblance of a wild beast? These madmen, dancing in the mire, and covered with mud, surrounded the King's coach. The groups that marched foremost, carried on long pikes the bloody heads of the life guardsmen, butchered in the morning.* Surely Satan himself first invented the putting of a human head at the end of a lance! The disfigured and pale features, the gory locks, the half open mouth, the closed eyes,—images of death, added to the gestures and salutations which the executioners made them perform, in horrid mockery of life, presented the most frightful spectacle that rage could have imagined. A troop of women, ugly as crime itself, swarming like insects, and wearing grenadiers' hairy caps, went continually to and fro, howling barbarous songs, embracing and insulting the life guards. This scene lasted for eight hours before the royal family arrived at the Place de Greve. They alighted at the Hotel de ville, their first resting place during protracted misery, that terminated some years afterwards in a horrible death. Thus ended the memorable 6th of October." The part which the Marquis bore in these transactions, has been variously represented, and his British enemies have found in them material for fresh calumnies. We have endeavored to give a true account of the matter, leaving the rea-

* It has been said that Lafayette allowed these horrible trophies to be paraded near the coach of the King. This is untrue. They could not approach the King's coach, and, what is more, Lafayette ordered them at once to be disarmed, as soon as he learned what they were bearing.

der to his own conclusions. It is too late to require much time to vindicate Lafayette from those aspersions. His character shines with increased luster each succeeding age, and will emerge from eclipse, as the sun gradually scatters the mists of morning and mounts upward to the zenith. The fact that, almost without bloodshed, he was enabled to control a mob which might otherwise have resulted in the most terrific anarchy, is sufficient to vindicate his activity in the melancholy events described.

The outbreak was quelled. The King and his household took up their residence in the Tuilleries, and the National Assembly held its sittings in Paris. Versailles, the seat of intrigue and luxury, was abandoned, and something done for the relief of the oppressed. The voice of the masses had been heard, and was producing its slow, but legitimate effect. Louis blindly endeavored to hush it, but in vain. Lafayette was zealous for freedom, though he did not swerve from his allegiance to his sovereign. He saw that France was not yet ready for a Republic, and that the nearest approximation which she could make, was by a constitutional monarchy, which would bind the king and people together in a united federation. Towards this all his efforts were directed, and, as the year 1790 opened, he caught glimpses of the realization of this sublime idea. The King distrusted him, and his associate members were, many of them, jealous of his growing popularity; but, true to himself, he did not pause in his mission. He saw the constitution growing under the hands of the Assembly, while they were shaking from the state the vipers of corruption which had fastened upon its vitality. The old rubbish of the feudal system, which, for ages, had penetrated with decay the national heart, was cleared away, and the King was no longer invested with supreme authority over the population of his realm. The executive, the legislative, and the judicial departments were successively scrutinized, and established after a new and more complete model. A free constitution, whose glorious principles sent fear to every despot in Europe, was, at length, established, notwithstanding the endeavor to crush the germ of liberty in its bud. Louis, vacillating as usual, would sometimes give assent to every proposition, and then blindly and stubbornly retract. Still progress was made, and before the anniversary of the rising of the people and the taking of the Bastile had recurred, the foundation of a republican representation had been laid.

The 14th of July was approaching, and it was determined to celebrate it in a manner worthy the anniversary of a nation's deliverance, of a nation's sovereignty. The municipality of Paris proposed that a confederation of the whole realm should take place in the capital, when the deputies sent by the eighty-three departments, the popular representation, the Parisian guard, and the monarch, should take the oath of allegiance to the constitution. The plan was hailed with enthusiasm over France, and immense preparations were immediately commenced for making the ceremony worthy of its great object.

The place selected for the festival was the Champ

de Mars, a spacious area extending from the Military School to the left bank of the Seine. In the midst of the plain an altar was erected, where the oath was to be administered, and around it an immense amphitheater was thrown up, where four hundred thousand spectators could sit and witness the grand ratification. Near the altar, in the center of the plain, and under an elegant pavilion, was erected a throne for the King, which, together with the seats for the Assembly by which it was flanked, was sprinkled all over with golden fleurs de lis. Balconies were erected for the Queen and court, and triumphal arches of great magnificence, spanned every entrance to the field. Upon the immense labor necessary, twelve thousand laborers were constantly employed, and still there was apprehension of failure in completing the work by the time appointed for the imposing pageant. The inhabitants then proposed to assist; enthusiasm soon animated the entire population, impelled by the one desire of preparing for the day irrevocably fixed for the ceremony. Men and women, high born and low, flocked together, and with perfect order and harmony, plied their busy hands. Churchmen, soldiers, elegant females, the nun from her convent, the monk from his cloister,—persons of all classes, took up the spade and pickaxe, and mingled amicably together. Says a writer of the time:—"The mind felt sinking under the weight of a delicious intoxication, at the sight of a whole people who had descended again to the sweet sentiments of a primitive fraternity."

Meanwhile, the federalists were beginning to assemble from all quarters of the kingdom, and were received, with open arms, by their *brethren* in Paris. Four days before the celebration, the different deputations met in the Hotel de Ville, to chose a president for the federation. Lafayette was the only man in the nation who could be selected for this office, and he was hailed President by acclamation. He wished to decline, but the Assembly would not excuse him. His faithful devotion to the people, had drawn the nation gratefully towards him, and the honor conferred upon him, was only a faint expression of the popular regard. Then from the rival power, came an equal honor. By a special act of the Assembly the King had been appointed for the day of the ceremony only, supreme commander of the entire National Guard. This office he delegated to Lafayette, who, by it, became high constable of all the armed men in the kingdom, and, in fact, controlled the destinies of France.

On the 13th of July, the confederates, with the Marquis at their head, waited upon the National Assembly and the monarch, to pay them their homage. The occasion was one full of interest, and gilded the dawn of liberty with new glories. In glowing terms, Lafayette addressed the members, and assured them of the gratitude of the nation for all they had done in her behalf. "You well knew," said he, "the necessities of France, and the will of Frenchmen, when you destroyed the gothic fabric of our government and laws, and respected only their monarchical principle;—Europe then discovered that a good king could be the protector of a free, as he had been the ground of comfort to an oppressed people. The rights of man are declared,—the sovereignty of the people acknowledged,—their power is representative,—and the bases of public order are established. Hasten, then, to give energy to the power of the state. The people owe to you the glory of a new constitution; but they require and expect that peace and tranquillity which cannot exist without a firm and effectual organization of government. We, gentlemen, devoted to the Revolution, and united in the name of liberty—the guarantees alike of individual and common rights and safety—we, called by the most imperative duty from all parts of the kingdom, founding our confidence on your wisdom, and our hopes on your services,—we will bear without hesitation, to the altar of the country, the oath which you may dictate to its soldiers.—Yes, gentlemen, our arms shall be stretched forth together, and, at the same instant, our brothers from all parts of France shall utter the oath which will unite them together. May the solemnity of that great day be the signal of the conciliation of parties; of the oblivion of resentments, and of the establishment of public peace and happiness. And fear not that this holy enthusiasm will hurry us beyond the proper and prescribed limits of public order. Under the protection of the law, the standard of liberty shall never become the rallying point of licentiousness and disorder. Gentlemen, we swear to you to respect the law which it is our duty to defend,—swear by our honor as freemen,—and Frenchmen do not promise in vain." To Louis he gave the unfeigned assurances of the loyalty of his people, and told him that he did not forget the rights of the sovereign, while he regarded those of the nation. "Sire," said he, "in the course of those memorable events which have restored to the nation its imprescriptible rights, and during which the energy of the people, and the virtues of their King, have produced such illustrious examples for the contemplation of the world, we loved to hail, in the person of your majesty, the most illustrious of all titles,—chief of the French, and King of a free people. Enjoy, sire, the recompense of your virtues, and let that pure homage which despotism could not command, be the glory and reward of a citizen king. The National Guards of France swear to your majesty an obedience which shall know no other limits than those of the law, and a love which shall only terminate with their existence."

The day of days at length came. Grayly broke forth the dawn of the 14th of July. In the words of a historian of the Revolution, "In spite of plotting aristocrats, lazy, hired spademen, and almost of destiny itself—for there had been much rain—the Champ de Mars is fairly ready. The morning comes, cold for a July one; but such a festival would make Greenland smile. Through every inlet of that national amphitheater—for it is a league in circuit, cut with openings at due intervals—floods in the living throng, covering, without tumult, space after space. Two hundred thousand patriotic men, and, twice as good, one hundred thousand patriotic women, all decked and glorified, as one can fancy, sit waiting in this Champ de Mars. What a picture, that circle of bright-dyed life, spread up there on its thirty-seated slope, leaning, one would say, on the thick umbrage of those avenue trees—for the stems of them are hidden by the height; and all beyond it mere greenness of the summer earth, with the gleam of waters or white sparklings of stone edifices. On remotest steeple and invisible village belfry stand men with spy-glasses. On the heights of Chaillot are many colored, undulating groups; round, and far on, over all the circling heights that embosom Paris, it is as one, more or less, peopled amphitheater, which the eye grows dim with measuring. Nay, heights have cannon, and a floating battery of cannon is on the Seine. When eye fails, ear shall serve. And all France, properly, is but one amphitheater; for, in paved town and unpaved hamlet men walk, listening, till the muffled thunder sounds audibly on their horizon, that they, too, may begin swearing and firing. But now, to streams of music, come confederates enough, for they have assembled on the Boulevard St. Antoine, and come marching through the city with their eighty-three department banners, and blessings, not loud but deep; comes National Assembly, and takes seat under its canopy; comes royalty, and takes seat on a throne beside it; and Lafayette, on a white charger, is here, and all the civic functionaries; and the confederates form dances, till their strictly military evolutions and manœuvres can begin. Task not the pen of mortal to describe them; truant imagination droops—declares that it is not worth while. There is wheeling and sweeping to slow, to quick, to double quick time. Sieur Motier, or Generalissimo Lafayette —for they are one and the same, and he, as General of France, in the King's stead, for twenty-four hours —must step forth with that sublime, chivalrous gait of his, solemnly ascend the steps of Fatherland's altar, in sight of heaven and of scarcely breathing earth, and pronounce the oath, "To King, to Law, to Nation," in his own name and that of armed France; whereat there is waving of banners, and sufficient acclaim. The National Assembly must swear, standing in its place; the King himself, audibly. The King swears; and now be the welkin split with vivats; let citizens, enfranchised, embrace; armed confederates clang their arms; and, above all, let that floating battery speak. It has spoken—to the four corners of France! From eminence to eminence, bursts the thunder, faint heard, loud repeated. From Arras to Avignon—from Metz to Bayonne—over Orleans and Blois—it rolls in cannon recitative; Puy bellows of it amid his granite mountains; Pau, where is the shell cradle of great Henri. At far Marseilles, one can think the ruddy evening witnesses it; over the deep blue Mediterranean waters, the castle of If, ruddy tinted, darts forth from every cannon's mouth its tongue of fire; and all the people shout, 'Yes, France is free!' Glorious France, that has burst out so, into universal sound and smoke, and attained the Phrygian *cap* of liberty."

In this brilliant festival Lafayette was the grand actor. Neither King nor Queen, not even the Assembly, nor the confederates, could awaken such acclamations as greeted him when he ascended the altar and took the prescribed oath. His popularity, however, did not intoxicate him, or make him love freedom the less. When the wish was indicated to him that he should be invested with the permanent command of the military force of the realm, high as such an honor would be, he would not for a moment listen to the suggestion. He urged the deputation, instead of thinking of him, to regard only the welfare of the common country, and not to blight the promise of brighter years. "Let not ambition," said he, "take possession of you; love the friends of the people, but reserve blind submission for the law, and enthusiasm for liberty. Pardon this advice, gentlemen; you have given me the glorious right to offer it, when, by loading me with every species of favor which one of your brothers could receive from you, my heart, amidst its delightful emotions, cannot repress a feeling of fear." As the confederates were about to leave Paris for their homes, they gave Lafayette the assurance of their grateful affection. "The deputies of the National Guards of France retire," said they, "with the regret of not being able to nominate you their chief. They respect the constitutional law, though it checks, at this moment, the impulse of their hearts. A circumstance which must cover you with immortal glory is, that you, yourself, promoted the law; that you, yourself, prescribed bounds to our gratitude."

The multiudes, intoxicated with excitement and hope, left the *campagne* to the silence of night and the light of the stars, while their fevered brain repeated in fantastic dreams the scenes of that jubilant day, which was too soon to be followed by the groans of a decimated and frantic people.

CHAPTER VIII.

SOLEMN PERJURY — LAFAYETTE'S POSITION — HIS LETTER TO WASHINGTON — JEALOUSY OF THE KING AND QUEEN — FLIGHT AND RETURN OF THE ROYAL FAMILY — THE KING SIGNS THE CONSTITUTION — LAFAYETTE RESIGNS HIS OFFICE AS COMMANDER OF THE NATIONAL GUARDS — AFFECTION OF THE GUARDS AND THE NATION FOR HIM — TESTIMONIALS OF ESTEEM — HE RETIRES TO CHAVAGNIAC — PETION IS ELECTED MAYOR OF PARIS — PREPARATIONS FOR WAR — LAFAYETTE IS CALLED UPON — HE ASSUMES THE COMMAND — MARCHES TO GIVET — TREASON — RETIRES TO MAUBEAGE — LETTER TO THE ASSEMBLY — APPEARS IN PARIS — RETURNS TO HIS ARMY — LAST EFFORT TO SAVE THE KING — THE REIGN OF TERROR — DECREE AGAINST LAFAYETTE — DIFFICULTIES WHICH SURROUND HIM — HE LEAVES THE ARMY.

The vacillating character of the French, was never exhibited more clearly than in the events which followed immediately the 14th July. Before the 1st of August the solemn oath seemed to have been forgotten, and King and people were again involved in the bitterness of strife. Old jealousies were revived,— former disputes were renewed, the same contentions which had previously existed, were burning again with the violence of a conflagration which, after a momentary check, glows the more intensely. Louis, in the enjoyment of his transient repose, resembled the human victim of pagan sacrifice, wearing garlands and feasting, before laid upon the bloody altar. To Lafayette was committed the care of the palace, and under his constant surveillance the King affected to feel himself a prisoner. The Queen, who had always distrusted the Marquis, influenced her lord to make peevish complaints concerning the manner of his attendance, to weaken, if possible, his popular favor. Lafayette, though he discerned this, yielded to the monarch's slightest wish, determining, whatever might be the course of others, that he would be faithful to his oath, "to defend the King and the constitution." The latter, he felt, could not stand without Louis, who, he knew, must fall without that instrument; he, therefore, defended both, as the only means of securing the interests of the state. Lafayette has been falsely accused of wavering here. There was a time when he seriously considered the question, whether a republic or a monarchy would the better promote the welfare of the people; after he had calmly decided in favor of royalty, he was consistent. He saw that his countrymen were not prepared for a Republic;—he believed that a constitutionally limited monarchy might be successfully administered, and acted accordingly. *He did not waver.* Though in the midst of trials,—constantly harassed by difficulties which would have overcome a weaker mind, meeting with darkest enmity, he stood like a rock amid the ocean, unmoved by the shock of the waves.

On the 26th of August, 1790, he thus writes to his cherished friend, Gen. Washington:—"We are disturbed with revolts among the regiments; and, as I am constantly attacked on both sides by the aristocratic and the factious parties, I do not know to which of the two we owe these insurrections. Our safeguard against them is the National Guards. There are more than a million of armed citizens; among them, patriotic legions; and my influence with them is as great as if I had accepted the chief command. I have lately lost some of my favor with the mob, and displeased the frantic lovers of licentiousness, as I am bent on establishing a legal subordination. But the nation at large is very thankful to me for it. It is not out of the heads of aristocrats to make a counter revolution. Nay, they do what they can with all the crowned heads of Europe, who hate us. But I think their plans will be either abandoned or unsuccessful. I am rather more concerned at a division that rages in the popular party. The club of the Jacobins, and that of '89,* as it is called, have divided the friends of liberty, who accuse each other, the Jacobins being taxed with a disorderly extravagance, and '89 with a tincture of ministerialism and ambition. I am endeavoring to bring about a reconciliation."

The King and Queen, unable to see that Lafayette was their friend, were careful to annoy him, while the loyalists, who hated him, malignantly joined in the assault upon his character. Disturbances were fomented by the court, with the design of throwing Paris into confusion, with the hope that, in the attempt to quell them, he might be overcome or assassinated. Failing in this, efforts were made upon a grander scale. It was determined that the royal family should elude the vigilance of their keeper, and flee from

---

* This club was afterwards called the Feuillans. It was instituted by Lafayette, and others, in the year 1789, for the purpose of counteracting the influence of the Jacobins.

Paris. This the King had long desired, for the fearful shadow of his doom, if he continued in the capital, was settling darkly upon his mind. A presentiment that he was destined to share the fate of Charles I. of England, strengthened hourly, and he had not the heart to meet it. A flight would ensure his own safety, and place him in a more advantageous position to treat with his refractory subjects. As the people placed great reliance upon his safe-keeping among them, his flight would attach odium to the Marquis, a result very desirable to his foes. Louis had fully resolved to break away from the oaths with which he bound himself, and to flee from the capital as soon as opportunity should be presented. On the 21st June, 1791, a plan, which had long been maturing, went into execution. In various disguises, one by one, the royal family left the palace by a private issue which communicated with the Carousel, crossed the Pont Royal, and, on the Quai des Theatins, entered the carriages which stood awaiting them, and were driven rapidly from Paris.

This was at midnight, but not till eight o'clock the next morning was it known in the city, and then the news flew over it with the rapidity of the wind. Lafayette was for a moment staggered at the tidings, but his calmness returned when he heard his own name shouted with execrations by the mob, assembling in lawless haste. Immediately dispatching an order for the pursuit of the fugitives, whom he supposed had been carried off by enemies of the public good, he repaired to the Hotel de Ville, and faced the throngs clamoring for vengeance upon his head, for having permitted the escape of the King. It was a moment that tried him to the center of feeling. The utter recklessness of a Parisian mob, none knew better than he; and there was nothing to assure him that the same fury which had proved fatal to others, might not be executed upon himself. "Down with Lafayette," —"Away with the traitor," were exclamations which met him as he approached, but his step faltered not, and his eye glanced over the vast multitude, as though he could sway it at will. The mob were awed to silence by his presence, more commanding than the eloquence of his lips, and he stood before them with his arms quietly folded, in the consciousness which the populace might discern, and read the evidence that *he* had not betrayed the people's trust. When he opened his lips, it was to make neither defense nor apology. Turning their attention to themselves, and the privileges for which they had struggled, he said, —"If you call this event a misfortune, what name would you give to a counter revolution which would deprive you of your liberty?" This simple expression accomplished vastly more than a formal explanation could have done. The crowd turned the tide of action, though in a very different direction from that Lafayette had intended. First one, then another, and then the multitude, as with the voice of one man, sent up the deafening shout, "Let us make Lafayette our King." Here was a new danger, though just the exclamation he would have rejoiced to hear had he been governed by the principles attributed to him by his enemies. His real patriotism and disinterestedness are fully seen in his answer,—"I thought that you professed a better opinion of me. What have I done that you do not believe me fit for something better?" It was enough. Shouts of "Long live the General" filled the air and tranquillity was again restored.

In the National Assembly, the flight of Louis was discussed, and a few charged Lafayette with conniving at it. The suspicion was however indignantly repelled, and many of the political enemies of Lafayette denounced even the insinuation. When it was understood that he was surrounded by a threatening multitude, at the Hotel de Ville, they sent a deputation from their own number, inviting him to proceed to their chamber, offering him an escort to protect him from the violence of the people. "I will order an escort for you," said Lafayette, "as a mark of respect; but, for myself, I shall return alone. I have never been in more perfect safety than at this moment, though the streets are filled with the people."

The prompt means taken for the arrest of the royal family were successful, and the unhappy fugitives, overwhelmned with mortification, were brought back to Paris. They were received without open insult, but with none of the honors which usually attend the reception of royalty. A decree had been passed by the Assembly suspending Louis from his kingly functions, and placing a guard over his person, together with that of the Queen and the Dauphin. This left France virtually without a monarch, for no provision was made for a successor. Lafayette, therefore, as Commander-in-Chief of the Guards, was, in fact, chief ruler of France. To none could the interests of the realm at this critical period, have been better entrusted. With fidelity he discharged his various duties. He was at the same time the friend of the King, and the servant of the state, and successfully managed to harmonize both of these seemingly conflicting positions, to the satisfaction of each of the parties concerned. Louis was his captive, but was made to feel restraint but lightly, while the people saw that every possible security was taken, to keep the noble prisoner safely. The confidence reposed in Lafayette at this period, he might have made subservient to his own self-aggrandizement, had he been a traitor, when the permanent supreme power was within his grasp. The fact that scrutiny can detect no aiming at undue authority, proves the purity of his character. How different his conduct from that of Bonaparte!

Mighty influences were now at work in the Kingdom. The Jacobin clubs which had spread over France, and numbered nearly 400,000 members, were taking the first steps towards the supremacy they afterwards gained. They were the uncompromising enemies of monarchy in any form, and advocated sternly a republic, regardless of consequences. To these was opposed the whole strength of the moderate revolutionists, who still held a majority in the Assembly. The Jacobins contended that Louis, by his flight, had voluntarily abdicated the throne, and that the people should elect a ruler in his stead. For such a step, neither the representatives nor patriots abroad were prepared, and consequently the restoration of Louis was designed. He assured the Assembly that he had no intention of fleeing from his kingdom; that he only wished to ascertain the sentiments of the people in reference to the constitution, and since he was satisfied that this was approved by his subjects, was himself ready to support it. The Assembly, therefore, removed the ban which they had laid upon him, declaring that Louis XVI was not culpable for his recent journey, and could not be brought to trial on account of it.

This decree raised a perfect storm of opposition. It was both decried in the legislative Hall and condemned on the public platform. Robespierre and Petion raised their voices loudly against it, and when it was ultimately passed, they declared their intention of appealing from the sovereignty of the Assembly to that of the people. The Jacobins seconded their opposition, and excited the populace to resistance. It needed but a spark to inflame the combustible materials; and this was like a fire-brand thrown into the magazine. Resentment sprung up every where, and the day after the bill passed, a great concourse gathered in the Champ de Mars to raise their solemn protest. Sedition was rife, but in the midst of anarchy, the man of the people, THE PATRIOT of the nation, suddenly appeared before them. Instead of obeying his orders to disperse, they turned to assail him for interfering with their proceedings. In the midst of the angry tide he proclaimed the principles of constitutional liberty, and recounted the oath they had taken there, hardly a year before; but in vain. Another spirit was in the ascendant, and the words fell powerless from his lips. Threats were muttered, and a musket was fired at his person. Though near the muzzle he escaped unharmed. The author of the attempt was arrested by the Guards and released by their commander, who was there to preserve life and quiet, at whatever hazard to himself. He was intent upon quelling the insurrection, and would not leave the place till he had done it. His plans were made and executed with firmness which at length drove the rioters from the field, though not till after blood had been shed, which was subsequently remembered against him.

This outbreak and other minor circumstances convinced the Assembly of the necessity of establishing the governent upon a stronger basis, and they hastened to a final revision of the constitution. This important instrument had been framed with great care, and though many of its provisions had been subjected to stormy debates, it was still adapted to heal the dissensions which tossed the nation. It was, therefore, soon completed, and submitted to Louis for his acceptance. "From that moment," says Thiers, "his freedom was restored to him; or, if that expression be objected to, the strict watch kept over the palace ceased, and he had liberty to retire whithersoever he pleased, to examine the constitutional act and to accept it freely. What was Louis XVI to do in this case? To reject the constitution would have been to abdicate in favor of a republic. The safest way, even according to his own system, was to accept it, and to expect, from time to time, those restitutions of power which he considered as due to him. Accordingly, after a certain number of days, he declared that he accepted the constitution. An extraordinary joy burst forth at this intelligence, as if, in fact, some obstacle had been anticipated on the part of the King, and his assent had been an unhoped for concession. He repaired to the Assembly, where he was received as in the most brilliant times. Lafayette, who never forgot to repair the inevitable evils of political troubles, proposed a general amnesty for all acts connected with the Revolution, which was proclaimed, amid shouts of joy, and the prison doors were instantly thrown open. At length, on the 30th of September, Thouret, the last president, declared that the Constituent Assembly had terminated its sittings."*

A few days afterwards, Lafayette, considering the purposes of his appointment fulfilled, and deeply desiring to retire into private life, resigned his office as Commander-in-Chief of the National Guards. His letter, stating his intentions, was kind and elevated. "To serve you until this day, gentlemen," said he, "was a duty imposed upon me by the sentiments which have animated my whole life. To resign now, without reserve, to my country, all the power and

* This Assembly had been in existence three years, and had enacted 1309 laws and decrees relative to legislation or to the general administration of the state.

influence she gave me for the purpose of defending her during recent convulsions,—this is a duty I owe to my well known resolutions, and it amply satisfies the only species of ambition I possess."

This was received with unfeigned regret. Lafayette was more than their leader, he was their idol. They gathered around him and desired him to continue at their head. When this was denied, they forged a sword from the bolts of the Bastile, and presented it, expressive both of their love and his worth in the crusade upon oppression. The municipality of Paris voted him a medal, emblematic of his saving the city so often from riot and bloodshed, causing a complimentary inscription to be placed on the bust of Lafayette, which had been presented to Paris twelve years before, by Virginia. Tokens of favor, no less pleasing, were showered upon him by individuals. Amid the honors of a grateful nation, he retired to his home, and was surrounded once more, with the joys of his quiet family circle. Ambition was satisfied, and he hoped that retirement would no more be disturbed by the tumults of political strife. When he learned that Bailly had resigned his office, and that he was placed as a candidate for the vacant mayorality of Paris, it gave him little satisfaction ; the news that he was defeated through the influence of the court, gave him less regret. The fact that Louis should exert himself so strenuously to promote the overthrow of his best friend is a singular proof of weakness and infatuation. Petion, whom the money of the King alone raised to the mayorship, was a decided Jacobin ; and the throne which Lafayette would have sacrificed his life to sustain, he would have overthrown in a moment. By giving him office, Louis hastened his own execution. The election of Petion placed the Jacobins in power, and their iron rule was soon felt. The Revolution would have stopped when the King signed the constitution, but for this; it was now destined to roll on till he was crushed beneath it. Bitterly did Louis XVI. afterwards rue the act when it was all too late to apply a remedy; and never yet did a King meet a fate more certainly brought upon him by his own suicidal weakness. Lafayette could not long indulge in the seclusion which he had chosen. France could not do without him, and an opportunity was soon presented again to engage actively in her service. The Revolution had driven many of the nobility from the kingdom, who, taking refuge with different foreign powers, endeavored to foment war against France. European politics were just then in a state which admitted of excitement, and these refugees soon kindled a blaze. The despots of many of the continental sovereignties caught the idea of stopping the Revolution by the sword, and they engaged in the struggle. The startling rumor reached Paris, that a large army was preparing for invasion; the difficulties of faction, in the city, were forgotten in view of the new and alarming calamity which threatened the country. The King united himself with the Legislative body in devising the mode of resistance. In December, 1791, the plans for defense were matured. Three armies of fifty thousand men each, were to meet on the Rhine, and

Lafayette, associated with Generals Luckner and Rochambeau, was appointed to command them. In proud array the armies commanding the whole frontier from Switzerland to Dunkirk, assured the invaders, that France, though distracted by Revolution, was yet a dreaded foe. The central army was assigned to Lafayette, who, fixing his head quarters at Metz, posted his defense, so as to command the whole line from the Meuse to the Moselle. The feelings with which he found himself again in military life are exhibited in the following extracts from a letter which he wrote to General Washington, from his rendezvous, at Metz, dated January 22d, 1792:

"This is a very different date from that which had announced to you my return to the sweets of private life;—a situation hitherto not very familiar to me, but which, after fifteen revolutionary years, I had become quite fit to enjoy. I have given you an account of the quiet and rural mode of living I had adopted in the mountains where I was born, having there a good house and a *late* manor,* now unlorded into a large farm, with an English overseer for my instruction. I felt myself very happy among my neighbors, no more vassals to me nor any body, and had given to my wife and rising family, the only quiet weeks they had enjoyed for a long time, when the threats and mad preparations of the refugees, and, still more, the coun-

---

* Here is an evidence that Lafayette carried out his professions, even when they interfered as in the present instance, with his individual rights.

tenance they had obtained in the dominions of our neighbors, induced the National Assembly and the King, to adopt a more rigorous system than had hitherto been the case.

"I had refused every public employment, that had been offered by the people, and, still more, had I denied my consent to my being appointed to any military command; but when I saw our liberties and constitution were seriously threatened, and my services could be usefully employed in fighting for our old cause, I could no longer resist the wishes of my countrymen; and as soon as the King's express reached my farm, I set out for Paris; from thence to this place; and I do not think it uninteresting to you, my dear General, to add, that I was every where on the road affectionately welcomed."

War was formally declared against Austria on the 20th of April, and offensive preparations commenced. The Netherlands were then under the dominion of Austria. The French Revolution had kindled a kindred spirit among them, and it was supposed the whole nation would joyfully welcome a French army which should offer means of deliverance from their old masters. A plan of action was matured by the Ministry, and, despite the cry of faction in Paris, it was sent to the Generals of the forces for enforcement. A part of this design was, that all the troops should be in motion about the same time, and form, if possible, a general rendezvous in the center of the Austrian Netherlands. The chief movement was entrusted to Lafayette, who, on the 24th of April, was ordered to collect his regiments and proceed to Givet, a distance of more than sixty leagues, by the 1st of May. This surprising requisition could only have been executed by the wonderful celerity with which Lafayette was accustomed to move his armies. Though his enemies hoped that he would not be able to accomplish it, when the day came he was at the post assigned, awaiting his further commands. The whole expedition was, however, destined to an inglorious close. While Lafayette was on his way to Givet, his enemies, who hated him more intensely than they loved the state, were plotting his ruin. A plan was laid upon a grand scale to draw off, by the blackest treachery, the extra divisions ordered to his aid, and so, by leaving him unsupported, force him to withdraw ingloriously from the field. They knew that he would not remain in the face of all Europe, with his handful of fifty thousand men; and that a retreat would be a bitter necessity to him. Their purpose was successful. At Givet, Lafayette learned with dismay that the two divisions which had been detached from Rochambeau's army had suddenly disbanded and fled in confusion, before seeing the enemy. His first design was to entrench himself in his present position and wait for further supplies; but a moment's consideration convinced him not only that it was impracticable, but enabled him to read clearly the causes which had led to the defection. No man could have acted more wisely than he at this juncture. Surrounded by secret and open foes; not knowing how far their machinations might have extended among his own men ; convinced that it would be madness to attempt to carry on the war alone, he yielded to the mandate of fate, and fell back with his men to his former post, making arrangements to act with efficiency at a moment's warning.

The news from Paris, soon convinced him that the conflict would not be carried on. Faction was again reigning in the city, and no party had sufficient power to control the machinery of war. With dismal forebodings, Lafayette turned his anxious eyes towards the capital, and read a premonition of fearful days in the portentous shadows which were slowly, but steadily, deepening over Paris and the entire kingdom. He saw Louis, too suspicious to abandon himself to any one of the parties, and too feeble to master them all, successively made the object, the tool and the victim of each. The Girondists, the Jacobins, and the Feuillans, were all striving for mastery ; and though the latter yielded tacitly to the King, it was only from fear, without confidence, while both of the former were undisguised in their opposition. They were equally at enmity with each other, and this spirit was unceasingly fanned by foreign agents ever anxious to spread disorder and ruin. Lafayette beheld the vial of political wrath fast filling, and knew it would shortly be poured upon the monarch's devoted head. Would that he had trusted me was his fervent exclamation, as courier following courier brought news that the plot was thickening around the person of him whom he had sworn, and was willing, to defend. He determined upon a *dernier* struggle to save the King,

From his camp at Maubeage, on the 16th June, 1792, he wrote his famous letter to the convention, in which he set forth plainly the condition to which the nation was reduced. In no measured terms he told them that the sword of Austria or of Europe, could not give so dangerous a blow to France as the jealousies and sharp contentions among her own citizens. He spoke of the Jacobins as enemies of the realm, and with far sighted sagacity predicted the results which would inevitably occur, if not speedily overthrown. "Can you dissemble even to yourselves," said he, "that a faction—and to avoid all vague demonstrations—the *Jacobin faction*, have caused all these disorders? It is that society which I boldly denounce; organized in its affiliated societies like a separate empire in the metropolis, and blindly governed by some ambitious leaders, this society forms a totally distinct corporation in the midst of the French nation, whose powers it usurps, by tyrannizing over its representatives and constituted authorities." He thus alluded to the King:—"Let the royal authority be untouched, for it is guaranteed by the constitution;—let it be independent, for its independence is one of the springs of our liberty;—let the King be revered, for he is invested with the majesty of the nation;—let him choose a ministry which wears the chain of no faction;—and if traitors exist, let them perish under the sword of the law."

No other man in France could have written such a letter, and none other known, would have dared to do it, if he could. An excitement, unequalled even in that time, succeeded its reception. The Jacobins had heretofore recoiled from a direct contest with Lafayette, but there was no longer retreat for them, or an alternative, save resistance. They met on the 18th of June, and though they knew with whom they had to deal, they entered upon the struggle for life or death. With one voice they took a solemn oath to destroy him, and they had never yet sworn in vain. They proposed that he should be sent to Orleans as a traitor;—that a price should be set upon his head, and that an edict should be issued, allowing any body who pleased, to murder him. Not content with open condemnation, their sleepless espionage was employed to influence the public mind. Their savage anathemas were not without effect. The Parisian mob, a faithless rabble, forgot his devotion to their safety, and turned their wrath upon him. With great adroitness the Jacobin leaders showed the people the expressions in his letter unfavorable to Louis, and made them believe that Louis and Lafayette were leagued against them. On the 20th of June, they rose in insurrection. Twenty thousand men of the lowest rank, armed with pikes and lances, paraded the streets of Paris, ready for slaughter. The Jacobins were among them to exasperate them to demoniac madness. Suddenly a shout arose, swelling to a deafening cry, and rolling in fearful reverberations over the city—"To the Tuilleries!" "To the Tuilleries!" "DOWN WITH THE KING!" The resistless wave rolled onward, sweeping every barrier opposing its progress. The guards of the palace fell back or were trampled, after an unavailing defense, beneath their feet. The calls of vengeance;—the yells of execration;—the curses loud and vehement, came to Louis, sitting in his chamber, with knell-like terror. Even then he felt as never before, that he was *a man*,—and determined to prove himself "every inch a King." He caught the spirit of the long line of monarchs whom he had succeeded, and, as the throng burst into his apartment, he met them with a dignity which made the leaders pause and recede. An outcry soon followed, but he was no longer to be intimidated by threats. If he could not save himself like a hero, he would at least die as became a Sovereign. His dignified demeanor awed the crowd, and his assurances that he was the friend of the people, hushed the tumult. The Assembly sent a deputation to his relief, who, crowding around him, rebuked the populace for the indignity offered to his majesty. Vergniaud and others, harangued the crowd, and persuaded them to retire, leaving the King again free from the dread of immediate violence, but with a rayless future before him.

On the 28th of June, Lafayette appeared in Paris. It was a bold step, but had been determined upon, when he learned the impression which his letter had made. The Assembly had charged him with a Cromwellian attempt at dictation, and he was there answering the slander by his silent attendance. He left his army, and came alone, a citizen to plead his own cause; asserting his innocence and asking punishment for the authors of the late outrages in the capital. He knew the power of the Jacobins, but did not hesitate, in their very citadel, to charge their crimes home, and demand the suppression of their clubs. He closed his speech in words well befitting him;—"Such are the representations submitted to the Assembly by a citizen, whose love for liberty, at least, will not be disputed."

His address was received with applause, but it was powerless in accomplishing the great object for which it was made. The Jacobin leaders, though awed, were not so easily crushed. In public and in private, —in the Assembly,—the streets, and in their clubs, he was decried as the enemy of liberty, and the betrayer of confidence he received from the people. He was charged with neglect of the public good, in leaving the camp at that period;—the journals represented his conduct as high treason;—he was called a liberticide, and a second Cromwell, with this difference, that he acted in concert with the King against the rights of the masses;—his effigy was burnt at the Palais Royal;—and he was accused of having proposed to march with his force to Paris. The direct charges he was able to meet and refute, but he could not remove the taint which the Jacobins were successful in indirectly casting upon him. It was not enough that he pointed to his past acts, and asking his enemies to specify his crimes, and prove them,—the Jacobins were fast becoming omnipotent in the state, and the fickle host which had lavished upon him the wealth of their adulation, were ready to pay homage at a rival shrine. Before two days had elapsed, Lafayette perceived the posture of things, and that it was useless to remain longer in the city. He waited upon Louis, and received his thanks, and on the 30th of

June, returned to his command. His mission had been a complete failure, and worse. He had not only been forced, but the enemies of himself and the kingdom had positively triumphed. For the first time in his life he was defeated, after having staked every thing on the issue. Though overcome in the contest, he was sustained by the consciousness that he had done all that man could do to relume the beacons of freedom which were fast expiring in the land.

But a new trial awaited him when he reached the army. His foes had been scattering the seeds of discord there, and he was already deserted by comrades in whom he had reposed uninterrupted confidence. He found that in his own camp he was no longer safe. Midnight hung upon his horison, and his career appeared to be near its goal. He remained at the head of the army, because he felt that he could not, at this juncture, abandon it, and watched with intensest interest the rapid developments of feeling in Paris.

THE REIGN OF TERROR, like a blind Polyphemus, was striding forward to erect the guileotine and decimate a kingdom; the heart of the patriot sunk within him, as he caught the monstrous outline, and read the dark mission of the lawless destroyer. On it came; it could not be stayed, but Lafayette resolved upon another struggle for his country's salvation. He believed that, the only probable attempt would be that of extricating the King from the crafty plots which pointed to his overthrow. A plan was matured by Lafayette for removing Louis from the capital and placing him in a position where he could command, rather than sue for, obedience. The 14th of July, the anniversary of the Federation, was approaching, and the plan was, that he should summon Generals Luckner and Lafayette to the city to participate in it, and when passed, to proceed to the Assembly in open day, and announce his intention of spending a short time at Compèigné. Lafayette was to provide a suitable escort for him, and when at Compèigné there were to be associated with this a detachment of militia and two regiments from the Marquis' chasseurs. These would afford him a sufficient body guard, and he could then, without fear, issue his proclamation, declaring his adherence to the constitution, and that all who opposed were traitors to the realm. The plan in its details was well arranged, and doubtless would have succeeded could the King have been prevailed upon to accept it. His true friends strongly urged him to put confidence in Lafayette, but the counter-revolutionists succeeded, and the proposal was rejected. Louis was a shipwrecked mariner, and now madly pushed away the last plank which could save him; yet he saw not that he was amid the waves, until beyond rescue.

Lafayette, finding his plans a failure, waited calmly the fatal result. Reports of conspiracy and intrigues, of misrule and the collision of parties, constantly reached his ears. Violent charges were made against him in the Assembly, but, prepared for the worst, they inflicted no pang. His name was associated with treason, and made the by-word of faction. Soon as his plan for the deliverance of Louis was known in Paris, the Jacobins boldly demanded his impeachment. A tempest, unknown before in that body, arose when this proposition was offered. The warm friends of Lafayette manfully spurned it, while his enemies supported it with slander and foulest abuse. The unstable crowd joined in the cry. But so flagrant injustice could not triumph yet. The last righteous act of that Assembly was done, when, on the 8th of August, they put aside the motions, and declared that Lafayette was still worthy of the confidence of the people of France.

Hardly had the courier borne to the Marquis this intelligence, before another arrived, bringing the terrible news of complete revolution in Paris. The 10th of August had arrived,—the birthday of the Reign of Terror. Faction had triumphed. The Jacobins, successful in rousing the people, an insurrection, wild and uncontrolable, rocked the metropolis. The royal palace was stormed; Louis forced to flee to the Assembly for protection; the masses, thirsting for blood, had begun the work of slaughter, afterwards carried on to its terrible consummation. The constitution was trampled under foot, and openly decried; monarchy was swept away like a floating bubble, and the King, himself hurled from his throne, was shut up in prison to await a mock trial and ignominious death.

Lafayette had, in anticipation of this, moved his army to Sedam, only two days march from Paris, and now formed the bold design of striking a blow for the restoration of order and the recovery of liberty. He distributed among his battalions a decisive letter, declaring the destruction of the constitution by a banditti, and the deposition of the King,—"Citizens," said he, "you are no longer represented; the National Assembly are in a state of slavery; your armies are without leaders; Petion reigns; the savage Danton and his satellites are masters. Thus, soldiers, it is your province to examine whether you will restore the hereditary representative to the throne, or submit to the digrace of having a Petion for your King."

For a brief time he hoped that this communication would be productive of good. The soldiery announced by their shouts of rage, that the tide of indignation was deep. The General had already disregarded the orders sent to him by the Assembly, and had put under arrest, the three commissioners deputed from that body, to enforce them. The first expression of his men was approbation, assuring him of cordial support. Their zeal soon subsided into apathy, and this gradually changed to secret, then open, defection. No other army could Lafayette depend upon, and even his chosen division contained enemies who were actively employed. Soon as the tidings of these disasters were received by the representatives, they at once passed a decree depriving him of his command and appointing Dumourier, an officer of their own interest, in his stead. Trial came upon trial—but, for a time, he concealed the critical posture of affairs. His path seemed crossed on every hand. "To have marched directly to Paris, would have exposed the King and his family to certain destruction; and in erecting the standard of revolt in the provinces, he would have been opposed by the other armies, and a civil war must inevitably have followed. In addition to these considerations, France was, at this moment, pressed on all sides by the enemy, and the idea of a capitulation with the presumptuous invaders of his country, struck him with horror. He was resolved, therefore, whatever might occur, neither to leave the frontiers destitute of defense, nor to lose his reputation by means of a disgraceful compact. But the oath that he had taken to support the constitutional King marked out a line of conduct from which he could not honorably swerve. He formd a plan to rally around him the neighboring departments, and to form, with some of the members of the constituted authorities, a kind of congress, to which he expected that many opposition members of the legislative body would unite themselves. Supported by the civil power, and seconded by the armies of the Moselle and the Rhine, he might have organized a powerful opposition, and reëstablished the constitution. But every circumstance necessary to the success of his project, failed together :—the enemy, on the threshhold of the empire, concentrated all his power ;—the versatile conduct of the King and court, destroyed all confidence, and rendered all his measures ineffectual ;—and the habits of the soldiery, had taught them to know no other power but the decrees of the Assembly ; every thing concerned in crushing an enterprise which the rapidity of events had not afforded him time to mature, whose success, if only partial, might have opened the gates of the frontiers to the enemy, and which it was impossible after the events of the 10th of August, completely to effect."

But the chief difficulty preventing the successful execution of the plan, lay in the state of his own forces. They began to comprehend his situation, and conflicting feelings were rife among them. But what tended most especially to weaken his hold over them, was the following order passed by the Assembly:

"NATIONAL ASSEMBLY, August 17, 1792.

"*Decree of accusation against M. de Lafayette.*

"I.—It appears to this Assembly, that there is just ground for accusation against M. de Lafayette, heretofore commander of the army of the north.

"II.—The executive power shall, in the most expeditious manner possible, carry the present decree into execution; and all constituted authorities, all citizens, and all soldiers, are hereby enjoined, by every means in their, to secure his person.

"III.—The Assembly forbids the army of the north, any longer to acknowledge him as a General, or to obey his orders; and strictly enjoins that no person whatsoever, shall furnish any thing to the troops, or pay any money for their use, but by the orders of M. Dumourier."

This decree was circulated through the army, and

the power of Lafayette over it was gone. The soldiers had become generally infected with the principles of the time, and the emissaries of the Jacobins, sent thither, had no difficulty in convincing them, that disobedience to his command was duty, and to recognize him officially longer, was to violate the laws. In this condition a single course remained to him. To attempt again to plead his cause before the bar of the Assembly, would, he knew, be worse than useless. To attempt to force the members to just terms, and to reëstablish the constitutional monarchy, by the might of arms, was beyond his power. To remain in camp was idle, and would subject him to needless danger. There was no alternative but flight, and this, with the greatest reluctance, he determined to embrace. Before, however, departing, he arranged every thing throughout the army, to prevent sudden surprise from the enemy, anxious even in that moment, for the welfare of a country which had basely discarded him. The preparations for his departure were made secretly, as is stated, to avoid increasing the number of his companions in exile. He would not draw away a soldier or officer from service, though it were to relieve with his presence the bitterness of voluntary banishment. Taking with him two or three trusty friends, he quietly left the camp on the morning of the 20th of August, before the dawn of day, and turned towards the Netherlands, to receive, in a hostile and foreign land, the safety which he could not find at home.

Unlike Washington, he had to deal with unprincipled men who, repudiating the religion of the Bible, raved like maniacs around the altar of Reason. Lafayette fled from their orgies and their wrath, with the natural repulsion, mingled with grief, that sent the Hebrew from the brutal inhabitants and volcanic fires of the cities of the plain.

CHAPTER IX.

Companions of Lafayette in his exile — He is stopped at Rochefort · Passports refused — Shameful treatment — Imprisonment — Delivered over by Prussia to Austria — Confinement at Olmutz — Refinement of cruelty — Sympathy felt for him — Efforts for his release — Conduct of Gouverneur Morris — Madame de Lafayette — Bollman and Huger's Attempt — Escape — Is taken and again thrown into prison — Increased cruelties — Conduct of Madame de Lafayette — With her two daughters she visits him in prison — Her heroism — Bonaparte — Final Release — Reception in Hamburg.

The companions of the Marquis were the two brothers, Louis and Victor Latour Maubourg, Bureau de Puzy, Alexandre Lameth, Auguste Masson, Rene Pillet, and Cardignan. They entered the Netherlands, from France, hoping to be able to proceed to America or to take up their residence in some European province, not then at war with France. They knew the hazard of falling in with the Austrian army, but, at the worst, they could be treated only as prisoners of war, and concluded this preferable to the peril in camp. On arriving at Rochefort after a rapid journey, they found themselves in the neighborhood of an advanced guard of Austrians. They could not proceed without passports, and could not retreat without danger of falling into the hands of the French. At the outskirts of Rochefort, de Puzy was sent forward to solicit passports, without disclosing the names or rank of those for whom they were designed. Count d' Harnoncourt, who then held command at this post, was a shrewd man, closely questioned de Puzy respecting his companions and their object in flying from France. Finding that they would be unwilling to join the refugees in the Austrian ranks, but they were patriots, d' Harnoncourt, detaining de Puzy, sent orders for the rest to advance. Refusal to comply with this command was out of the question, and soon Lafayette was among the foes of the Republic, and under the piercing gaze of the commandant. Contrary to his hopes he was instantly recognized, and d' Harnoncourt, of course, would not allow them now to pass till he had communicated with his superior officer. With some empty expressions of respect, he told them it was impossible for them to depart until the next day, and that before, it was necessary to obtain the requisite permission from General Moitelle, then stationed at Namur. A messenger was dispatched to that place, with the important intelligence that Lafayette was a prisoner, and de Puzy accompanied him to solicit, in person, the continuance of their journey. Arriving at Namur he was ushered into the presence of the Austrian General, whose dull eye kindled with a strange fire when he learned the purport of his errand. He could hardly believe his senses when he heard that d' Harnoncourt held in safe keeping, at Rochefort, the bravest general against whom the allied armies opposed to France were called to contend. "What!" said he, "Lafayette? Lafayette? Run instantly and inform the Duke of Bourbon of it," said he to one of his officers. "Lafayette? Set out this moment and carry this news to his royal highness at Brussels," he added to another, and on he went, issuing his orders and muttering the word *Lafayette*, until, before the astonished de Puzy could interpose a word, the news had been dispatched to half the princes and generals in Europe, that Lafayette was a captive with the allies. Passports were, of course, refused, and on the 21st of August the prisoners were conducted to Namur, to gratify the commandant's curiosity, and to learn how the laws of nations and of war may yield to a selfish policy, fogetful of every principle of right in the furtherance of base and narrow ends. Lafayette found he was a close prisoner, and, besides, indignities were offered which made him blush for his human fellowship with those who insulted him. It was hinted to him that he might purchase a mitigation of his hardships, by revealing the condition and military resources of France, and giving to the allied armies such other information as would aid them in their proposed invasion. This was too much for the high spirit of the Marquis. He thought of Arnold, and thus linking that name with his, made his heart leap with a glow of indignation. Prince Charles, who visited him to open the subject, shrunk with shame before the man who spurned treachery as infinitely more dreadful than death itself. The Austrians did not know their prisoner. They had heard of his patriotism, but it was unmeaning to the dull ears upon which despotism had poured its notes of arrogance and the sound of fetters. They supposed that he must be governed by motives like their own, and marvelled at the reverse. From Namur the captives were conducted to Nivelles where further contempt was borne. A commissioner waited upon them from the Duke of Saxe Teschen, leader of the Austrian forces at Brussels, to demand, in due form, for the King of France, it was said, the treasure which Lafayette was supposed to have taken with him in his flight. Such a demand was at first received as an undignified joke, but when the signs of authority were displayed, and the commissioner gave assurance of his earnestness, Lafayette met him with mingled indignation and scorn. "I am to infer then," said he, with cutting emphasis, "that if the Duke of Saxe Teschen had been in my place he would have stolen the military chest of the army. Tell him that the Generals of the King of France were taught in a different school of morals."

From Nivelles, Lafayette was conducted to Luxembourg, where an attempt was made to assassinate him by some of the French refugees. Escaping from this, he was reserved for a severe and almost hopeless captivity. His captors, disregarding entirely the claims of justice and humanity and the laws of nations, treated him like a feared and hated serf. A correspondence was had between the courts of Vienna and Berlin, by which it was finally decided that he should be given over to the Prussians, for more cruel confinement. The hand tingles with shame when called to record the fact; but truths more humiliating and abhorrent, lie in the subsequent transactions. Despotism gloated over the wrongs inflicted on freedom's champion, though it quailed at heart before the spirit which he breathed. As the carrion kite may assail the eagle through the bars of his cage, and fly screaming with alarm when they meet in the free air.

At Luxembourg, the captives were placed in a common cart, closely guarded, and hurried to Wessel, on the Rhine, within the Prussian domain. The news of their approach collected the populace along their way, to salute with coarse and unfeeling taunts the very man who was a martyr to their rights. The guard made no effort to prevent it. Lafayette entered the prison at Wessel, without having allowed his foes occasion for exultation. A thrill ran along his frame while the heavy manacles were locked upon his hands and feet, but when he heard the dungeon doors turn upon their hinges, and the bolts drop into their sockets, his accustomed tranquillity returned.

Nature, however, yielded. The cold damp air of his cell, added to the hardships through which he had passed, brought on sickness which, for a time, precluded hope of recovery. Day by day his strength wasted, but no mitigation of his confinement was allowed him. Once the King of Prussia offered him aid if he would assist in the plans forming against France; but he met the message with the scorn it merited, and bade the officer who brought it, return to his master and tell him that he was yet Lafayette.

The King seemed determined to exhaust his ingenuity in increasing the burden of incarceration. Enraged by the contempt of his noble prisoner, he added blacker infamy to his character by transferring him to a gloomier abode. The dungeons of Wessel were not dark enough to suit the monarch's malignity; he determined to make them so. Without warning, Lafayette and his friends were thrown into the cart which brought them to Wessel and hurried away. No intimation of the object of this removal was given, till the sombre towers of Magdebourg rose in the distance, and they were told that its chill caverns were to be their home. No intelligence was received respecting their families, but reports of the reign of terror were repeated, to torture them with solicitude for France and all they cherished upon her soil. As they entered the loathsome vault, they were told to bid adieu for ever to the world.

Here they lived for a year, if their wretched existence could be called life. No ray of comfort was permitted to play upon the cold pavement, nor hope of deliverance to illumine the future. Desolate and despairing, they lay; the only news from the outward world was such as would augment their misery. Frederic William occasionally sent to learn if their sufferings were sufficiently intense, and then found pastime in new acts of fiendish despotism. Despairing of making him yield, and fearing that the peace which he was concluding with France would require the surrender of Lafayette, he caused him, with Maubourg and de Puzy, to be transferred to the Austrians. Austria was ready to perfect what her neighbor had begun. The darkness which rested upon her;—the despotism which reigned in every part of her dominions;—the brutalizing system of serfdom;—the narrow mindedness and bigotry which prevailed in her councils, and guided her whole policy, fitted her for the work of torturing Lafayette, as the same admirable traits have qualified her, in our own times, to crush Hungary and break the heart of Kossuth; and which had their impersonation in Haynau. Austria has always been consistent with herself. She has never *grown*. She has always beat time, while the advancing nations, by her side, have been pressing onward to light and liberty. This very day she lies like a blot upon the face of Europe. Around her, still hang the shadows of the dark ages. Her despotism has preserved for her people a hierarchy, which, in turn, makes the chains of tyranny firmer, though more galling, and lays upon the nation an incrustation of hoary abuses.

Olmutz was selected by Austria for the prisoners, and they were carried thither. "Though placed within the same castle, and occupying cells in the same corridor, the friends were as completely guarded against all intercourse with each other, and all knowledge of each other's condition, as if an ocean or a continent separated them. As they entered their cells, it was declared to each of them, that the would never come out of them alive,—that they would never see any thing but what was enclosed within the four walls of their respective cells,—that they would hold no communication with the outer world, nor receive any kind of information of persons or things there,—that their jailers were even prohibited from pronouncing their names,—that in the prison reports and government dispatcnes, they would be referred to only by the number of their cells.—that they would never be suffered to learn any thing of the situation of their families, or even to know of each other's existence;—and, that, as such a situation of hopeless confinement would naturally incite to suicide, knives and forks, and all other instruments by which they might do violence to themselves, would be thenceforth withheld from them."

This was Austria's improvement upon the cruelties at Magdebourg. The walls of his dungeon were twelve feet thick, and the only mode of either entrance or egress, was through two doors, one of iron, the other of wood, nearly two feet thick; both of which were covered with bolts and bars. Into the cell the air was admitted only through an opening in the walls two feet square, secured at each end by transverse massive iron bars. Without, and directly under this loop hole, was a broad ditch, covered with water only when it rained, at other times constantly sending forth a poisonous effluvium from its stagnant pools. The dimensions of his room were eight or ten paces deep, by six or eight wide, and its whole furniture consisted of an old worm-eaten table, a broken chair, and a bed of rotten straw filled with vermin. A miserable allowance was brought to him twice a day, with which to eke out his loathesome existence; books were almost wholly excluded, and without a voice to greet his ear save the gruff tones of the jailer, life, bitter life, wore away.

He whose name was written so deeply upon the

hearts of two nations, was not forgotten. The news of his imprisonment spread wherever he was known—and where was he not known?—awakening feelings corresponding with the differing estimate of his career. In the United States grief attended the tidings. They had watched with profound interest his course during the French struggle, and had felt an affectionate pride in seeing that the dawn of liberty, which had risen to noontide upon their broad land, was brightening around him in his native Gaul. Sympathy was elicited in his behalf, and efforts put forth to obtain his release. It did not become a free people to remain inactive while the form which "rode on the battle's edge" for them, was pining under the weight of fetters. While Lafayette was at Magdebourg, the American minister in France, learning that he was in need of money, took the responsibility of directing the banker of the United States, at Hamburgh, to advance him ten thousand florins; an act which Congress afterwards ratified, under the head of military compensation. The condition of the Marquis was subduing to the spirit of Washington. His private feelings urged him to take every step to liberate his friend, while his public duty, as the President of a neutral nation, forbade him to interfere. With pain he was compelled to refuse, for friendship, to compromise his public duty. But while, as President, he maintained the neutrality of the nation, as a man his influence went strongly for the Marquis' release. "I need hardly mention" he wrote to Mr. Pinckney, then in Europe, "how much my sensibility has been hurt by the treatment this gentleman has met with, or how anxious I am to see him liberated therefrom; but what course to pursue, as most likely and proper to aid the measure, is not quite so easy to decide on. As President of the United States, there must not be a commitment of the government by any interference of mine; and it is no easy matter, in a transaction of this nature, for a public character to assume the garb of a private citizen, in a case that does not relate to himself. Yet such is my wish to contribute my mite to accomplish that desirable object, that I have no objection to its being made known to the Imperial ambassador, in London, who, if he thinks proper, may communicate it to his court, that this event is an ardent wish of the people of the United States, to which I sincerely add mine. The time, the manner, and even the measure itself, I leave to your discretion; as circumstances, and every matter which concerns this gentleman, are better known on that than they are on this side of the Atlantic."

To the Emperor of Germany, General Washington also wrote as follows:

"It will readily occur to your majesty, that occasions may sometimes exist, on which official considerations would constrain the chief of a nation to be silent and passive, in relation even to objects which affect his sensibility, and claim his interposition as a man. Finding myself precisely in this situation at present, I take the liberty of writing this private letter to your majesty, being persuaded that my motives will also be my apology for it.

"In common with the people of this country, I retain a strong and cordial sense of the services rendered to them by the Marquis de Lafayette; and my friendship for him has been constant and sincere. It is natural, therefore, that I should sympathize with him and his family in their misfortunes, and endeavor to mitigate the calamities which they experience; among which, his present confinement is not the least distressing.

"I forbear to enlarge on this delicate subject. Permit me only to submit to your majesty's consideration, whether his long imprisonment, and the confiscation of his estates, and the indigence and dispersion of his family, and the painful anxieties incident to all these circumstances, do not form an assemblage of sufferings which recommend him to the mediation of humanity? Allow me, sir, on this occasion to be its organ; and to entreat, that he may be permitted to come to this country, on such conditions and under such restrictions, as your majesty may think it expedient to prescribe.

"As it is a maxim with me not to ask what, under similar circumstances, I would not grant, your majesty will do me the justice to believe, that this request appears to me to correspond to those great principles of magnanimity and wisdom, which form the basis of sound policy and durable glory.

"May the Almighty and Merciful Sovereign of the universe keep your majesty under his protection and guidance."

But not only in America, in Europe also, there were

similar demonstrations. In the British House of Parliament, Wilberforce, and Fox, and Sheridan, were active in his behalf, though bigotry unsubdued, would then tarnish his fame. A number of the leading papers in London and Hamburgh, commenced a series of articles, exposing in the most cutting language, the infamous conduct of Prussia and Austria, to the scorn of all Europe. Their perfidy in detaining a prisoner, contrary to the rights of nations and of humanity, was condemned with an indignant eloquence and a scathing sarcasm, which goaded the tyrants, till they spoke in their own defense. They declared that Lafayette's freedom was incompatible with the safety of the present governments of Europe; and this was the plausible apology for inquisitorial cruelties. Though France indirectly caused his present calamities, she still possessed noble souls. Madame de Stael, with her characteristic energy, wrote upon the subject to Gouverneur Morris, who, after he was superseded as minister to France, by Mr. Munroe, traveled through Germany and Austria, and in various ways endeavored to procure the liberation of Lafayette. In her letter she says:—"What I have to task of you is so much in accordance with your own feelings, that my letter will only repeat to you their dictates in poorer expressions. You are traveling through Germany, and, whether on a public mission or not, you have influence, for they are not so stupid as not to consult a man like you. Open the prison doors of M. de Lafayette. Pay the debt of your country. What greater service can any one render to his native land, than to discharge her obligations of gratitude? Is there any severer calamity, than that which has befallen Lafayette? Does any more glaring injustice attract the attention of Europe? I speak to you of glory, yet I know a more elevated sentiment is the motive of your conduct." *

It was at this period that the virtues and heroic devotion of Madame de Lafayette shone conspicuously forth. Naturally of a retiring and gentle disposition, possessing all the attractions of female loveliness, she was better fitted for the quiet charm of the family circle than to move in the wider sphere which her rank required. History pours no clearer radiance upon female character; possessing so gentle, so pure, yet strong affections, true modesty, unaffected symplicity and ingeniousness, combined with a discretion which could preserve her dignity and maintain a becoming reserve, consistent with the freedom and confidence which distinguished her. When the thunder-bolt fell at her feet, breaking up her family circle and withering her domestic hopes, her friends expected to see her fall like a smitten flower. But like the blossom, bowed by dew drops of evening, she raised her head with a new strength derived from the

* The conduct of Mr. Morris is worthy of all praise. He not only spared no sacrifice for the Marquis, he also acted a magnanimous part towards his suffering family. To Madame de Lafayette, when she was confined by order of the French authorities, to her residence in Chavagnac, he loaned from his private funds, one hundred thousand livres, and afterwards, when she was brought to Paris and imprisoned, it was through his intercession alone that liberty was restored.

visitation, and the tears that fell shone in the radiance of her resignation and love, as dew glows in the light of the morning. While the sympathy of friends was unbounded she was called upon to act, and she nobly fulfilled her mission. Her husband was a prisoner, and to the Prussian monarch; and she addressed a petition whose every line portrayed, distinctly, the injustice he was committing. In that petition, she says "He, in whose favor I implore the mercy of your majesty, has never known crime. Faithful to his King, when he could no longer be of service to him he left France. At the moment when he was made prisoner he was crossing the low countries to take refuge in America. He believed himself under protection of the law of nations, and he trusted to it with so much the more confidence, as the generous sentiments of your majesty were not unknown to him. I may, perhaps, be blind to the character of a beloved husband, but I cannot deceive myself in being persuaded that your majesty will grant the prayer of an unhappy woman." The agony, occasioned by her husband's imprisonment, was hardly increased by the evils which the French government added to her misfortunes. The feeling for his safety rose above all personal considerations, and she seemed unaware of her danger as a victim of the Reign of Terror. He was in all her thoughts; and she would have given life, gladly, to save his. The following letter she wrote, in 1792, to Washington. Describing the situation of Lafayette and herself, she thus pleads for them both. "He was taken by the troops of the

Emperor, although the King of Prussia retains him a prisoner in his dominions. And while he suffers this inconceivable persecution from the enemies without, the faction which reigns within keeps me a hostage at one hundred and twenty leagues from the capital. Judge, then, at what distance I am from him. In this abyss of misery, the idea of owing to the United States and to Washington the life and liberty of M. de Lafayette, kindles a ray of hope in my heart. I hope every thing from the goodness of the people with whom he has set an example of that liberty of which he is now made the victim. And shall I dare speak what I hope? I would ask of them, through you, for an envoy, who shall go to reclaim him in the name of the republic of the United States, wheresoever he may be found, and who shall be authorized to make, with the power in whose charge he may be placed, all necessary engagements for his relief, and for taking him to the United States, even if he is there to be guarded as a captive. If his wife and his children could be comprised in this mission, it is easy to judge how happy it would be for her and them, but, if this would, in the least degree, retard or embarass the measure, we will defer still longer the happiness of a reünion. May heaven deign to bless the confidence with which it has inspired me. I hope my request is not a rash one. Accept the homage of the sentiments which have dictated this letter, as well as that of attachment and tender respect."

It was exceedingly trying for Washington, to be unable to comply with that request. Public sentiment in the United States was strong in favor of Madame

Lafayette's suggestion, and the President had to resist both this and the full tide of his own emotions in sustaining the honor of the nation. He wrote to Madame Lafayette, kindly and tenderly, assuring her of his sympathy and stating that, while he could not commit his official character or involve the country in embarassments, he would still do his utmost as a private individual, to procure a deliverance, which he desired ardently as herself.

After Lafayette's last transfer, all knowledge of his place of confinement was excluded from his friends. Austria meant that his existence should be strictly a living death. They, however, believing him to be yet alive, did not pause in their endeavors, but perseveringly sought to discover his dungeon. At length a generous and daring spirit assumed the task, both of finding where he was confined, and of rescuing him if possible. This was Dr. J. Erick Bollman, a young German physician, who had just received his degree of Doctor of Medicine from the University of Gottingen. Though personally unacquainted with Lafayette, he was an enthusiastic admirer of him, and had made several ineffectual attempts to save him from royal ferocity. Not disheartened, he sold his books to procure means for his journey and set off for Hamburgh. He was here introduced to a wealthy banker, by the name of Sieveking, who entered zealously into his plans, and advanced him money sufficient to carry them out.* The following account has been mainly

* See Port Folio, vol. XXII. We have made free use of this account, it being the best and most authentic one ever published.

taken and condensed from a narrative of his projects and adventures, as written by Dr. Bollman himself:

Leaving Hamburg, he assumed the character of a traveler in pursuit of knowledge, and began his wary and difficult enterprise. Traversing Germany, he learned that Lafayette, after having been surrendered to the Austrian government, had been borne away on the route towards Olmutz. With this knowledge he selected, near the frontier, a place of temporary retreat, in case he should succeed in rescuing the captive; and having made all necessary preliminary arrangements, proceeded on to Olmutz. The utmost caution was indispensable to success, for the Austrian police, at all times more vigilant than that of any country in Europe, was now unusually active. Its Argus eyes were towards every quarter of the state, and all direct inquiry respecting the object of his search would inevitably have been noticed, and led to a suspicion which would have destroyed his plans before they had attained the maturity of promise.

Dr. Bollman acted with admirable care and circumspection. He ascertained that several state prisoners were confined in the citadel of Olmutz, under a mystery which rendered it highly probable to him, that Lafayette was among them. Acting upon this supposition, the doctor visited the hospital and sought an acquaintance with the first surgeon, rightly judging from reports which he had gathered respecting the health of the captives, that this officer must be in the habit of attending upon them.

The surgeon proved to be an upright man, of good

sense and feeling. The acquaintance seemed to be mutually agreeable, and after several interviews, when the conversation turned on the effect of moral impressions on the constitution, Dr. Bollman, who had skillfully guided to this issue, abruptly drew a pamphlet from his pocket and remarked :—" Since we are on the subject, you attend to the state prisoners here, Lafayette is among them, and his health is much impaired. Show him this pamphlet. Tell him a traveler left it with you, who lately saw, in London, all the persons named in it, his particular friends ;—that they are well, and continue attached to him as much as ever. This intelligence will do him more good than all your drugs."—At the same moment, he laid the pamphlet on the table, and perceiving that the surgeon hardly knew what to reply, changed the conversation, and shortly left him.

Thus far every thing had worked finely. The manner of the surgeon convinced Bollman that Lafayette was at Olmutz, and he well knew that if he should receive the pamphlet, he would devise means to improve the opportunity. Calling at the hospital as before, but without himself renewing the subject, in a few days, the surgeon mentioned to him of his own accord, that he had given the pamphlet to Lafayette, who wished to learn some further particulars respecting the situation of one or two of the individuals named in it. Upon hearing this, the doctor, appearing to have accidentally about him some white paper, but which, in fact, had been prepared for the emergency, sat immediately down and wrote a few lines in reply to the inquiries made, finishing with the sentence,—"I am glad of the opportunity of addressing you these words, which, *when read with your usual warmth*, will afford to a heart like yours, some consolation." The paper had been previously written over with sympathetic ink, and the italicized words were a sufficient hint to the quick-minded Lafayette. Applying heat to the paper, he read, with a throbbing heart, its secret language, and learned that there was a great soul near him, who was ready to peril every thing to effect his escape. The method by which this could be done, could only be pointed out by the prisoner, and with hope again awakening his energies, he sat down to fix on a plan, and communicate it to his generous friend outside.

To guard against suspicion, Dr. Bollman, on the day following this, left Olmutz and proceeded to Vienna, where he remained a considerable time, but confiding his design to no person whatever. Here he had a carriage constructed, in which were contrived convenient places for conveying, secretly, a variety of articles, such as rope-ladders, cords, and tools which would be necessary for cutting iron bars, and for similar purposes. These general preparations being made, he visited several gentlemen on their estates in Moravia, and took an opportunity of again touching at Olmutz, where he called on the surgeon, who returned him the pamphlet formerly left for Lafayette. On examining it, he found to his inexpressible joy, that the margin had been written over with sympathetic ink; from which he learned that the captive, on account of his enfeebled state of health, had at length obtained permission to take an airing, on certain days, in a carriage, accompanied by a military guard; and that the best and easiest mode to restore him to liberty, would be to attack the guard on one of these excursions.

All this was satisfactory to Dr. Bollman, and having ascertained for his guidance, that Lafayette, in taking his ride, sat in an open carriage, with an officer by his side, a driver on the box, and two armed soldiers standing behind, he returned to Vienna to complete his plans for this new phase in the adventure. As it was necessary to have at least one coadjutor in the undertaking, he fixed upon a kindred spirit, one predisposed in all his sympathies to favor the bold measure which he contemplated. This was Francis Kinlock Huger, the son of Col. Huger, of South Carolina, at whose house Lafayette first lodged when he landed in America. He was a young man of uncommon talent, decision and enthusiasm; who entered into the whole plan, and devoted himself to its execution with the most romantic earnestness.

Having agreed upon a mode, they publicly announced their intention of returning to England together. Two saddle horses were purchased, and engaging a steady groom to attend them, they set out on their journey. Thus, sometimes sending the groom a station or two forward with the carriage; at others, leaving him to bring up the horses slowly, while they pushed onward in the carriage, they arrived at Olmutz.

These were the only two persons on the continent, except Lafayette himself, who had the slightest suspicion of any arrangements for his liberation, and neither of these persons knew him by sight. When they reached Olmutz, the doctor immediately visited the surgeon, and, knowing the day when the captive was to take his ride, mentioned to him the same day as the one on which he intended to continue his journey. On that day, Nov. 8th, 1794, the groom was dispatched, at an early hour, to Hoff, a post town about twenty-five miles distant, with orders to have fresh horses in readiness, at four o'clock. As neither of the parties knew the other, it had been concerted between them, that, to avoid all mistakes, when the rescue should be attempted, each should take off his hat and wipe his forehead in token of recognition.

Their horses were now ready at the inn, and Mr. Huger feigned some business near the town gate, in order to watch the moment when the carriage should pass. As soon as he saw it, he hastened back to the inn and communicated the news to the Doctor. The two then mounted, followed the carriage at some distance, armed only with a pair of pistols, and those not loaded with ball. Their success was to depend upon the surprise, as, under the circumstances of the case, they considered that it would be not only unjustifiable, but useless and imprudent, to take any person's life.

At length they quickened their pace and rode past the carriage, and then, slackening, allowed it again to go ahead, while they seized the opportunity as it was passing, to exchange signals with the prisoner. At two or three miles from the gate, the carriage left the high road and passed into a less frequented tract in the midst of an open country. Every motion was now watched by the two horsemen, with the intensest interest. Presently the carriage stopped, and Lafayette and the officer got out and walked, arm and arm, to give the former more opportunity for exercise. The carriage with the guard drove slowly on, but remained in sight. This was evidently the time for the attempt, and galloping up, the doctor threw the reins of his horse to Huger, and instantly sprang to the ground by the side of the officer and Lafayette. At the same moment the latter seized hold of the officer's sword, but before he could draw it from the scabbard, the officer had seized it also, and the scuffle began. Bollman sprang upon the officer, who had caught hold of Lafayette, and, in the melee which ensued, the three came together to the ground, the officer roaring as loudly as he could for help, and the guard, on hearing it, instead of coming to his assistance, fleeing to alarm the citadel. Huger, passing the bridles of the two horses over one arm, with his other hand thrust his handkerchief into the officer's mouth to stop his noise, and Bollman kneeling upon him, managed to keep him to the ground, while Lafayette extricating himself from his grasp, sprang to his feet once more a free man.

Thus far all had gone admirably, and would now have resulted well, but one of the horses taking fright at the scene and noise, had reared, slipped his bridle and ran off. The doctor, still keeping down the officer, handed a purse to Lafayette and bade him mount the remaining horse and save himself now by flight. Huger told him in English to go *to Hoff*, but he, mistaking what was said to him for a more general direction *to go off*, delayed a moment to see if he could not assist them — then went on — then rode back, still unwilling to leave them, and finally, urged anew, galloped away and was out of sight in a minute.

As soon as this was accomplished, the two heroes left the officer without further violence, and recovering the horse which had escaped, they both mounted him, intending to follow and assist Lafayette. But this animal, less docile and attractable than the other, which had been trained to carry two persons, refused to perform this task, reared, bounded, and presently threw both. Huger immediately exclaimed, "This will never do! The Marquis wants you. Take the horse, therefore, and push on, and I will take my chance on foot across the country." The doctor did so, but his companion, who now had little chance of escape, was soon seized by the peasants, who had witnessed the scene, and conducted back to Olmutz. These accidents defeated the design, wisely planned, and, so far as they could foresee results, judiciously and prudently attempted. Dr. Bollman easily arrived at Hoff; but not finding Lafayette there, and being anxious to receive some intelligence of him, although he might readily have secured himself by proceeding to Tarnowitz, he lingered about the frontiers, till the next night, when he, too, was arrested, by order of the Prussian authority, at the requisition of Austria.

Lafayette remained unpursued. He had taken a wrong road, which led to Jagerscloff, a place on the Prussian frontier, and followed it as long as his horse could proceed. He was within a few miles of the boundary of Austrian rule, and perceiving that his horse could go no further, he accosted a peasant, whom he overtook on the road, not far from the village, and under some pretext, offered him money if he would procure him another horse and attend him to the frontier. The man apparently agreed, and went to the village for the horse, though his suspicion was awakened by the appearance of the stranger. He promptly returned, but he came with a force which arrested the astonished fugitive, and, despite his entreaties and offers of gold, he was led into the village, carried before a magistrate, recognized by an officer from Olmutz, and before three short days of liberty had gladdened his heart, he was loaded with chains, and carried back to his dungeon with little hope now that his obscure and ignominious sufferings could be terminated except by death.*

He found, in the treatment to which he was subjected, that he had not yet been permitted to conceive the extent of that cruelty which despotism was

* Bollman and Huger, after having endured the harshest treatment and strictest confinement, for over eight months, were at length liberated through the powerful intercession of an Austrian nobleman, a personal friend of the former

able to inflict. "The irons were so closely fastened around his ankles, that for three months he endured the most excruciating torture. During the winter 1794–5, which was extremely severe, he was reduced almost to the last extremity by a violent fever, and, yet, was deprived of proper attendance, of air, of suitable food, and of decent clothes. In this state he was allowed nothing for his bed but a little damp and moldy straw, and was closely confined by a chain around his waist, which was fastened to the wall, and barely permitted him to turn from one side to the other. No light was admitted into his cell, and he was even refused the smallest allowance of linen. Worn down by disease and the rigor of the season, he became miserably emaciated.

To increase his miseries, almost insupportable mental anxieties were added to his physical distresses. He was made to believe that he was only reserved for a public execution, and that his chivalrous deliverers had already perished on the scaffold; while, at the same time, he was not permitted to know whether his family were still alive, or had fallen under the revolutionary axe, of which, during the few days he was out of his dungeon, he had heard such appalling accounts."

The attempted rescue, though unsuccessful in its immediate result, was yet productive of beneficial effects. It gave to Europe and the world a clue to the place of his confinement, and, consequently, added definiteness and vigor to the plans which were already maturing for his deliverance. It stirred anew the heart of his devoted wife, who, as soon as she was free from the restraints imposed by the terrorists, determined to present her plea, in person, before the Emperor of Austria, strong in the faith of affection that her petition could not be denied, when urged with all the arguments of her woman's love. Sending her son George to America, to the care of Washington, and assuming for herself the name of Mrs. Mortier, she set out for Vienna, with American passports, and accompanied by her two daughters, in disguise. Anastasia, the elder of these, was then sixteen, and Virginia, the younger, thirteen years of age.

The Emperor before whom she presented her request was Francis I., a nephew of the unfortunate Marie Antoinette, who possessed, in addition to the prejudices growing out of his position, the hostility to Lafayette which had been cherished by the ill-fated Queen of France. It was, therefore, with no willing ear that he listened to the petition, although pressed with a force and eloquence which none could use but a wife pleading for the husband of her youth. He told her that his "hands were tied," so that he could not liberate him; but, at length, moved by her entreaties, he granted her request that herself and daughters might be permitted to share his terrible captivity. In order to yield as little as possible, this permission was itself made as near a prohibition as the nature of the case would admit. They were assured, that if they entered the prison they could never come out alive, and that if they went they were to leave behind them every thing which could in the least degree minister to their comfort, by alleviating the woe which must reign unbroken within the walls of an Austrian dungeon.

Harsh as these provisions were, and well calculated as they must have been to deter ladies accustomed to all the refinements and luxuries of life, they were still accepted without hesitation. The cold bosom of the Emperor thrilled with a new sympathy as these brave spirits left his presence, voluntarily to shut themselves out from the world and assume the horrors of a hopeless captivity, for the sake of mitigating another's sorrows. Touched with regret, it is possible that even then he would have given orders for the release of Lafayette, had it not been as he himself said, that his "hands were tied." We shall make no attempt to picture the meeting which took place between Lafayette and his wife and daughters. Imagination can better furnish the scene than words describe it. Those dungeon walls never rung to such melody, as when the dearest objects of earthly love greeted the lonely captive in his cell. Joy, pure and hallowed, was the first emotion, and the prison became a palace in that outgush of emotion which flowed from reciprocal sympathy and affection. What was either prison or palace, in such a moment, to them?

The complicated horrors and sufferings of their loathsome confinement, were too much for the delicate frame of Madame de Lafayette, already worn down by previous suffering and anxiety. Yet, for sixteen months, she endured it all cheerfully, adhering firmly to her resolution to perish, if she must, by her husband's side. Her gradual emaciation and growing feebleness were not, however, unnoticed by the fond eye of him whom she had come to bless, and, alarmed for her safety, he urged her to write to the Emperer, and petition for an egress of at least two weeks from the prison, that she might breathe a purer air and obtain that medical assistance her sinking health so urgently demanded. This she at length did, and then waited for two months longer before a reply was deigned to her simple and humble request. It was a matter of grave consultation among the lords at Vienna, how they might answer in the keenest form of cruelty, the petition of a suffering and pure-minded woman, whose only crime was that she was the wife of Lafayette and shared in the hatred which her husband felt to oppression. After due deliberation, it was determined with a refinement of brutality, that her request should be granted on condition that she should never appear in the capital nor return to the prison. Was this former provision adopted because they felt that they would be ashamed to meet her afterwards?

These conditions Madame de Lafayette spurned as indignantly as she would their authors. She told the officer who laid them before her, that rather than leave the prison on such terms, she would remain there even should she be called to die in the loathesomeness of her captivity. An answer being required in writing, she seized a pen and wrote the following resolve, every line of which illustrates the truth of Madame de Stael's remark, that "the history of female virtue and female heroism presents nothing more rare in excellence, than the life and character of Madame de Lafayette."

"I owed it to my family and my friends, to ask the assistance necessary for my health;—but they know that the conditions attached to it cannot be accepted by me. I never can forget that, while we were both on the point of perishing—I by the tyranny of Robespierre, my husband by the physical and moral sufferings of his captivity—I was not permitted to receive any news of him, nor he to learn that his children and I still existed. I will not expose myself to the horrors of a new separation. Whatever may be the state of my health, or the inconvenience of this residence to my daughters, we shall gratefully avail ourselves of his imperial majesty's goodness in permitting us to share my husband's captivity in all its details. NOAILLES LAFAYETTE."

No complaint afterwards fell from the lips of this heroic woman, and no further trial made by the sufferers to escape the privations which were drawing their curtain of gloom fearfully around them. Sad enough was their lot, but it was better than separation and endured without a murmur. To aggravate their sorrow, the two daughters were guarded in separate dungeons, for sixteen hours of each day, and the eight hours which the family were allowed to spend together, were liable to constant interruptions by the busy interference of the functionaries of the prison. The clothes of the captives were only partially allowed renewal, though worn, tattered and filthy;—their food was barely enough to satisfy hunger, and of the coarsest kind;—the air which they breathed was noxious with effluvia; the light of heaven was rarely permitted to cheer the dreary archway around them;—and thus the weary months passed away, increasing in horror by the infernal skill of the jailers inventing new methods of heartless persecution.

But Providence, whose mysterious and wise purposes send adversity and prosperity, had not determined that Lafayette and his family should perish so. Austria could spurn the entreaties of America, and England, and France; she could frown at the words of reproach repeated over the continent, but she quailed when the tidings of Napoleon's vast designs and victorious career, sent alarm through her imperial chambers; she heard the voice of "the conqueror of Italy" in menacing tones. Her Italian provinces were snatched from her grasp almost before she knew that they were endangered, and, with her power humbled, she saw the victorious feet of the hero of Lodi steadily encroaching on her domains. Her generals were unable to stand before him, and, after defeats and disasters had followed in rapid succession, her armies put to rout, and her fair possessions disappearing, she was at length compelled to sue for peace. Negotiations were opened at Leoben, but the triumphant Napoleon would grant no peace until Austria had set at liberty every foreign prisoner confined for political offences. It was expressly stipulated by Bonaparte, that the dungeon doors of Olmutz should be opened to Lafayette and his companions in captivity. The language of Bonaparte was such as could not be misunderstood, and she dared not refuse, though for a long time she evaded the point, and sought to do so wholly by other concessions. But Napoleon had made his demands from which nothing could induce him to yield. He told the Austrian envoys, who met him at Leoben, that the release of Lafayette and his companions must be granted, and bade them signify to the cabinet at Vienna, "that the speedy liberation of the prisoners at Olmutz, was the most unequivocal pledge which his imperial majesty could give to the French republic, of his desire to bring to a happy issue a negotiation that essentially interested the welfare of both nations, and the tranquillity of Europe." As the commissioners still equivocated and delayed, Bonaparte, losing his temper one day, seizing a valuable tea service, which stood upon the sideboard, and which had been presented by the Empress Catharine to one of the commissioners, dashed it upon the floor before them, exclaiming, "War is declared, but remember, that in less than three months I will demolish your monarchy as I dash in pieces this porcelain." It was enough; the treaty was signed, and the Austrian government was bound, upon national faith, to set the prisoners free.*

* Austria was unwilling to acknowledge even then that she had been forced to submission. It was a remark of one of her ministers, Baron Thugut, that "Lafayette was not liberated at the instance of

On the 23d of September, 1797, Lafayette, after an imprisonment of over five years, and his wife and daughters, after having been confined with him for twenty-two months, were allowed again to look upon the light and breath once more the pure air of heaven. The emotions of that family then mock the power of language. An officer awaited them at the gates to escort them to Hamburgh, where they were to receive their formal discharge from John Parish, Esq., the worthy American consul, who had long been devoted to their escape. Their reception in Hamburgh is related by Mr. Parish himself.

"The Marquis' departure from Olmutz was notified to M. de Buol and myself, and I concerted measures for his being delivered over to me in my own house. Every thing was so arranged as to have the ceremony performed as quickly and secretly as possible, and the 4th of October was fixed for this reception. Mr. Morris and I dined that day with the minister Baron de Buol. I left them at four o'clock, in order to be at home when they arrived. An immense crowd of people announced their arrival. The streets were lined, and my house was soon filled with them. A lane was formed to let the prisoners pass to my room.

France, but merely to show the Emperor's consideration for the United States of America." The influence of the American President may have had its weight, and if so,—as another has remarked,—it is not a little singular that his release should have been effected by the co-operation of the two most conspicuous men of their age. one the founder of a republic, the other of a despotism,—George Washington and Napoleon Bonaparte.

Lafayette led the way and was followed by his infirm lady and two daughters. He flew into my arms; his wife and daughters clung to me. A silence, an expressive silence, took place. It was broken by an exclamation of, "my friend! my dearest friend! *my deliverer!* See the work of your generosity! My poor, poor wife, hardly able to support herself!" And, indeed, she was not standing, but hanging on my arm, imbued with tears, while her two lovely girls had hold of the other. The scene was extremely affecting and I was very much agitated. The room was full and I am sure there was not a dry eye in it. I placed the Marchioness on a sofa; she sobbed and wept much, and could utter but few words. Again the Marquis came to my arms, his heart overflowing with gratitude. I never saw a man in such complete ecstacy of body and mind. He is a handsome man, in the prime of life, and seemed to have suffered but little from his confinement. It required a good quarter of an hour to compose him.

"In the midst of this scene the minister joined us. I introduced the Marquis and his family to him, and then requested that the ceremony about to be performed, might be in a private room, and desired that the rest of the company might remain where they were.

"The minister, and his secretary, with the officer of the escort, Mr. Morris and *the prisoner*, retired with me to an inner apartment, where M. de Buol, after a very handsome address to *the prisoner*, stated the particular satisfaction he had in delivering him over to a friend who loved and respected him so much. He then addressed me, and after some flattering compliments, reminded me of my engagement to the Emperor, to have the Marquis removed out of Germany in ten days, which I again promised to fulfill, when he told Lafayette that he was now completely restored to liberty."

In rapture he could exclaim with the English Bard,—

"O ye loud Waves! and O ye Forests high!
  And O ye Clouds that far above me soared!
Thou rising Sun! thou blue rejoicing sky!
  Yea, every thing that is and will be free!
  Bear witness for me wheresoe'er ye be,
  With what deep worship I have still adored
  The spirit of divinest Liberty!

CHAPTER X.

Lafayette in private life again — Two years in Holstein — Visits Batavia — Overthrow of the French Directory — Napoleon appointed First Consul — Lafayette appears in Paris — Chagrin of Bonaparte — Mutual understanding — Lafayette retires to La Grange — His intercourse with Bonaparte ceases — Death of Madame de Lafayette — Banishment of Bonaparte to Elba — Elevation of Louis XVIII to the French throne — Escape of Bonaparte — He appears in Paris — Bonaparte and Lafayette — Reverses at Waterloo — Abdication — Lafayette at La Grange — Is again elected to the Chamber of Deputies — Revisits America — Incidents of his tour — Returns to France — Another Revolution — Death of Lafayette — His Character.

The first act of Lafayette after his release was to obey the dictates of a grateful heart by writing and expressing his cordial acknowledgements to those who had so generously aided in his restoration. His next step was to procure a temporary retreat, where the sinking health of Madame de Lafayette might be restored, and which should be a home till the shores of his own native land should again welcome his footsteps. The terms of release implied, as we have seen, that he should leave the Austrian jurisdiction within ten days; and as the Directory had not yet invited him to return, he was compelled to select his residence upon neutral ground; accordingly Holstein, a dependency of the King of Denmark, was chosen. In this territory, at the little town of Welmoldt, he enjoyed relaxation and repose. His own patrimony had been confiscated, but he was now relieved from pecuniary embarassment by a bequest ot tour thousand pounds which had been made him by two English ladies as a token of their sympathy. With his son George, returned from America, his family circle was complete, and two years of uninterrupted pleasure glided by at Welmoldt. His time was occupied partly with agriculture, partly with literature and general science, and partly in arranging his "Historical Fragments," embracing the political incidents and events of his past life. From the agitations which were still rocking Europe and which Napoleon was beginning to guide, he kept studiously aloof. He desired to quit European politics, at least for a time, and if it could be, to revisit America and take up his abode among the people of his early fame and affection. He communicated his wishes to Washington, but was dissuaded from immediate action on account of difficulties of a serious and delicate nature which had just arisen between the French Directory and the government of the United States.

In the year 1799 the Batavian republic, in gratitude for his services rendered in 1787, sent him a formal invitation to visit that state, which he accepted; and soon after left Holstein for Utrecht. He was here received with marked attention. The government and citizens conspired to render him the full tribute of their grateful affection; and in renewing his intercourse with many of his former friends whom he now met, he began to *feel* that his manacles were removed. Still he was not at home. Amid the delights with which he was surrounded, he was yet an exile

The French Directory still refused to erase his name from the list of the proscribed, and France was therefore shut against him. Germany was forbidden ground. He could not return to Holstein, for Russia was just then meditating an invasion of that province. His way was not yet clear to America. England, though she might not forbid him a refuge, could not afford him a hospitable reception. As he had before written when confined at Magdebourg: "To the dangers of an escape from these barriers, guards and chains, are added those of a flight through the enemy's country, and an asylum. From Constantinople to Lisbon, from Kamschatka to Amsterdam, (for I am not in favor with the house of Orange,) only bastiles await me. The forests of the Hurons and the Iroquois are peopled with my friends. The despots of Europe and their courts, are savages to me. Though I am not beloved at St. James, that is a nation of laws; but I would avoid a country at war with my own."

In the latter part of the year 1799, occurred those memorable events in Paris which overthrew the government of the Directory; established the Consulate, and placed the victorious Napoleon at the head of affairs in the Republic. Though he had secured the freedom of Lafayette, he was averse to his returning, aware that his own aspirations and plans could never harmonize with those of so earnest a patriot. The Marquis, unsuccessful in his applications, suspected that all was not right in Bonaparte's professions of attachment either to freedom or himself. Sensible of the obligations which he owed to Napoleon, he did not suffer his gratitude to blind his mind or delude his heart. Soon as he heard at Utrecht that the Directory was no more, he made a decisive stroke to regain his privilege. Before the first Consul could have time to take action upon his case ; before the joy of the people over the silent guileotine and dethroned Robespierre, could have subsided, he determined to appear in Paris and demand in person the restoration of his citizenship. Arriving at Paris he immediately announced his arrival in the following note to Napoleon.

"From the day when the prisoners of Olmutz owed their liberty to you, to this, when the liberty of my country lays me under still greater obligations to you, I have thought that the continuance of my proscription was not expedient for the government, or for myself. Accordingly, I am now in Paris. Before going into the country, where I shall meet my family — before even seeing my friends here, I delay not a moment to address myself to you ; not that I doubt that I am in my appropriate place, wherever the republic is founded upon worthy bases, but because both my duty and my feelings prompt me to bear to you in person the expression of my gratitude."

Bonaparte was taken completely by surprise. The "man of the people" had outgeneralled the "conqueror of Italy." He could not outwardly express dissatisfaction, for he had just sworn to be faithful to those principles which the whole life of Lafayette had illustrated. To refuse the claim would be directly hostile to his professions, while to admit it, would be to subject all his actions to the surveillance of a man whose presence he feared. In the first few interviews between them, Lafayette and Bonaparte understood each other perfectly, though the latter endeavored to gloss over his ambitious aspirations. Lafayette abhorred dissimulation, and was perfectly frank in the expression of his opinions. Soon as he learned those of the Consul, he did not hesitate to denounce them to his face. He admired Napoleon's military glory, but shrank with disgust from the selfish, lawless passion for fame that reigned in the citadel of his soul. The homage which he felt for his resplendant genius, did not so dazzle as to prevent him from discerning his vast designs. While Lafayette's request was unanswered, the two held long and frequent conversations upon the interests of the country; but no sooner was it received than it became equally agreeable to them both, that the Marquis should leave Paris for the comparative obscurity of country life. La Grange, an inheritance of Madame de Lafayette, which had been confiscated during the Revolution, was now restored by order of the new government, to its original possessors. It was a beautiful estate, comprising about a thousand acres, situated in the fertile district of La Brie, about forty miles east of Paris. At this delightful retreat, the family of Lafayette became once more united upon their native soil. Secluding himself from political strife, and, with a spirit which the dungeons of Olmutz had not tamed, refu sing inflexibly to bow before imperial authority, he gave himself exclusively to the endearments of domestic life, and the pursuits of literature and science. Napoleon, who would have gained his adherence, plied every means at his command. He proffered him the dignity and emoluments of a membership in the new Senate which he was constituting, but as he could not accept this without appearing to lend support to the government, it was resolutely declined. The post of ambassador to the United States was then offered him, but this he felt bound to refuse for very different reasons. He felt himself almost as much a citizen of America as of France, and he could not indulge the thought of going there as a stranger, to watch with a jealous eye over the rights of his own country.

In 1802, he met at a dinner party Lord Cornwallis, the newly appointed British Minister to France, and in reply to his lordship's queries, he assured him that his attachment to freedom was firm and uncompromising as ever. The conversation turning upon Napoleon's administration, and the question being asked Lafayette whether this was consonant to his ideas of liberty, he boldly replied, that it was not. Court spies were not long in carrying this to Napoleon, who was enraged. The next time they met, he did not conceal his resentment. "Lord Cornwallis pretends," said he, "that you are not yet corrected."

"Of what?" demanded Lafayette, "of my love of liberty? What should disgust me with that? The extravagances and crimes of terrorist tyranny have only served to make me hate more heartily every arbitrary regimé, and attach myself more strongly to my principles."

"But you have spoken to him of our affairs," said the consul, without concealing his rage.

"No one is further than myself," replied Lafayette, "from seeking a foreign ambassador to censure what is passing in my own country; but if he ask me if this is liberty, I must answer, No."

"I must say to you, General Lafayette," said Bonaparte,—"and I perceive it with pain, that, by your manner of speaking of the acts of the government you give its enemies the weight of your name."

"What more can I do?" was the firm reply,—"I live in the country in retirement, I avoid as far as I can, occasions of speaking of public affairs; but when any one demands of me if your administration of the government, is conformable to my ideas of liberty, *I shall say that it is not. I wish to be prudent, but I cannot be false.*"

The towering ambition of Napoleon, not content with uncertain greatness, desired to have his office conferred upon him for life. The legislative body submitted the question to the people, who, dazzled by the splendor of Napoleon's military achievements, voted to sanction this appointment. When Lafayette was called upon to vote, he replied: "I cannot vote for such a magistracy, until public liberty has been sufficiently guaranteed. Then will I give my vote to Napoleon Bonaparte." In the following letter, dated

La Grange, May 20th, 1802, he thus addressed the First Consul:

"GENERAL,—When a man, penetrated with the gratitude which he owes you, and too much alive to glory not to admire yours, has placed restrictions on his suffrage, those restrictions will be so much the less suspected when it is known that none more than himself would delight to see you chief magistrate for life of a free republic. The 18th Brumaire saved France, and I felt that I was recalled by the liberal professions to which you have attached your honor. We afterwards beheld in the consular power that restorative dictatorship, which, under the auspices of your genius, has achieved such great things, less great, however, than will be the restoration to liberty. It is impossible that you, General, the first in that order of men, (whom, to quote and compare it, would require me to retrace every age of history,) can wish that such a revolution, so many victories, so much blood and miseries, should produce to the world and to ourselves no other results than an arbitrary system. The French people have too well known their rights to have entirely forgotten them. But perhaps they are better able to recover them now with advantage than in the heat of effervescence; and you, by the power of your character and the public confidence; by the superiority of your talents, your situation and your fortune, may, by reëstablishing liberty, subdue our dangers and calm our inquietudes. I have no other than patriotic and personal motives in wishing for you, as the climax of our glory, a permanent magistrative post; but it is in unity with my principles, my engagements, the actions of my whole life, to ascertain, before I vote, that liberty is established on bases worthy of the nation and of you. I hope you will now acknowledge, General, as you have already had occasion to do, that to firmness in my political opinions are joined my sincere wishes for your welfare, and profound sentiments of my obligations to you."

This memorable, manly and characteristic letter was never answered. Napoleon withdrew entirely from Lafayette and surrounded himself only with those advisers who would have no scruples in carrying forward his plans. All intercourse between them was suspended, and they did not meet again till after Napoleon's sad reverses, in 1814, had taught him to feel the wisdom of those counsels once rashly slighted.

The years passed pleasantly by Lafayette; the world had not forgotten him, and by visiting him in his seclusion, or less directly, the distingué manifested their appreciation of his worth. Many of the British whigs who had nobly defended him in Parliament, personally paid their respects to him at La Grange. A number of his friends from America went to see him, and entreated him to make his permanent abode within a Union cemented in part by his own blood. President Jefferson seconded these requests and prepared the way for him honorably to become an American citizen by offering to appoint him governor of the newly acquired territory of Louisiana. The heart of the General was touched by these tokens of affection, but he felt constrained to remain in France as long as there was the slightest hope of her political elevation. Though every thing seemed lost, yet he discerned radiance athwart the gloom. As he expressed it in his letter to Mr. Jefferson: "For me to pronounce the sentence; to proclaim it, as it were, by a final expatriation, would be a concession so contrary to my sanguine nature, that unless I were absolutely forced, I know not the land, however disadvantageous, and still less can I imagine the hope, however unpromising, which I could totally and irrevocably abandon."

But the tranquillity of La Grange was mournfully interrupted. A terrible calamity, in 1807, fell with desolating weight upon that household. During the barbarous confinement in Austria, the constitution of Madame de Lafayette had received a shock which it could not bear. Disease, slow but certain, had fastened upon her frame and hastened her to the grave. The raptures of re-union could not divert, though they cheered, her pathway to the tomb. Lafayette saw her cheek paling; her eye growing dim; her step becoming less elastic; and the thought which these warnings awakened was one of agony. On the 24th of December she gave him her last smile, and breathing a prayer that he might have "the peace of God," she closed her eyes in death's gentlest slumber. "She died," says Mr. de Segur, "surrounded by a numerous family, who offered up ardent prayers to heaven for her preservation. When unable to articulate, a smile played upon her lips at the sight of her husband and children, who bathed her death-bed with tears. Devoted to her domestic duties, which were her only pleasure; adorned by every virtue; pious, modest, charitable, severe to herself, indulgent to others, she was one of the few whose pure reputation has received fresh luster from the misfortunes of the Revolution. Though ruined by our political storm, yet she scarcely seemed to recollect that she had ever enjoyed ample fortune. She was the happiness of her family, the friend of the poor, the consoler of the afflicted, an ornament to her country, and an honor to her sex."

The emotions which tossed the heart of Lafayette under this bereavement, he himself has partially expressed in the following extract from a letter to his friend Masclet. "I willingly admit," says he, "that under great misfortune, I have felt myself superior to the situation in which my friends had the kindness to sympathize; but at present, I have neither the power nor the wish to struggle against the calamity which has befallen me, or rather, to surmount the deep affliction which I shall carry with me to the grave. It will be mingled with the sweetest recollections of the thirty-four years, during which I was bound by the tenderest ties that, perhaps, ever existed, and with the thought of her last moments, in which she heaped upon me such proofs of her incomparable affection. I cannot describe the happiness which, in the midst of so many vicissitudes and troubles, I have constantly derived from the tender, noble and generous feeling, ever associated to the interests which gave animation to my existence."

These feelings were perennial. The widowhood of his heart was no transient thing; it darkened the world till *he* sank to rest. "One day during his last illness," writes a constant attendant upon him, "I surprised him kissing her portrait, which he always wore suspended to his neck in a small gold medallion. Around the portrait were the words, 'I am yours,' and on the back was engraved this short and touching inscription: 'I was then a gentle companion to you! —in that case—bless me.' "

In the year 1814 passed another act in the rapidly shifting drama of French politics. The ruling dynasty was changed. The allied powers of Europe had broken the rod of Napoleon, and banished him to Elba, while Louis XVIII. was seated upon the throne of his fathers. Amid these excitements Lafayette stood a reserved but not unobservant spectator. He did not regret the fall of Bonaparte, for he had seen him striding rapidly forward to an uncompromising despotism. He did not rejoice in the elevation of Louis, for this only brought upon the stage again the old evils of Jacobinism, from which he and the nation had already suffered so frightfully. The fact, that Louis derived his power and was maintained in his position by the enemies of the realm, was especially repugnant. During the brief reign of this monarch, Lafayette appeared once at court, and though graciously received by the King, he retired to La Grange and did not repeat the visit. He could do nothing for France, and his only course was to mark the tide of affairs; persuaded that republican principles would yet have a glorious resurrection.

Louis XVIII. remained in possession of his throne for scarcely eleven months. The "man of destiny" had not yet fulfilled his prescribed career. In the month of February, 1815, he contrived to elude the vigilant watch at Elba, and on the first of March he landed upon the shores of France. From Cannes, where he first planted his foot, the news of his arrival spread as on lightening wing, awakening the mingled emotions of gladness and consternation. With scarcely a thousand soldiers, he started for Paris, confident that he should be able to drive his rival from the throne, and take again the scepter. His march was a triumph. Bands of men, actuated by the enthusiasm which he could inspire at will, flocked to his standard. The force sent out to oppose his progress, joined his ranks, with the hearty shout "*vive l'empereur.*" Marshal Ney, "the bravest of the brave," with all the troops under his command, hastened to swell his army. Grenoble and Lyons opened their gates at his approach, while with victorious and rapid strides, the exiled Emperor neared the walls of Paris. Louis heard of his approach at first with amazement, and then with despair. One by one, he saw the props on which he had relied, sinking away from beneath him, until before the 18th of March, his last army had yielded to the magic of Napoleon's presence, and he found himself alone. His only resource was in flight, and on the 20th of March he forsook the capital, which was immediately entered by Napoleon, who, assuming the reins, recommenced his imperial reign.

Lafayette could not interfere, but looked on with absorbing interest. He was not unnoticed by the Emperor. Napoleon knew that power regained, might be wrested from his grasp, unless its foundations were laid more broadly in concessions which the progressive democratic principle demanded. He accordingly gave his pledges, and then sent his brother Joseph to sound Lafayette, and secure his allegiance. Honors were offered him;—all the dignity that Bonaparte could bestow was laid at his feet, but he refused to compromise principle, or attach himself to the fortunes of the Corsican. An hereditary peerage was reëstablished by Napoleon, and Lafayette pressed to take his seat as a member, with the intimation that his name was first on the list of peers. His reply to the ex-king of Spain, who had urged this, was significant:—"Should I ever again appear on the scene of public life," said he, "IT CAN ONLY BE AS A REPRESENTATIVE OF THE PEOPLE." The peerage was refused, and Lafayette, urged by the inhabitants of his district, accepted the appointment as their representative to the elective body, instituted to sit in connection with the peers.

In this capacity he appeared before his country, ready to show forth the same immutability of integrity, and the same energy "as was possessed by him to whom America raised statues ere manhood had shed its down upon his cheek;—to whom the military spirit of France devoted a sword of victory, formed out of the dungeon bars of the Bastile which he had broken. As a member of the chamber of deputies, he exhibited to his country a bright, untarnished model of the true, pure, incorruptible constitutionalists of 1789, whose views for the liberty and happiness of their country had been successively and effectually frustrated, by the sordid selfishness of antiquated privilege, by the factious intrigues of sanguinary democracy,—and by the aspiring views of bold, boundless and despotic ambition."

His course in the chamber during the first stage of his renewed appearance there, was very unobtrusive. He sought no prominence, either to favor or oppose any new measure. He considered France invaded, and as a good citizen, voted for all the supplies needful for defense; but in no way implicated himself in Bonaparte's gigantic designs. It was not till after the overthrow at Waterloo, that his voice was heard from the tribune, expressing sentiments which had not been breathed in that place, since they had fallen from his own lips twenty years before. He insisted that Napoleon should abdicate, but indulged in no invectives, and uttered no reproaches upon fallen greatness. In all the mortifying scenes through which the Emperor was now compelled to move, Lafayette treated him with generous sympathy and kindness. He stipulated in the Assembly that the liberty and life of Napoleon should be guaranteed by the nation, and endeavored to obtain for him two frigates to conduct him safely to the United States before falling into the hands of the allies ; but it was too late. Napoleon's star of destiny was declining, yet his heart was touched by the attentions of him from whom he had least expected them.

After the fate of Napoleon was sealed, Louis XVIII. was again forced by the allies upon the French, contrary to the wishes both of Lafayette and themselves. Resistance was however impossible, for a million of foreign bayonets environed him, and Lafayette again returned to La Grange. His retirement continued unbroken for four years, when, in 1819, he was elected to the chamber of deputies, from the departments of La Sarthe and Meaux. The King had manifested that steady encroachment upon the rights of the people characteristic of the Bourbons, and Lafayette opposed the arrogance of Louis. He attacked despotic claims with a freedom of speech that went to the palace. The minions of the King were resolved to crush him. They hoped to find him guilty of conspiracy ; they watched his words for a traitorous meaning ; but he continued hurling his fulminations against tyranny, utterly regardless of the consequences to himself. The King bore it awhile, but patience was never a Bourbon virtue, and Louis XVIII. certainly did not excel his predecessors in this particular. In 1823 he ordered his Solicitor General to accuse Lafayette of treason. The charge was publicly made in the chamber of deputies, and, for a few minutes, was received with profound silence by that body. At length Lafayette slowly arose, and with perfect self-possession, took his stand upon the tribune. For a moment he said nothing, but with his arms folded across his manly breast, he coolly surveyed the assembly. Then, with composure and without denying the charge, he said :—"In spite of my habitual indifference to party accusations and animosities, I still think myself bound to say a single word upon this occasion. During the whole course of a life entirely devoted to liberty, I have constantly been an object of attack to the enemies of that cause, under whatever form, despotic, aristocratic, or anarchic, they have endeavored to combat it. I do not complain, then, because I observe some affectation in the use of the word *proved*, which the Solicitor General has employed against me; but I join my honored friends in demanding a public inquiry, within the walls of this chamber, and in the face of the nation. Then, I and my adversaries, to whatever rank they belong, may declare, without reserve, all that we have mutually had to reproach each other with, for the last thirty years."

From such a challenge his accusers recoiled and none was willing to accept it. They loved darkness rather than light. The charge melted speedily away before the threatening aspect of a public inquisition. Lafayette was acquitted, but the government, by bribery and intrigues, defeated his reëlection. He was at length prepared for his contemplated project of revisiting America. France and the United States were at peace; he was free from any extraordinary care; and his waning years reminded him that his voyage must be speedily, if ever, accomplished. He had struggled to establish a republic upon both continents; foiled at home, he yearned to repose under the goodly tree which he had planted and watered abroad; whose boughs were waving broad and high in the sunlight of human well-being. Universal joy spread over America at the intelligence. President Monroe promply wrote him, offering to place a national frigate at his service to convey him to the United States. He no longer hesitated, and declining Mr. Monroe's offer, he set sail from Havre, on the 12th of July, 1824, in an American merchantman, accompanied by his son George Washington, and his private secretary Mr. Levasseur. The citizens of Havre were prepared to give a public demonstration of their admiration of Lafayette, but the government had ordered its police to stop it and repress any signs of respect by the immense multitude assembled to witness his embarkation. But three hearty cheers broke spontaneously from the host, as the sails of the Cadmus were spread, and the wind bore the vessel from port.

On the 15th of August, the Cadmus arrived in the harbor of New York, after a pleasant passage of thirty-one days. It was on the morning of the Sabbath; and, with a becoming respect for the sacredness of the day, he accepted the invitation of Vice President Tompkins to land upon Staten Island, and remain at his mansion till the following day. With unutterable emotion he set his feet upon the freest soil in the world, endeared by grand and touching memories.

It was a rich draught of pleasure, and all the magnificence of his reception afterwards did not augment the gladness of this first moment of his landing.

The arrangements for his reception in the city were ample; and early on Monday morning salutes were fired, and the bells commenced ringing their glad peals of welcome. The whole town was alive with expectation, and soon the bay, from New York to Staten Island, was covered with boats anxious to catch the first sight of the nation's guest. At nine o'clock in the morning, the committee appointed by the Corporation, the Officers of the Army and Navy, the Major-Generals and the Brigadier-Generals of the Militia, the President of the Chamber of Commerce, and the committee from the Society of Cincinnati, set out to escort him to the city. All the steamboats proffered their services to accompany the escort, magnificently dressed for the occasion, with flags and streamers of every land, they presented a pageant new and altogether imposing. The Battery was crowded with spectators; Castle Garden was filled, and every boat that arrived to take its station teemed with excited throngs. Amid the display of the scene, the steamboat Chancellor Livingston, which was to receive the Marquis, presented a singular appearance; her only decoration being the flag of the United States and that of New York. This was a delicate compliment to Lafayette. He needed not the ornaments of tinselled splendor. He was received with military honors; but the wild huzza, which rose from thousands when he stepped on board, drowned the music and the roar of cannon. Among the company on board were several revolutionary soldiers, who had been by his side in the smoke of battle, and forgetful of ceremony they rushed forward to embrace their old companion in arms. The greeting was equally warm with him, and tears fell from "eyes unused to weep," while those veterens were embracing. Just then, the bands, which had been playing, "See the conquering hero comes," struck into the favorite French air, "*Ou peut-on etre mieux qu'au sein de sa famille,*"* and the immense flotilla moved forward. Far as the eye could reach, the venerable Marquis saw joyful faces, and heard the acclamations of the two hundred thousand participants of that gala day.

Landing at the Battery, he entered Castle Garden, and partook of refreshments provided, and then taking his set with General Morton, in an elegant barouche, drawn by four white horses, a way was slowly opened through the multitude, to the City Hall. All along Broadway the pavements, the roofs and windows, were crowded by a dense assemblage, among whom the eye of the illustrious visiter rested upon no sorrowful face.

At the City Hall he was appropriately welcomed by the Mayor, and then received the congratulations of distinguished citizens, who pressed forward to offer their salutation. Now and then, one of his former comrades would press through the crowd, and grasping his hand, give by his flowing tears a welcome which his faltering tongue refused to speak.

For four days he remained in New York ; on the

* "Where can one be better than in the bosom of his family."

20th, he left for Boston, attended by a large concourse of citizens, who thronged his way for miles. His course was along Long Island Sound, and his reception by the different towns on the southern borders of Connecticut, was evidence of the general enthusiasm awakened by his arrival. At Fairfield, an elegant table was prepared at the Hotel, by the young ladies of the town, who gained great honor by the manner in which it had been prepared. "The decorations of the table were planned on a style of the greatest elegance ; the dishes were quite enveloped with evergreens and scattering flowers ; and the due proportions were observed in the succession of viands, as well as in the harmony and contrast of colors, which maintained a kind of silent correspondence, from the opposite sides of a splendid cone that occupied the center. On taking their seats at the table, the guests might have supposed themselves invited to a feast of wreaths and flowers, studded with the 'crimson hail' of winter greens, cranberries and amare dulcis. The table was like the bed of some fairy's enchanted garden, so entirely did the decorations overshadow and conceal the rich collation beneath. When this verdant veil was removed, the scene was changed as suddenly as at the dissolving of a spell, and the company could not repress their surprise. The General expressed his gratification at this specimen of female taste, and regretted that it should be so quickly destroyed, to gratify that of the gentlemen."

On the 24th, he reached Boston, where his reception was exceedingly brilliant. Under the shadow of Bunker Hill and Faneuil Hall, his soul kindled with the fire which burned nearly half a century before.

Such was the uniformly splendid reception, that to have described one scene, will be to have pictured all. He traveled most of the country, and with daily increasing pleasure, saw evidences of thrift and prosperity. In the southern and western portion of the country, he went over an area of over 3000 miles in extent, which was a pathless desert when he last visited the new world, but which now displayed to his astonished vision, nine new states, from whose flourishing towns a free, virtuous, and intelligent people, poured forth to invoke blessings on his head. Every new city, every improvement that he witnessed, every indication of advancing greatness, was testimony to the wisdom and purity of his youthful choice. His mind often went back to scenes of early hardship, and as he contrasted them with the brightness of the present, he rejoiced in the harvest, a thousand fold, upon the bloody sowing. His visit was during an excited Presidential contest, when the friends of Adams, Jackson, Clay and Crawford, were in the field, and the country was in a flame of party strife. Few elections have been more warmly fought, and he looked on a passive, but deeply interested, observer. He beheld the elements of order; the law and the constitution exerted their silent authority. The same men who to-day, in party hostility met like foes, to-morrow would mingle their congratulations. It was a spectacle which made him sigh over the scenes of the Old World. It was a beautiful exhibition of the practical workings of principles which his benevolence would have scattered around the globe.

It is often said that republics are ungrateful, but the United States have given a bright exception to this charge. Congress bestowed upon him two hundred thousand dollars, and a township of land, as a partial testimony to the value of his Revolutionary services.

His reception by Congress was peculiarly gratifying. The first act passed by it after organization, was one of public welcome to him. A committee of twenty-four members, was appointed to wait upon the General, and invite him to visit Congress upon such a day as he might choose to designate. On the day appointed, he entered the Hall of Representatives, which had been tastefully decorated, where the Senators and Members of the House had assembled to receive him. Every one rose on his entry, and remained standing while the rich tones of Mr. Clay, the Speaker of the House, pronounced the following eloquent address :—

"General,—The House of Representatives of the United States, impelled alike by its own feelings, and by those of the whole American people, could not have assigned to me a more gratifying duty, than that of being its organ to present to you cordial congratulations upon the occasion of your recent arrival in the United States, in compliance with the wishes of Congress, and to assure you of the very high satisfaction which your presence affords on this early theater of your glory and renown. Although but few of the members who compose this body, shared with you in the war of the Revolution, all have a knowledge from impartial history, or from faithful tradition, of the perils, the sufferings, and the sacrifices, which you have voluntarily encountered, and the signal services, in America and in Europe, which you performed for an infant, a distant, and an alien people ; and all feel, and own, the very great extent of the obligations under which you have placed our country. But the relations in which you have ever stood to the United States, interesting and important as they have been, do not constitute the only motive of the respect and admiration which this House entertains for you. Your consistency of character, your uniform devotion to regulated liberty, in all the vicissitudes of a long and arduous life, also commands its highest admiration. During all the recent convulsions of Europe, amidst, as after the dispersion of, every political storm, the people of the United States have ever beheld you true to your old principles, firm and erect, cheering and animating, with your well known voice, the votaries of liberty, its faithful and fearless champion, ready to shed the last drop of that blood, which here you so freely and nobly spilt in the same holy cause.

"The vain wish has been sometimes indulged, that Providence would allow the Patriot, after death, to return to his country, and to contemplate the intermediate changes which had taken place—to view the

the forests felled, the cities built, the mountains leveled, the canals cut, the highways constructed, the progress of the arts, the advancement of learning, and the increase of population. General, your present visit to the United States is the realization of the consoling object of that wish. You are in the midst of posterity! Every where you must have been struck with the great changes, physical and moral, which have occurred since you left us. Even this very city, bearing a venerated name, alike endeared to you and to us, has since emerged from the forest which then covered its site. In one respect, you behold us unaltered, and that is in this sentiment of continued devotion to liberty, and of ardent affection and profound gratitude to your departed friend, the Father of his country, and to your illustrious associates, in the field and in the cabinet, for the multiplied blessings which surround us, and for the very privilege of addressing you, which I now exercise. This sentiment, now fondly cherished by more than ten millions of people, will be transmitted, with unabated vigor, down the tide of time, through the countless millions who are destined to inhabit this continent, to the latest posterity."

The reply of Lafayette was full of feeling. Said he :—

"Mr. Speaker,—While the people of the United States, and their honorable Representatives in Congress, have deigned to make choice of me, one of the American veterans, to signify in his person, their esteem for our joint services and their attachment to the principles for which we have had the honor to fight and bleed, I am proud and happy to share those extraordinary favors with my dear revolutionary companions—yet, it would be, on my part, uncandid and ungrateful not to acknowledge my personal share in those testimonies of kindness, as they excite in my breast emotions which no words could adequately express.

"My obligations to the United States, sir, far exceed any merit I might claim. They date from the time when I had the happiness to be adopted as a young soldier, a favored son of America. They have been continued to me during almost half a century of constant affection and confidence, and now, sir, thanks to your most gratifying invitation, I find myself greeted by a series of welcomes, one hour of which would more than compensate for the public exertions and sufferings of a whole life.

"The approbation of the American people and their Representatives, for my conduct during the vicissitudes of the European Revolution, is the highest reward I could receive. Well may I stand 'firm and erect,' when, in their names, and by you, Mr. Speaker, I am declared to have, in every instance, been faithful to those American principles of liberty, equality and true social order, the devotion to which, as it has been from my earliest youth, so shall it continue to be to my latest breath.

"You have been pleased to allude, Mr. Speaker, to the peculiar felicity of my situation, when, after so long an absence, I am called to witness the immense improvements, the admirable communications, the prodigious creations of which we find an example in this city, whose name itself is a venerated palladium; in a word, all the grandeur and prosperity of these happy United States, which, at the same time they nobly secure the complete assertion of American Independence, reflect on every part of the world the light of a far superior political civilization.

"What better pledge can be given of a persevering national love of liberty, when those blessings are evidenlty the result of a virtuous resistance to oppression, and the institutions founded on the rights of man and the Republican principal of self-government. No, Mr. Speaker, posterity has not begun for me—since in the sons of my companions and friends, I find the same public feelings, and permit me to add, the same feelings in my behalf, which I have had the happiness to experience in their fathers.

"Sir, I have been allowed, forty years ago, before a Committee of a Congress of thirteen States, to express the fond wishes of an American heart. On this day I have the honor, and enjoy the delight, to congratulate the Representatives of the Union, so vastly enlarged, on the realization of those wishes, even beyond every human expectation, and upon the almost infinite prospects we can with certainty anticipate.

"Permit me, Mr. Speaker, and Gentlemen, to join, to the expression of those sentiments, a tribute of my lively gratitude, affectionate devotion, and profound respect."

The House of Representatives then adjourned, and the Speaker descended from his chair, and gave his hand affectionately to the agitated veteran. The members gathered round, and, as one by one they gave their greeting, Lafayette felt, that amid all the triumphs he had enjoyed, none had surpassed this. A scene as impressive occurred in the Senate chamber.

Among the incidents of Lafayette's tour, was his visit to the tomb of Washington, which is thus described by his private secretary and constant attendant :—

"Leaving Washington and descending the Potomac, after a voyage of two hours, the guns of fort Washing announced that we were approaching the last abode of the Father of his country. At this solemn signal, to which the military band accompanying us responded by plaintive strains, we went on deck and the venerable soil of Mt. Vernon was before us; at this view an involuntary and spontaneous movement made us kneel. We landed in boats and trod upon the ground so often worn by the feet of Washington. A carriage received General Lafayette, and the other visitors silently ascended the precipitous path which conducted to the solitary habitation of Mt. Vernon.

"Three nephews of General Washington took Lafayette, his son, and myself, to conduct us to the tomb of their uncle; our numerous companions remained in the house; in a few minutes after, the cannon of the fort, thundering anew, announced that LAFAYETTE rendered homage to the ashes of WASHINGTON. Simple and modest as he was during life, the tomb of the citizen hero is scarcely perceived amid the sombre cypresses by which it is surrounded. A vault slightly elevated and sodded over, a wooden door without inscriptions, some withered and some green garlands, indicate, to the traveler who visits this spot, the place where rest in peace the puissant arms which broke the chains of his country. As we approached, the door was opened; Lafayette descended alone into the vault, and a few minutes after re-appeared with his eyes overflowing with tears. He took his son and me by the hand and led us into the tomb, where by a sign he indicated the coffin of his paternal friend, alongside of which was that of his companion in life, united to him in the grave. We knelt reverently near his coffin, which we respectfully saluted with our lips, and rising threw ourselves into the arms of Lafayette and mingled our tears with his."

The year, which he had allotted for his visit, passed rapidly by in well nigh uninterrupted festivity and rejoicing. But such scenes could not last forever, and on the 6th of September, 1825, the anniversary of his birth day, Lafayette enjoyed his last fete in America. This was at the house of President Adams, in Washington, and on the following day, "the old man eloquent," in the presence of a large concourse of citizens, made the farewell address in the name of the American people and government. The closing part of this was in the following highly finished strain.

"The ship is now prepared for your reception, and

equipped for sea. From the moment of her departure, the prayers of millions will ascend to heaven that her passage may be prosperous, and your return to the bosom of your family as propitious to your happiness, as your visit to this scene of your youthful glory has been to that of the American people.

"Go, then, our beloved friend — return to the land of brilliant genius, of generous sentiment, of heroic valor; to that beautiful France, the nursing mother of the twelfth Louis and the fourth Henry; to the native soil of Bayard and Coligni, of Turenne and Catinat, of Fenelon and d' Aguesseau. In that illustrious catalogue of names which she claims as of her children, and with honest pride holds to the admiration of other nations, the name of Lafayette has already for centuries been enrolled. And it shall henceforth burnish into brighter fame; for if, in after days, a Frenchman shall be called to indicate the character of his nation by that of one individual, during the age in which we live, the blood of lofty patriotism shall mantle in his cheek, the fire of conscious virtue shall sparkle in his eye, and he shall pronounce the name of Lafayette. Yet we, too, and our children, in life and after death, shall claim you for his own. You are ours by that more than patriotic self-devotion with which you flew to the aid of our fathers at the crisis of their fate; ours by that long series of years in which you have cherished us in your regard; ours by that unshaken sentiment of gratitude for your services, which is a precious portion of our inheritance; ours by that tie of love, stronger than death, which has linked your name, for the endless ages of time, with the name of Washington.

"At the painful moment of parting from you, we take comfort in the thought, that wherever you may be, to the last pulsation of your heart, our country will ever be present to your affections; and a cheering consolation assures us, that we are not called to sorrow most of all that we shall see your face no more. We shall indulge the pleasing anticipation of beholding our friend again. In the meantime, speaking in the name of the whole people of the United States, and at a loss only for language to give utterance to that feeling of attachment with which the heart of the nation beats, as the heart of one man—I bid you a reluctant and affectionate farewell."

Visibly moved, Lafayette thus replied:

"Amid all my obligations to the General Government, and particularly to you, sir, its respected Chief-Magistrate, I have most thankfully to acknowledge the opportunity given me, at this solemn and painful moment, to present the people of the United States with a parting tribute of profound, inexpressible gratitude.

"To have been in the infant and critical days of these States adopted by them as a favorite son, to have participated with them in the toils and perils of our unspotted struggle for independence, freedom, and equal rights, and, in the foundation of the American era, of a new social order, which has already pervaded this, and must, for the dignity and happiness of mankind, successively pervade every part of the other hemisphere, to have receivea at every stage of the Revolution, and during forty years after that period, from the people of the United States, and their representatives at home and abroad, continual marks of their confidence and kindness, has been the pride, the encouragement, the support of a long and eventful life.

"But how could I find words to acknowledge that series of welcomes, those unbounded and universal displays of public affection, which have marked each step, each hour of a twelve months' progress through the twenty-four States, and which, while they overwhelm my heart with grateful delight, have most satisfactorily evinced the concurrence of the people in the kind testimonies, in the immense favors, bestowed on me by the several branches of their representatives, in every part, and at the central seat of the confederacy?

"Yet gratifications still higher await me, in the wonders of creation and improvement that have met my enchanted eye, in the unparalleled and self-felt happiness of the people; in their rapid prosperity and insured security, public and private; in a practice of good order, the appendage of true freedom and a national good sense, the final arbiter of all difficulties, I have had proudly to recognize a result of the republican principles for which we have fought, and a glorious demonstration to the most timid and prejudiced minds, of the superiority over degrading aristocracy or despotism, of popular institutions founded on the plain rights of man, and where the local rights of every section are preserved under a constitutional bond of union. The cherishing of that union between the States, as it has been the farewell entreaty of our great paternal Washington, and will ever have the dying prayer of every patriot American, so it has become the sacred pledge of the emancipation of the world, an object in which I am happy to observe that the American people, while they give the animating example of successful free institutions in return for an evil entailed upon them by Europe, and of which a liberal and enlightened sense is every where more and more generally felt, show themselves every day more anxiously interested.

"And now, sir, how can I do justice to my deep and lively feelings, for the assurances, most peculiarly valued, of your esteem and friendship, for your so very kind references to old times, to my beloved associates, to the vicissitudes of my life, for your affecting picture of the blessings poured by the several generations of the American people, on the remaining days of a delighted veteran, for your affectionate remarks on this sad hour of separation, on the country of my birth, full I can say of American sympathies, on the hope so necessary to me of my seeing again the country that has deigned, near a half a century ago, to call me hers! I shall content myself, refraining from superfluous repetitions, at once, before you, sir, and this respected circle, to proclaim my cordial confirmation of every one of the sentiments which I have had daily opportunities publicly to utter, from the time when your venerable predecessor, my old friend and brother in arms, transmitted to me the honorable invitation of Congress, to this day, when you, my dear sir, whose friendly connections with me date from your earliest youth, are going to consign me to the protection, across the Atlantic, of the heroic national flag, on board the splendid ship, the name* of which has been not the least flattering and kind among the numberless favors conferred upon me.

"God bless you, sir, and all who surround us. God bless the American people, each of their states, and the federal government. Accept this patriotic farewell of an overflowing heart; such will be its last throb when it ceases to beat."

On the same day Lafayette embarked at the head of the Potomac, on the frigate which had been set apart to convey him to France, and the following morning, the Brandywine weighed anchor and spread her sails to the breeze. Sadness fell upon the heart of Lafayette, as his eye caught the last glimpse of the receding shore, for he knew that he should never behold it again. His family met him at Havre, and his tenants flocked forth like children around a parent, as he drew near La Grange. May he never leave us again, was the fervent wish breathed by the humblest attendant. Engaged in lighter employments which his age demanded, surrounded by pleasing associations, he hoped that his tempest-tossed

* The Brandywine — alluding to the battle in which he was first wounded. An exceedingly fine compliment.

bark might now glide peacefully and smoothly over the deep, into the eternal haven. Along his eventful career, he glanced without regret, and looked onward to death, desiring to go with a still and untroubled spirit.

But the clouds which had been for generations gathering in the firmament, had not yet spent their fury upon his devoted land. The moanings of another-tempest were heard. Charles X. was on the throne of France, and madly dashing on to despotism, while the volcanic elements were gathering strength, hourly, *under his insane administration.* Lafayette saw the coming crisis, and once more accepted a seat in the Chamber of Deputies. He hoped to guide, if he could not avert, the storm. For two or three years he labored incessantly, and with former activity, to prevent the calamity, by inducing a different order of things in the government. Charles distrusted him with Bourbon prejudice ; the Ministry hated him ; and his endeavors were ineffectual to accomplish permanent change. The management of public affairs grew constantly worse, and the people, driven at last to desperation, resolved again to take redress into their own hands. In 1830, this was done. In July of that year, was the Revolution of "THE THREE DAYS" accomplisned. Before the infatuated Monarch had dreamed of danger, the crown was rudely torn from his brow, and the scepter snatched from his hand for ever. The terrible lesson which had been taught in the fate of Louis XVI., Charles X. blindly refused to learn, until he was in the hopeless vortex.

His overthrow was rapid, but unmarked by the atrocities of the previous Revolution, which filled the sluices of Paris with blood. Lafayette was called to the command of the National Guards, and the people clamored for a Republic; insisting that their tried friend should be their chief magistrate. With disinterested patriotism, which never shone more radiantly than on the present occasion, he felt that France was not ready for a Republican form of government; and that he had not, sufficiently, the confidence of all parties, to secure a harmonious result, should he assume the reigns of sovereignty. This was therefore declined, and his own choice fell upon Louis Philippe, Duke of Orleans, whose entire course of life had so far exhibited a uniform and consistent attachment to free principles, fitted as a member of the royal family to reconcile in his person the conflicting interests of the nation. "I know only one man," said Lafayette to him, "who can bring France to a Republic, and you are that man."

Owing very much to Lafayette's influence, opposed by his friends, Louis Philippe was duly chosen Lieutenant General of the nation, which title was subsequently changed to "Citizen King of the French." In this appointment we admire the self-sacrificing spirit of Lafayette, but we cannot affirm what subsequent events have fully denied,—the wisdom of the choice. During his life he maintained an outward show of respect for his King, who, soon after his elevation, gave unmistakable signs that his footsteps also were in the beaten path of absolutism and tyranny.

His fate has been an additional warning to despots, and adds another page to those annals from which the kings of the earth should learn wisdom.

We must now come to the close of the earthly existence of him whose character and career we have endeavored, in the preceding pages, to portray Though blessed with a constitution which had sustained burdens insupportable to ordinary frames, he had to yield to accumulated disease and old age. An attack of ischury, to which he was predisposed, met him on the 2d of February, 1834, and soon gave warning of fatality. He gradually sunk, and neither the skill of physicians, the assiduities of friends, nor the sympathies of nations, could stay the Destroyer. "On the 20th of May," says one of his attending physicians, "about one o'clock in the morning, the gravity of the symptoms increased. Respiration, which, for the last eight and forty hours had been much impeded, became still more difficult, and the danger of suffocation was more imminent. Drowsiness, delirium, and prostration of strength, became more decidedly pronounced, and at twenty minutes past four o'clock in the morning, Lafayette expired in our arms.

"A few moments before he breathed his last, Lafayette opened his eyes, and fixed them with a look of affection on his children, who surrounded his bed, as if to bless them, and bid them an eternal adieu. He pressed my hand convulsively, experienced a slight degree of contraction in the forehead and eyebrows, and drew in a deep and lengthened breath, which was immediately followed by a last sigh. His pulse, which had not lost its force, suddenly ceased to beat. A murmuring noise was still heard about the region of the heart. To produce re-animation, we employed stimulating frictions, but in vain; the General had ceased to exist. His countenance resumed a calm expression — that of peaceful slumber."

Thus died LAFAYETTE, in the seventy-seventh year of his age. We would that we might catch, in these closing scenes, the evidences of a Christian faith, but this we are unhappily denied. The cheering hopes of Heaven were not present to gild his pathway to the sepulchure. Lafayette needed these, without which all other virtues are dim and powerless in such an hour. If to the noble qualities which he possessed, "had been added," as another has remarked, "the pure faith and sublime hopes of the Gospel, nothing would have been wanting to complete the portraiture of *a perfect man*."

A universal sadness spread over France, and many parts of Europe, at his death. As the tidings were borne across the Atlantic, sorrow, like the shadow of a total eclipse, swept over the Union; the *penumbra* of that which followed the decease of George Washington.

A Kingdom and a Republic joined in a funeral wail for "the MAN OF TWO WORLDS," emphatically, because he had drawn the hemispheres together in the growing brotherhood of our common humanity

Such as we have described him, was Lafayette. The events which were crowded into his long life, illustrate his character better than a critical analysis could give its strong and beautiful elements. The two revolutions through which he passed, remind us of the course of some great rivers, which, quietly emerging from their own solitude among the highlands, flow on to a battlement of rocks, where in a foaming concentration of power, is revealed the manifold hues and sublime law of their onward current. Lafayette came to our shores from his early home of luxury, and entered the vortex of revolution. Doubtless there was something of youthful romance in the bold adventure. But when the purity and grandeur of his purpose, whose guiding law was affection for Freedom, was revealed in his marvelous success, Washington heard the echo of his own mighty spirit, and the people hailed the Marquis, as worthy to be folded in the same mantle with the man who stood in isolated dignity upon a continent—with the nations at his feet in their involuntary homage. Retiring to La Grange, the heroic nobleman was, for a brief period, behind the scenes again. But at the frantic cry of his country he appears amid the fearful meeting of awakened millions in civil war. The same bright and majestic march of being under the inner force of patriotic fervor, was disclosed, and won the admiration of all. We do not recollect another instance of a "PROTECTOR," ungoverned by fixed religious principles, whose character is so unsullied, and whose name binds perpetually together, in historical annals, two centuries and two worlds!

www.ingramcontent.com/pod-product-compliance
Lightning Source LLC
LaVergne TN
LVHW020124110826
845151LV00001B/271

9781425541040